Beginning Spring 2

From Novice to Professional

Dave Minter

Apress®

Beginning Spring 2: From Novice to Professional

Copyright © 2008 by Dave Minter

ISBN-13 (pbk): 978-1-59059-685-2

ISBN-10 (pbk): 1-59059-685-4

ISBN-13 (electronic): 978-1-4302-0493-0

ISBN-10 (electronic): 1-4302-0493-1

Printed and bound in the United States of America 9 8 7 6 5 4 3 2 1

Lead Editor: Steve Anglin
Technical Reviewer: Kris Lander
Editorial Board: Steve Anglin, Ewan Buckingham, Tony Campbell, Gary Cornell, Jonathan Gennick, Jason Gilmore, Kevin Goff, Jonathan Hassell, Matthew Moodie, Joseph Ottinger, Jeffrey Pepper, Ben Renow-Clarke, Dominic Shakeshaft, Matt Wade, Tom Welsh
Project Manager: Kylie Johnston
Copy Editor: Sharon Wilkey
Associate Production Director: Kari Brooks-Copony
Production Editor: Gwen Burda
Compositor: Susan Glinert Stevens
Proofreader: Linda Seifert
Indexer: Toma Mulligan
Artist: Kinetic Publishing Services, LLC
Cover Designer: Kurt Krames
Manufacturing Director: Tom Debolski

Distributed to the book trade worldwide by Springer-Verlag New York, Inc., 233 Spring Street, 6th Floor, New York, NY 10013. Phone 1-800-SPRINGER, fax 201-348-4505, e-mail orders-ny@springer-sbm.com, or visit http://www.springeronline.com.

For information on translations, please contact Apress directly at 2855 Telegraph Avenue, Suite 600, Berkeley, CA 94705. Phone 510-549-5930, fax 510-549-5939, e-mail info@apress.com, or visit http://www.apress.com.

The source code for this book is available to readers at http://www.apress.com.

To my parents

Contents at a Glance

Contents

About the Author

DAVE MINTER has adored computers since he was small enough to play in the boxes they came in. He built his first PC from discarded, faulty, and obsolete components, and considers that to be the foundation of his career as an integration consultant. Dave lives in London, where he helps large and small companies build systems that "just work." Currently he is developing a bizarre new type of web application server for FatMoggy Ltd. He is a co-author of three other Apress books: *Building Portals with the Java Portlet API*, *Pro Hibernate 3*, and *Beginning Hibernate*.

About the Technical Reviewer

 From the moment his parents gave him a Spectrum 48K for his seventh birthday, it became clear that **KRIS LANDER** was always going to be an early adopter when it came to technology. Upon leaving school, with a computer addiction and a mild vitamin A deficiency, he decided to turn his childhood passion into a serious vocation, embarking on a degree in software engineering from the University of Wales.

Kris's constant thirst for emerging Java technologies has become a trademark throughout his professional career. A Java Web Enterprise (J2EE) specialist from day one and developer of applications using Spring since 2003, Kris has worked on many large-scale IT projects for corporate blue chip and successful new technology companies on both sides of the Atlantic. Based and brought up in London, in his spare time he enjoys good food and music production.

Acknowledgments

I would like to thank the staff at Apress, who as always have displayed their impeccable efficiency and good humor throughout the creative process. Particular thanks are due to Kylie Johnston for keeping the book on schedule, to Sharon Wilkey for knocking my errant grammar back into shape, and to Steve Anglin for accepting the proposal (and listening to my tiresome complaints about marketing jargon).

I am very pleased that my erstwhile colleague Kris Lander could spare the time to perform the technical review of this book. He's an expert Spring consultant, and the book would be far poorer without his corrections and suggestions. Thanks, Kris.

Thanks also to Luke Taylor for assistance with the chapter on Spring (Acegi) Security and supplying tea-related remote banter via Internet messenger.

Finally, I am particularly grateful to Manville Harris Photography for supplying the author's photograph.

Introduction

The Spring framework is a stunningly good piece of software. Building enterprise software is a difficult exercise at the best of times, and there are numerous common problems that developers consistently encounter. Spring smooths over or eliminates a remarkable number of these problems.

Spring's clean design and accommodating approach to existing standards and libraries has resulted in a spectacular rise in its popularity among Java developers. Spring can be retrofitted to old projects and is now often used as the foundation for new development. If you haven't yet encountered Spring, you probably will do so very soon.

Although Spring is well designed and documented, getting bootstrapped in the basics of the framework can still be difficult. This book aims to get Java developers up and running with Spring as quickly as possible by tying the abstract and conceptual discussions to concrete examples in code.

Who This Book Is For

This book assumes an understanding of the basic Java technologies; you must know the core Java Standard Edition (JSE) libraries and you should also be reasonably experienced in working with XML files in order to follow the configuration examples. It will be helpful if you are already familiar with the Maven build tool, but experience with this is not essential.

You are not expected to have any prior knowledge of Spring. The reader I had in mind when writing the book is someone who is about to start work on a Spring-based project, who has just joined a Spring-based project, or who has heard about some of the good things that Spring has to offer and is contemplating using Spring. This book should help you get your bearings and get cracking.

You will not need to purchase any commercial software in order to learn or use Spring because the framework is open source software.

Experienced users of Spring should still find some useful information in the later chapters, and I think even expert developers may find Chapter 7 on Acegi security helpful.

How This Book Is Structured

The first three chapters of this book cover the basic introductory matter. Complete newcomers to Spring should read these chapters in detail before embarking on any of the other examples or investigating the code samples.

The rest of the chapters cover the basic components of Spring that most developers will use regularly. Developers who have already worked with Spring and are looking for more information on the subject will find these to be of more immediate interest than the first three introductory chapters. Readers who are familiar with Spring 1.*x* but not Spring 2 should probably at least skim through Chapter 3 because there are some additions to the XML configuration syntax in Spring 2.

Expert developers are not really the target of this book, but they may find some items of interest in the later chapters, particularly Chapter 7 and the appendix. The chapter contents in more detail are as follows:

- Chapter 1 outlines the basic purpose and architecture of the Spring framework, and introduces inversion of control (IOC) and aspect-oriented programming (AOP) techniques. This chapter also provides a whirlwind tour of the basic components discussed in this book.

- Chapter 2 introduces the sample application. It presents a rationale for the application, a simplified specification for it, and walks you through the build process. This chapter also introduces the Maven 2 build tool.

- Chapter 3 provides a detailed explanation of inversion of control and loose coupling, and explains why they are such useful techniques. This chapter also explains some of the core Spring classes and Spring's XML configuration file syntax.

- Chapter 4 explains how Spring can be used to create interchangeable DAO classes based on different persistence mechanisms. Complete examples are provided for plain JDBC-based and Hibernate-based database access.

- Chapter 5 shows how various Spring features can be used to create an application's service layer. The use of AOP is explained both in enforcing transaction management and for other purposes.

- Chapter 6 introduces the use of Spring to build the web tier of an application. The Spring Model View Controller (Spring MVC) and Spring Web Flow libraries are explained with examples.

- Chapter 7 introduces Spring Security (also known as Acegi security). The various filters and other components used in a Spring Security–protected application are explained. The example demonstrates how to provide authentication, authorization, and channel security services.

- Chapter 8 shows how Spring can be used to send e-mail, a common task that is relatively difficult without the advantages of the Spring framework. The examples demonstrate the use of Spring to send plain text, formatted (HTML) text, and formatted text with attachments.

- Chapter 9 explains how Spring can be used to make an application's service layer remotely accessible over the network. Client and server examples are provided using various protocols, including remote method invocation (RMI) and SOAP.

- Chapter 10 demonstrates the best ways to unit-test your Spring-based application code. It demonstrates an approach to unit-testing the DAO classes created in Chapter 4, explains the use of the EasyMock mock control library, and introduces some of the Spring mock classes provided to ease your testing.

- The appendix is an installation guide and introduction to the Spring IDE plug-in for the Eclipse development environment. The support for editing XML files, including autocompletion features, are explained, as are the various file creation wizards, and the graphical views and editors for other configuration files.

Downloading the Code

The source code for this book is available from the Apress website (www.apress.com). The source code is provided as a complete Maven project (see Chapter 2).

Contacting the Author

I strive for accuracy and clarity, but of course I don't always attain them. If you don't understand something that I've written, you think I've made a mistake, or you think I've omitted some important material. please feel free to send a note to me directly at dave@paperstack.com.

You can read articles on Spring and Java technologies, including occasional code samples and useful libraries, on my blog at geeklondon.com.

CHAPTER 1

An Introduction to Spring

The first time I encountered Spring was when a client asked me whether I knew anything about it. I didn't and said so, but that's always my cue to go find out about a technology. Next time, or so my reasoning goes, I should at least be able to reel off a definition.

Most of the documentation I could find stressed two basic points: that Spring supported inversion of control (IOC) and that it was a lightweight framework. I found this enormously puzzling because although the various sources discussed these features, none of them addressed the question of why these features were desirable.

The situation has improved somewhat since then. Most introductions to the Spring framework do make at least a gesture toward discussing the merits of the feature set rather than merely listing it. Even so, while this chapter is my chance to impart a respect for the technical accomplishments of the Spring authors, I also intend to explain just why some of those technical features are so valuable.

Two years after having to express total ignorance of Spring, I find myself using it every day because it allows me to build applications far more productively (and enjoyably) than I could have done before. I have found working with Spring to be enormously rewarding and I hope you will too.

Frameworks

I don't think there is any hard and fast definition of what does or does not constitute a framework. My rule of thumb definition would probably be that it's a *framework* if in general it invokes your code rather than your code invoking it—but there are plenty of self-professed frameworks that fall outside my rather narrow definition.

Certainly Spring is a framework by this definition. I discuss one aspect of this in the next section, "Inversion of Control," but this is not the only sense in which Spring could be said to be a framework, and indeed it is not compulsory for you to use Spring in this way; stand-alone applications can easily take advantage of various components of Spring.

A broader sense of *framework* defines it as a structure used to solve a complex technical issue. Again Spring qualifies, though it might be better to think of it as a framework of frameworks. For example, the Hibernate Object Relational Mapping (ORM) framework provides a solution to the complex technical problem of persisting objects from your object model into a relational database. Spring provides a set of tools to aid you in integrating Hibernate with the other parts of your applications—and Hibernate is only one of many frameworks and libraries that Spring provides support for.

Lightweight, another ill-defined term, can be taken as implying the lack of a need for a Java Platform, Enterprise Edition (Java EE) component stack, as the impact on your application's memory footprint, as the impact on your application's disk (and thus download) footprint, and as the degree to which you can discard unnecessary components. I do not think that the term *lightweight* has any real value, but in all of these areas Spring excels. Indeed, to a large extent it was created as a reaction against the weight of the Java EE component stack, though it is able to take advantage of Java EE features when this is desirable.

Spring is therefore an environment within which your code can operate, a set of libraries for solving certain types of problems, and a set of libraries for assisting you in interacting with numerous other frameworks. However you define the buzzwords, Spring is a fine example of a useful framework.

Inversion of Control (IOC)

A familiar problem to application developers is creating the application glue code—code that doesn't do much other than set up preexisting components and manage the data that is being passed between them. Typically, the problems arising from this concern exhibit themselves in monolithic brittle factory classes that become dependencies for large parts of the application and are virtually impossible to test in isolation.

At its heart, Spring is primarily a framework for enabling the use of IOC (also known as *dependency injection*). This is not to diminish Spring's other features, but rather to highlight the importance of IOC in addressing the problem of tangled dependencies. In this section, I will try to explain IOC's value.

Dependency Lookup

Typical application logic traditionally does something like the following to obtain a resource:

```
Foo foo = FooFactory.getInstance();
```

Here we have obtained the resource (an instance of Foo) by invoking a static method on a singleton factory class. Alternatively, we might construct the desired resource directly:

```
Foo foo = new FooImpl();
```

Or we might look up the resource in a Java Naming and Directory Interface (JNDI) context:

```
Context initialCtx = new InitialContext();
Context environmentCtx = (Context) initCtx.lookup("java:comp/env");
Foo foo = (Foo)environmentCtx.lookup("Foo");
```

I'm sure you can think of dozens of other ways that you can acquire resources, but most of them will have two things in common: your application logic is in control of exactly what resource is acquired, and you create a hard dependency on some other class in the process. This approach is known as *dependency lookup.*

In these three examples, we create dependencies upon the FooFactory class, upon the FooImpl implementation class, and upon the various classes of the JNDI application programming interface (API).

The Problem with Dependency Lookup

You could reasonably ask why dependency lookup is a bad thing. Obviously these techniques all have value. Certainly we aren't going to give up use of the new operator anytime soon. The disadvantage arises when we choose to reuse code that has a hard dependency on one set of classes in another context where they are less appropriate.

For example, consider some application code that acquires its database Connection object by use of the DriverManager's factory methods, as is typical for a stand-alone application (see Listing 1-1).

Listing 1-1. *Acquiring Connection Resources by Using Factory Methods*

```
public void foo() {
   Class.forName("org.hsqldb.jdbcDriver");
   Connection c =
     DriverManager.getConnection("jdbc:hsqldb:timesheetDB","sa","");
   PreparedStatement ps =
     c.prepareStatement("...");
   ...
}
```

When we come to migrate this code into a web application where database resources are normally acquired by JNDI, we must modify the code. Ideally, we would keep all of the database connection acquisition logic in one place so that we need to change only one class, rather than changing all classes where the connection object is used. We can do this by providing a factory class, as shown in Listing 1-2.

Listing 1-2. *Simplifying Connection Acquisition by Using Another Factory*

```
public void foo() {
   Connection c = ConnectionFactory.getConnection();
   PreparedStatement ps =
      c.prepareStatement("...");
   ...
}
```

Alternatively we could do this by supplying the connection object to any classes that need to use it, as shown in Listing 1-3.

Listing 1-3. *Simplifying Connection Acquisition by Parameterization*

```
public FooFacility(final Connection c) {
   this.c = c;
}

private Connection c;

public void foo() {
   PreparedStatement ps =
      c.prepareStatement("...");
   ...
}
```

Of these two latter approaches, at first glance the ConnectionFactory class looks more appealing because it has a reduced footprint in our class. On the other hand, we still have a hard dependency on the external class. Our changes to ensure compatibility within different environments are certainly reduced—now we will have to amend only ConnectionFactory— but this class is still required, and in environments where there is already a strategy for connection acquisition, it will add complexity to add another class with the same responsibility. You would naturally want to replace calls to our custom ConnectionFactory with calls to the existing factory (or vice versa), but this brings us back to our original problem: having to modify code when moving our logic to a new environment.

Dependency Injection as a Solution

If we use the parameterized version of the code, we have removed the need to modify the code in any environment because we have removed the hard relationship with the classes that create the Connection object. To use the correct terminology, we have *decoupled* our class from the *dependency* required to appropriate the connection.

The problem with decoupling the logic in this way is that it potentially creates a tedious requirement to provide the connection whenever we wish to use this logic. Using the appropriate terminology, this is the problem of how to *inject* the dependency. This is exactly the problem that Spring IOC solves: it makes the problem of supplying dependencies to classes so wonderfully simple that we can take full advantage of the benefits of decoupling.

I explain in detail how you inject dependencies by using Spring and how this mechanism works internally in Chapter 3.

Dependency Injection as an Aid to Testing

I have explained how tight coupling causes problems when we want to move our application logic from one environment to another, but there is a special case of this issue that makes IOC's advantages dramatically apparent. This is the problem of unit testing.

Writing unit tests is an art in itself. The well-written test concentrates on a single component of the system and tests all of its behavior as thoroughly as possible. However, when a class is tightly coupled to other parts of the application, testing that class in isolation becomes impossible.

By encouraging loose coupling, it becomes easier to eliminate irrelevant classes from the test, often by providing mock objects in place of heavyweight implementations. I discuss unit and integration testing in more detail in Chapter 10.

An Agile Framework

A variety of successful software development techniques have become known collectively as *agile programming*. Initially having a very loose definition, agile development became codified in the "Agile Manifesto" (www.agilemanifesto.org) presented by a number of software development luminaries.

There are now several formal methodologies such as Scrum and Extreme Programming (XP) that follow agile approaches. The precise value of the full collection of techniques used is debatable, and some shops that pay lip service to agile methodologies don't follow through on all of the agile edicts. Nonetheless, the agile approach is becoming ever more popular, and even in isolation the individual techniques of agile programming are certainly proving their worth. The need to issue frequent deliverables and the encouragement of refactoring present challenges to traditional environments, where tight coupling between components makes for difficulty in achieving the rapid rate of change that Spring can accommodate easily. Spring is not in and of itsclf an *agile* framework (there's no such thing) but it does lend support to some of the agile development techniques in various ways.

The ease of testing a cleanly decoupled Spring application accommodates the Test-Driven Development (TDD) approach. Spring espouses the Don't Repeat Yourself (DRY) principle. This encourages developers to create logic once and only once. Wherever possible, boilerplate code has been abstracted away into standard helper and library classes, and there are utility classes available to encourage developers to adopt the same approach for their own implementations. Code constructed in accordance with the DRY principle makes refactoring easier, as changes to application logic are localized.

Aspect-Oriented Programming (AOP)

Aspect-oriented programming (AOP) describes an approach to a set of problems that do not fit naturally into the object-oriented programming (OOP) approach to problem solving. AOP is not particularly new, but in the Java world it is only with the introduction of tools such as AspectJ and Spring AOP that it has gained a mainstream audience.

Unfortunately, AOP introduces its own terminology, which Spring AOP has adopted for the sake of consistency with existing tools. The concepts are remarkably simple, however, even when the underlying implementation is complex.

The use of an AOP framework allows a solution to a problem to be applied before and after the invocation of various externally identified method calls. This is a gross approximation to the depth of AOP, which I discuss in far more detail in Chapter 5, but it should be sufficient for this introductory chapter.

Almost all Spring developers will want to take advantage of existing AOP libraries in Spring to apply to their own applications. The most typical example of this is the declarative transaction management library. In a conventional Java application, a service layer method's transaction management might be handled something like this:

```
public class AccountServiceImpl
    extends ServiceImpl
    implements AccountService
{
    public Account createAccount() {
        try {
            beginTransaction();
            Account account = dao.save(new Account());
            commitTransaction();
            return account;
        } catch( Exception e ) {
            rollbackTransaction();
        }
    }
}
```

With the use of declarative transaction management, the method implementation can be reduced to this:

```
@Transactional
public class AccountServiceImpl
    extends ServiceImpl
    implements AccountService
{
    public Account createAccount() {
        return dao.save(new Account());
    }
}
```

Instead of duplicating the begin/commit/rollback logic in all of our service layer implementation classes, we use a Spring AOP annotation to declare that a transaction must begin when we enter any of the implementation class's methods and that it should be committed when they complete. We also accept the default behavior that causes unchecked exceptions emitted by the method to roll back the transaction. The syntax of all this is remarkably compact.

Because Spring provides all of the AOP libraries necessary to carry out the transactional behavior identified by our annotation, no further configuration is required.

■Note I think this is a big enough deal that it's worth reiterating: a tiny annotation removes the need for any explicit transaction management anywhere else in your application.

AOP can be applied anywhere that you have a set of requirements that apply without regard to the object model across otherwise unrelated parts of your application. Indeed, functionality that addresses these concerns is essentially the definition of an *aspect*. The commonest uses of AOP are therefore in managing transactions, guaranteeing security, and providing auditing and logging information. These are all supported by existing Spring AOP libraries, to such an extent that typical Spring developers will never need to create their own AOP libraries. Even so, Chapter 5 covers the creation of simple AOP tools along with the alternative XML-based syntax and use of the AspectJ framework.

Libraries

Spring doesn't just provide a bare framework and leave other libraries to their own concerns. Instead it provides wrappers to accommodate other design philosophies within its own framework.

All of the standard parts of Java EE are supported. You can therefore manage JTA transactions, connect to databases, enforce security, send e-mail, schedule operations, manage JMX services, generate reports, write PDF files, and in fact do pretty much anything you are likely to want to do.

For the rare case that falls outside Spring's coverage, Spring is emphatically based around the use of Plain Old Java Objects (POJOs) and allows for the initialization of almost any preexisting class that can be invoked from conventional code. It is trivially easy to integrate even the most cumbersome of legacy code.

In practice, the Spring philosophy is so alluring that developers familiar with Spring are likely to add wrappers (again a variety of classes exist to assist with this) to existing code to give it a more Spring-like external appearance—when they can resist the temptation to rework the internals of the offending library.

Spring and Web Applications

In some ways, Spring was created both as an attempt to sidestep the overbearing requirements of Java EE and also to gain some of its advantages. The problem with Java EE historically was that although it provided a lot of excellent features, it was difficult to use these in isolation, forcing developers to choose between the heavyweight complex Java EE environment and simpler but limited alternatives. Spring bridges this gap by allowing developers to pick and choose the most appropriate parts of Java EE for their applications. It applies this approach to a variety of other libraries and toolkits, and adopts the same philosophy to its own internal design.

Java EE is and was primarily a platform for server programming. Spring can be used entirely independently of the server environment, but it provides strong support for server programming and particularly for web application building.

Spring MVC

My commercial exposure to the Spring framework in general arose through a specific requirement that we use the Spring Model View Controller (Spring MVC) framework to build the web component of an application, so I have something of a soft spot for it.

A Spring MVC application is cleanly divided between views, controller classes, and the model. The views are typically JSPs, though they can use a variety of other technologies. A suite of controller classes are provided that cover everything from the creation of basic forms to fully fledged "wizard" classes that allow you to walk a user through filling in a complex form. The implementation of the model is up to you, but typically consists of a service layer in turn calling into data access objects (DAOs) for persistence requirements.

As with all good frameworks, Spring MVC does not force you to use session scope to maintain state (ensuring good scalability). While the controllers take advantage of inheritance to provide most of their functionality, it is trivially easy to implement a controller interface and aggregate in existing controller behavior, allowing your own controller classes the option to aggregate or inherit external functionality. Most other web frameworks are not as liberal.

The transfer classes (form beans) in Spring MVC are conventional POJOs, and the validation framework is both POJO-based and simple to configure.

Spring Web Flow

Spring Web Flow can be seen as a complement to the existing Spring MVC framework, as it uses the existing view resolvers and a specialized controller to provide its functionality. Web Flow allows you to model your application behavior as a state machine: the application resides in various states, and events are raised to move the application between these states. That may sound a bit weird if you haven't seen this sort of model before, but it's actually a pretty well-accepted approach to designing certain types of web applications.

Web Flow allows you to design modules of your web application as complex user journeys without arbitrary end points. Whereas Spring MVC is ideal for simple linear form-based problems, Spring Web Flow is suited to more-dynamic problems. The two can be mixed and matched as appropriate.

The additional advantage of building an application by using Web Flow is the ease of design—state machines are easy to model as diagrams—combined with the fact that a Web Flow application can readily be packaged for reuse in other projects.

The web component of our example application is built using a combination of Spring MVC and Spring Web Flow so you will have an opportunity to gauge the relative merits of these two related approaches to web application design.

Spring Portlet MVC

Of specialized interest to Portlet developers is the Spring Portlet MVC framework. Portlet containers (portals) allow you to build a larger web application up from a set of smaller subcomponents that can reside together on the same web page. Portals usually provide a set of standard infrastructure capabilities such as user authentication and authorization. A typical portal is supplied with a large suite of standard portlets to allow users to read e-mail, manage content, maintain a calendar, and so on. This makes them attractive for creating in intranets or for customer-facing websites, where a set of basic services can be supplemented by a small suite of custom-written tools to provide an integrated environment without the expense and time constraint of creating an entirely bespoke system.

Spring Portlet MVC provides an exactly analogous version of the Spring MVC framework for working within a JSR 168–compliant portlet environment. Although Spring Portlet MVC builds on the JSR 168 portlet API, the differences between Spring Portlet MVC and Spring MVC are much easier to accommodate than the differences between the portlet API and the servlet API that underlie them.

In addition to minimizing the technical differences between the portlet and servlet APIs, Spring Portlet MVC provides all of the facilities to the portlet environment that Spring MVC provides to the servlet environment.

Other Frameworks

While it introduces some delightful frameworks of its own, Spring also plays nicely with existing frameworks. There is full support for the use of Apache Struts, JavaServer Faces, and Apache Tapestry in the framework. In each case, suitable classes are provided to allow you to inject dependencies into the standard implementation classes.

Where possible, several approaches are offered for users who may be working under additional constraints. For example, the Struts framework can be Spring enabled by configuring your actions using either `DelegatingRequestProcessor` or `DelegatingActionProxy`. The former allows closer integration with Spring, but the latter allows you to take advantage of Spring features without giving up any custom request processors that you may be using (Struts does not allow you to configure multiple request processors).

Similar support is available for most commonly used frameworks, and the approaches used for these transfer well to any other web framework that uses standard Java features and that provides for a modicum of extensibility.

Other Issues

A typical example of Spring's helpfully catholic perspective is in its support for creating DAO classes. Spring provides a common conceptual approach of template and helper classes that you will examine in more detail in Chapter 4. Specific classes are provided for the various database persistence tools, including plain JDBC, but also ORM tools such as Hibernate, iBATIS, and TopLink.

Security is addressed by the Acegi Spring Security component. This provides a comprehensive suite of tools for enforcing authentication and authorization in a web application. I discuss the Spring Security framework in Chapter 7.

Spring has a wealth of other features that are not specific to any one framework, but which are enormously helpful. There is support for a suite of view technologies, including traditional JSPs but also encompassing XML, PDF files, Apache Velocity, and even Microsoft Excel spreadsheets.

Support for features such as the Jakarta Commons file-upload utilities and the notoriously tricky JavaMail API turn otherwise problematic tasks into relatively simple configuration options.

Documentation

Documentation does not normally appear on the feature list of any framework, and open source tools have a mediocre reputation for their documentation. Typically, developers are more interested in writing interesting software than in explaining to the uninitiated how to take advantage of it. Spring is a breath of fresh air in this respect. The documentation for Spring itself is well written and comprehensive.

The Spring Javadoc API documentation is particularly well thought out, another happy surprise for developers too used to seeing the minimum of autogenerated API references. For example, the Javadoc for the Spring MVC framework discusses the purpose of the various classes, methods, fields, and parameters in depth, but it also contains invaluable discussion of the life cycle of the controller classes.

Spring is a formidable product, without doubt. Because it ties together such a diverse suite of libraries and other frameworks, it inevitably has some murky corners and contains some pitfalls for unwary novices. This book aims to address those issues and help you up the steeper part of Spring's learning curve. After you have bootstrapped a basic understanding of the design and philosophy of Spring, you will have a wealth of documentation and other resources available to you.

All of the documentation for the Spring framework is available from the Spring website at `http://springframework.org`, and you can get help from a thriving community of other Spring users in the forums at `http://forum.springframework.org`.

Other Tools

While Spring is primarily a set of libraries constituting a framework, I should mention the tools typically used when working with Spring, and the support that is available for them.

Maven

Spring does not require specific support from its build environment. Still, Spring's broad spectrum of support for external libraries can lure a developer into creating a project that has a complicated dependency tree. I would therefore recommend the use of a tool providing support for dependency management. For the examples in this book, I have used the Maven 2 project to manage dependencies, and it is gratifying to note that the files in the default Maven repository are well maintained for the Spring framework. Users of other dependency management tools that take advantage of Maven repositories will also benefit from this good housekeeping.

Spring Integrated Development Environment (IDE) Plug-in

Spring uses XML files for its configuration, and all current integrated development environments (IDEs) will provide basic support for maintaining correct XML syntax. Most IDEs now also provide a modicum of additional support for Spring configuration files.

The examples in this book were all built using the Java Development Tools edition of the Eclipse IDE. Eclipse does not provide innate support for Spring beyond its XML capabilities, but it is trivial to install the Spring IDE plug-in for Eclipse. This provides intelligent sensing of the attributes in bean configuration files, and a wizard for creating the contents of a basic Spring 2 project. I provide a walk-through of the basic features of this plug-in in the appendix.

Conclusion

Spring is more than the sum of its parts. Although some of the subcomponents of Spring are important projects in their own right (Spring MVC is the example that springs to mind), Spring's major contribution is that it presents a unifying concept. Spring has a definite philosophy of design, and wrappers are provided for libraries that deviate from this philosophy. To a large extent, when you have learned to use one library within the Spring API, you will have equipped yourself with a large part of the mental toolkit that is required to use all the others.

Rather than worrying about the time it will take to use a new technology, Spring developers for the most part can be confident that they will know how to configure and interact with the tools it comprises. The freedom to integrate tools into an application without the fear of spiraling complexity encourages us away from the tyranny of Not Invented Here syndrome. In short: Spring makes you more productive.

In the next chapter, you'll look at the sample application that we'll be using to illustrate the use of the Spring framework as a whole, and then in subsequent chapters I'll take you through the individual features and show you how they are used to build the application.

CHAPTER 2

■ ■ ■

Presenting the Sample Application

In this chapter, I present you with our sample application, a simple online timesheet. My aim is to present good working examples of all the topics that we discuss in this book. That is not to say that every fragment of code that you see in the text will exist somewhere in the sample application, but rather that all the techniques that I recommend will have their place in the code. In practice, a code sample is likely to be excluded only where it is illustrating a poor practice.

Rationale

I have chosen the online timesheet for the example for several reasons:

- It is a simple concept, familiar to any office worker.

- It translates well into a web-based application.

- It requires a persistent store of data.

- It requires some basic authentication and authorization.

Collectively these features allow me to showcase all of the important features of Spring, such as the web framework, the integration with the Hibernate persistence framework, and the Acegi security layer.

Architecture of the Sample Application

I have split the timesheet application into the standard set of layers shown in Figure 2-1. As well as being an uncontroversial way of slicing up an application, these layers correspond well with the suites of Spring classes that are required to build a web application.

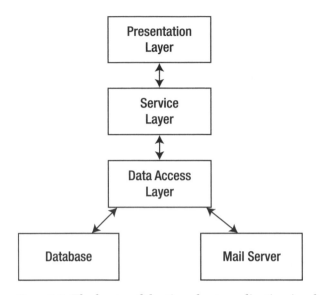

Figure 2-1. *The layers of the timesheet application implementation*

Actually the layers of Figure 2-1 present something of a mixed metaphor, as I have added two architectural components (the database and mail server) that are not normally thought of as being application layers in their own right.

The Presentation Layer

The presentation layer of the application includes all of the components that are primarily concerned with presenting the application to the user. The example application has several presentation aspects to it: the login pages, the user administration pages, and the timesheet management pages. The specific implementation can vary, and Spring is very accommodating of external standards, but for the sake of simplicity I have implemented these by using the Spring MVC and Spring Web Flow libraries for the controllers and JavaServer Pages (JSPs) to render the output (the views). The presentation layer is discussed in depth in Chapter 6.

The container for the web application that I have used in my examples is Apache Tomcat version 5.5, which is downloadable from the Apache website at http://tomcat.apache.org.

You will need to ensure that you have the Tomcat manager application installed (this is included in the default Tomcat installation) to allow the application build to manage web application deployments. You also will need to configure an administrative username and password for the manager application, usually by editing the tomcat-users.xml file in the conf subdirectory of the Tomcat installation directory.

The Service Layer

The service layer represents the business logic of the application. All operations from the presentation layer pass through the service layer. Indeed, ideally the presentation layer is a relatively thin veneer of functionality on top of the service layer. The service layer is often exposed to other external mechanisms that need to have direct access to the logic of the application—for example, an application may make the methods of all or part of the service layer available via SOAP so that third parties can create their own clients to the system.

The service layer itself is then a combination of business logic and an aggregation of necessary data access layer components. In my simple timesheet application, this means that you will see a lot of service layer methods as simple as (or simpler than) the example in Listing 2-1.

Listing 2-1. *A (Simple) Service Layer Method*

```
public void updateTimesheet(final Timesheet timesheet) {
   timesheetDao.update(timesheet);
   emailDao.sendTimesheetUpdate(timesheet);
}
```

This may seem pointless—it's natural to wonder why the two DAO method calls cannot be incorporated directly into a presentation layer method—but there are advantages. The service layer method can be exposed to the outside world without needing to reveal the existence (and implementation detail) of the two DAOs. And the method provides a simple place in which to put transactionality. If the timesheet update fails, we don't want to send the e-mail, and conversely if the e-mail cannot be sent, we should not update the timesheet.

The issues around building a business service layer and transactionality are discussed in full detail in Chapter 5.

The Data Access Layer

The data access layer is our interface with underlying data stores. The timesheet application limits these underlying components to a single database and a single mail server. This is not an unrealistic example (many real applications have exactly this structure) but there are numerous other mechanisms that could be used, such as data-queuing systems and event-logging systems.

The DAO provides an abstraction of the underlying data source. In principle, an implementation based around a relational database can be replaced with a flat-file–based implementation (or vice versa) without any impact on the functionality of the rest of the application. More realistically, a specific database could be substituted with minimal impact to the rest of the design.

The benefits around a possible substitution of implementation can be overstated; swapping out a database isn't that frequent an occurrence. The real benefit of introducing the DAO layer is the way that it constrains certain types of complexity (database operations) to small classes. This makes debugging much simpler, and this is the advantage of the layered approach in general. A bug can be readily tracked to the layer it originates in (often its characteristics will be such that it is easy to infer its origin), and the limited complexity of the layer then makes analysis of the bug much simpler.

The Database and Mail Server

The two architectural components shown in Figure 2-1 are the database and the mail server. These are applications in their own right, standing outside your Spring application implementation.

I have assumed that the mail server is available to you already. If you can send and receive e-mail, you already have access to one, and I think that is a reasonable assumption for readers of this book.

The database is another matter. You may have no database readily available or you may have several. Installing a database (let alone administrating one) can be a complex task in itself, and I have therefore decided to use the HSQL (previously known as Hypersonic) embedded database. This can be used in several modes:

- Stand-alone as a network-accessible database manager

- Embedded as an in-memory database

- Embedded as a flat-file–based database

The full documentation for the HSQL database can be obtained from the website at `http://hsqldb.sourceforge.net`.

I use the database in only the two embedded modes: in-memory for the benefit of unit tests (so that the database can be repeatedly created and destroyed without affecting subsequent tests) and as a flat-file–based database for running the example application.

Because I am using the database in embedded mode, I only need to obtain the library files in order to configure the database, and I do this by pulling it in as a Maven dependency (see the "Maven" section later in this chapter) so you don't need to explicitly download anything! If you want to use another database that's already available to you when running the example application, this is discussed in detail in Chapter 4.

Specification

You should always have a specification. Without one, you don't know exactly what you are building, and many an application goes hopelessly over budget or over deadline or both because insufficient time was spent specifying what the application actually needed to do.

That is not to say that a specification is set in stone. No project ever emerges with quite the design that the architect had in mind when he started work. The specification should be changed as its inadequacies and misconceptions become clear.

This is not a book on design, so the full-blown specification that I worked from in building the example application would be overkill. Moreover, it has some eccentric requirements, because they were bent by the need to illustrate architectural detail where the normal situation is reversed.

Given these constraints, I have limited my specification to a couple of use case scenarios explaining how a typical user might interact with the site. For information on how a real specification should be put together, I recommend reading the four-part article "Painless Functional Specifications" by the always excellent Joel Spolsky in *Joel on Software* (Apress, 2007) and on his website at `http://joelonsoftware.com`.

Scenario 1

Jane is the administrator of the company intranet site. To add a new user, John Strange, to the application, she goes to the login page and enters the readily guessable default login details (`admin/setec`). Upon logging in, she selects the Administration menu option and is presented with a list of the existing users. She selects the Add New User menu option.

On the resulting Create User page, which you can see in Figure 2-2, she sets the username (`jstrange`) and clicks Preview User. She checks that the name has been entered correctly and clicks the Save User button. Looking at the list, she can see that John's username has been added and so she chooses Logout from the main menu.

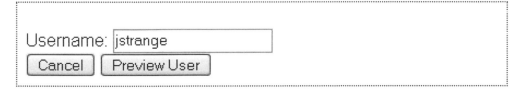

Figure 2-2. *The Create User page*

Scenario 2

John Strange is new to the company and has been asked to fill in his timesheet for his first day's work. Jane has sent him an e-mail with his login details (jstrange/password) and he enters these into the login page. Upon logging in, he is presented with the (empty) home page and chooses Manage Timesheets from the menu.

As a new user, he has no timesheets listed on this page, so he chooses Create Timesheet from the menu. This presents him with the page shown in Figure 2-3.

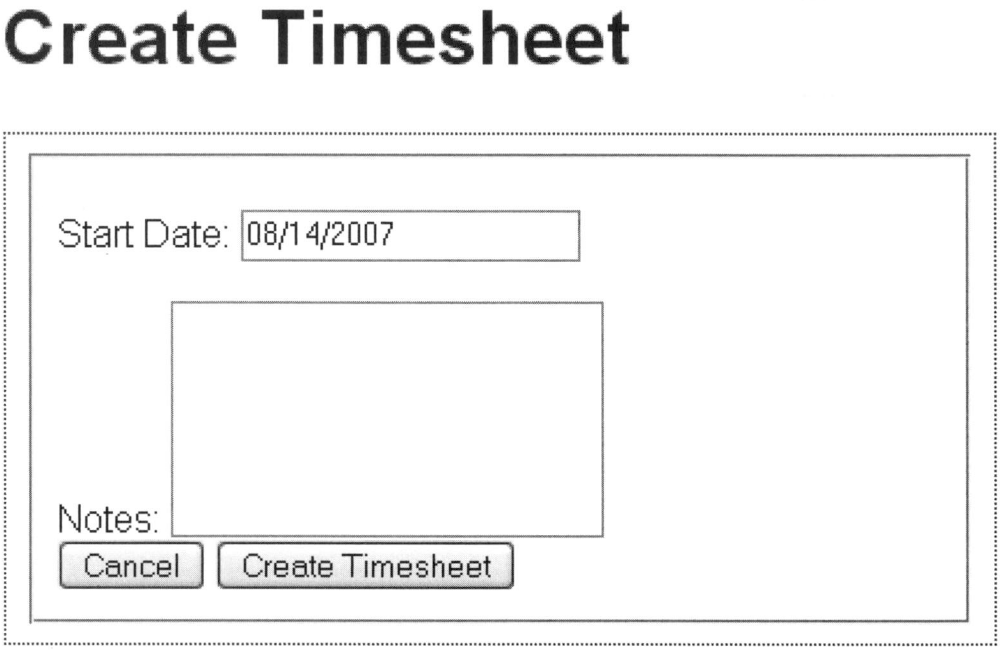

Create Timesheet

Start Date: 08/14/2007

Notes:

Cancel   Create Timesheet

Figure 2-3. *The Create Timesheet page*

He enters a note stating that this is his first timesheet and clicks the Create Timesheet button. He is returned to the Manage Timesheets page, where his timesheet now appears in the list. Selecting this timesheet, he can now see his (empty) timesheet. He selects the Add Period command in order to add his day's working details. He amends the start and finish time to match his working day (entering the office at 9 a.m. sharp and leaving at 7 p.m. in order to look keen on his first day). He adds a note explaining that this is his first day, and as he is an agency worker sets his rate to $40 an hour (standard pay). He will now see the updated view of the timesheet shown in Figure 2-4.

View Timesheet

Owner: jstrange

Timesheet# 10

Created on: 08/14/2007

Starts on: 08/14/2007

Notes:

| Home |
| Logout |
| Add Period |
| Update Timesheet |
| Delete Timesheet |

Start	Finish	Note	Rate	Type	
08/14/2007 09:00	08/14/2007 19:00	First day's work.	40	Standard	Delete Period

Figure 2-4. *The View Timesheet page*

The system returns him to the Manage Timesheet page, where he selects the link to the timesheet again and checks that his changes have been recorded correctly. After he is satisfied that they are, he chooses Logout from the menu and goes home (even though it's only 5 p.m.).

Maven

The example application project was built and managed by using the Maven 2 software project management tool. Maven provides a large number of facilities, in a sense a limitless number because it is extensible, but the important ones that we are concerned with are related to managing the build. I decided to use Maven 2 for this process primarily because it eliminates the need to include minutely detailed lists of the JAR files that must be downloaded when building an application.

Setting Up a Maven Project

Maven provides a mechanism for creating template projects with appropriate directories to be populated with code and configuration files. For example, to start a new typical Java project, you would issue the command in Listing 2-2.

Listing 2-2. *Creating an Archetypical Java Project*

```
mvn archetype:create -DgroupId=com.apress.timesheets
  -DartifactId=timesheets-core
```

Running this command then creates the set of directories shown in Listing 2-3.

Listing 2-3. *The Files Contained Within the Project*

```
./timesheets-core/pom.xml
./timesheets-core/src/main/java/com/apress/timesheets/App.java
./timesheets-core/src/test/java/com/apress/timesheets/AppTest.java
```

These represent the configuration of the project, an example application, and an example unit test for the application. By far the most important of these is the pom.xml file containing the project configuration (*POM* stands for *Project Object Model*).

If you are more familiar with the Apache Ant tool, you may make the mistake of assuming that the pom.xml file is equivalent to a build.xml file used by Ant and that the two tools therefore serve the same purpose. This would be misleading, however. The two tools have some analogous features, but their mechanisms are different. For example, an Ant build file contains explicit definitions of everything that is to be done to perform a build, whereas a POM file omits everything except the *differences* from the default behavior.

The POM file shown in Listing 2-4 contains no explicit instructions on what should happen when the project is built, but it contains sufficient information to build the default project generated by the Maven archetype command.

Listing 2-4. *The pom.xml File Generated by the Command in Listing 2-1*

```
<project
xmlns="http://maven.apache.org/POM/4.0.0"
xmlns:xsi="http://www.w3.org/2001/XMLSchema-instance"
xsi:schemaLocation="http://maven.apache.org/POM/4.0.0 ➥
http://maven.apache.org/maven-v4_0_0.xsd">
  <modelVersion>4.0.0</modelVersion>
  <groupId>com.apress.timesheets</groupId>
  <artifactId>timesheets-core</artifactId>
  <packaging>jar</packaging>
  <version>1.0-SNAPSHOT</version>
  <name>timesheets-core</name>
  <url>http://maven.apache.org</url>
```

```
  <dependencies>
    <dependency>
      <groupId>junit</groupId>
      <artifactId>junit</artifactId>
      <version>3.8.1</version>
      <scope>test</scope>
    </dependency>
  </dependencies>
</project>
```

The only build-related configuration detail is related to the type of file that should be produced by a full build. In Listing 2-4, this will be a JAR file called `timesheets-core-1.0-SNAPSHOT.jar` (composed from the `artifactId`, `version`, and `packaging` elements of the POM file).

To generate this file, the install target should be invoked with the command `mvn install`. The output of this target will then be installed into the local repository. To perform a build from scratch, you can add the clean target thus: `mvn clean install`.

The most important section of the file is the `dependencies` element containing a list of dependency elements. These are the libraries that your application will utilize. So, in the generated code there is a dependency on the JUnit library at version 3.8.1 that will be used only when running unit tests (that is, it will not be included in the output of any builds). Dependencies will be downloaded from the repositories available to your build, starting with the local repository; and if not available from there, an attempt to download from the remote repository will occur (or any other repositories you may add to the POM configuration).

In the example application, you will not need to specify the contents of the POM files because they have already been provided for you. However, if you want to build on the examples or create an application from scratch, you should spend some time reading about the Maven build tool on the Maven website at `http://maven.apache.org`.

The Maven Repository

Repositories are configurable, and by default you will be using two. One is the online repository at the ibiblio archive, and the other is a local repository on the file system. By configuring entries in the POM files, you can remove these and/or add others.

The purpose of a repository is to hold libraries, or rather build artifacts that are typically JAR libraries. The local repository is created when you first run the Maven tool and is typically stored in a directory called `.m2` within your home directory. The period prefixing it is a Unix convention that causes the directory to be omitted from normal directory listings, and the *m2* stands for *Maven 2*. So, for example, on my Linux and Windows workstations, these directories are, respectively, as follows:

```
/home/dcminter/.m2
C:\Documents and Settings\Dave Minter\.m2
```

The remote repository serves as a consistent location from which to obtain library files. For example, a tool such as Hibernate will use dozens of other libraries: XML parsing libraries, logging libraries, code generation libraries, and so on and so forth. Each of these has its own packaging conventions, its own website, and its own versioning discipline. Maven's repositories are standardized, allowing the download of a particular library version to be automated, and they often contain additional information identifying the library's own dependencies.

You can browse through the contents of the ibiblio repository (the default remote repository) on the web at http://mirrors.ibiblio.org/pub/mirrors/maven2/.

The local repository serves several purposes. It acts as a cache, avoiding the need to load files from the remote site every time you perform a build. It allows you to store libraries in one place instead of copying them into every project that you are working on (and thus keeping the project itself uncluttered). Last, it acts as a store for the output of your own builds, allowing you to avoid the need to copy JAR files between projects.

The local repository directory is managed by the Maven tool. You do not normally have to add or remove files directly—with one exception. The standard place to store settings that are unique to your machine is the settings.xml file in this directory. Typically this might contain the connection details for your database, or paths to development servers.

Obtaining Maven

Maven can be downloaded from the Apache Maven website at http://maven.apache.org as a zip file. You will need to unzip this onto the local file system and put the unzipped package's bin directory into your command path. If you do not already have a JAVA_HOME environment variable pointing to your JDK install directory, you will need to add one. Maven commands are always issued as parameters to the mvn command (a batch file and shell script are provided in the Maven bin directory, so you will be able to use the same command on Unix and Windows platforms regardless).

Downloading, Configuring, and Building the Sample Application

You can download the source code for the example application as a zip archive from the Source Code/Download area of the Apress website at http://apress.com/book/view/1590596854. Unpack this into a suitable directory. The root timesheets folder contains the files and folders listed in Table 2-1.

Table 2-1. *Files and Folders in the Source Code Archive*

Name	Description
pom.xml	Configures Maven to build the six subprojects.
repository	Contains some library files that are not available on the public repository sites and that will not initially be available from your local repository. By specifying this directory as an *additional* repository, we remove the need to explicitly download and install JARs into your local repository (in the .m2 directory).
timesheets-aop	Contains the examples of AOP programming from Chapter 5.
timesheets-client	Contains the client code for the remoting examples in Chapter 9.
timesheets-core	Contains the core components of the example application, including the DAO implementation (Chapter 4), the service layer (Chapter 5), and various interfaces.
timesheets-coupling	Contains some examples from Chapter 3.
timesheets-email	Contains the e-mail examples from Chapter 8.
timesheets-webapp	Contains the web application itself (Chapter 6), much of the security configuration (Chapter 7), and the server-side remoting examples (Chapter 9).

To build the web application and deploy it to your web server, you will need to provide Maven with some specific configuration details by creating or modifying your settings.xml file. Listing 2-5 shows the entries to provide.

Listing 2-5. *The settings.xml Configuration File with Some Placeholder Values*

```
<?xml version="1.0"?>
<settings xmlns="http://maven.apache.org/POM/4.0.0"
    xmlns:xsi="http://www.w3.org/2001/XMLSchema-instance"
    xsi:schemaLocation="http://maven.apache.org/POM/4.0.0
                        http://maven.apache.org/xsd/settings-1.0.0.xsd">
    <profiles>
        <profile>
            <id>standard-config</id>
            <properties>
                <timesheet-smtp-server>
                    smtp.example.com
                </timesheet-smtp-server>
                <timesheet-mail-sender>
                    timesheets@example.com
                </timesheet-mail-sender>
```

```
            <timesheet-mail-recipient>
                test@example.com
            </timesheet-mail-recipient>
            <timesheet-context-path>
                /timesheet
            </timesheet-context-path>
            <timesheet-tomcat-manager-url>
                http://localhost:8080/manager
            </timesheet-tomcat-manager-url>
          </properties>
        </profile>
    </profiles>
    <servers>
      <server>
        <id>timesheet</id>
        <username>admin</username>
        <password>adminpassword</password>
      </server>
    </servers>
    <activeProfiles>
        <activeProfile>standard-config</activeProfile>
    </activeProfiles>
</settings>
```

You will need to change the two lines shown in bold in Listing 2-5. These are, respectively, an SMTP server to use when the application sends e-mail, the recipient of the e-mails sent by the application server, and the administrative username for the manager application on your Tomcat server.

Some of the other values in this file assume that you are using the default application configuration. If you are not, you will need to modify the appropriate entries. For example, if you were running your Tomcat server on port 80 instead of port 8080, you would need to alter the value of the timesheet-tomcat-manager-url element from http:// localhost:8080/manager to http://localhost:80/manager or http://localhost/manager.

With the settings file configured, you can build the source code by issuing the command mvn install in the root timesheets directory. With your Tomcat server running, you can install the web application by using the command mvn tomcat:deploy and can uninstall it by using the command mvn tomcat:undeploy.

Eclipse

If you want to work on the code in the example application from Eclipse, you can generate suitable configuration files by running the command mvn eclipse:eclipse from the directory containing the top-level POM file. This will set up the `.project` and `.classpath` files within the project, and you will then be able to import the Maven projects into Eclipse. Note that you will need to set the `M2_REPO` classpath variable in Eclipse. This can be configured by using the Control Panel reached by choosing the Window ➤ Preferences ➤ Java ➤ Build Path ➤ Classpath Variables menu option. Figure 2-5 shows the resulting dialog box.

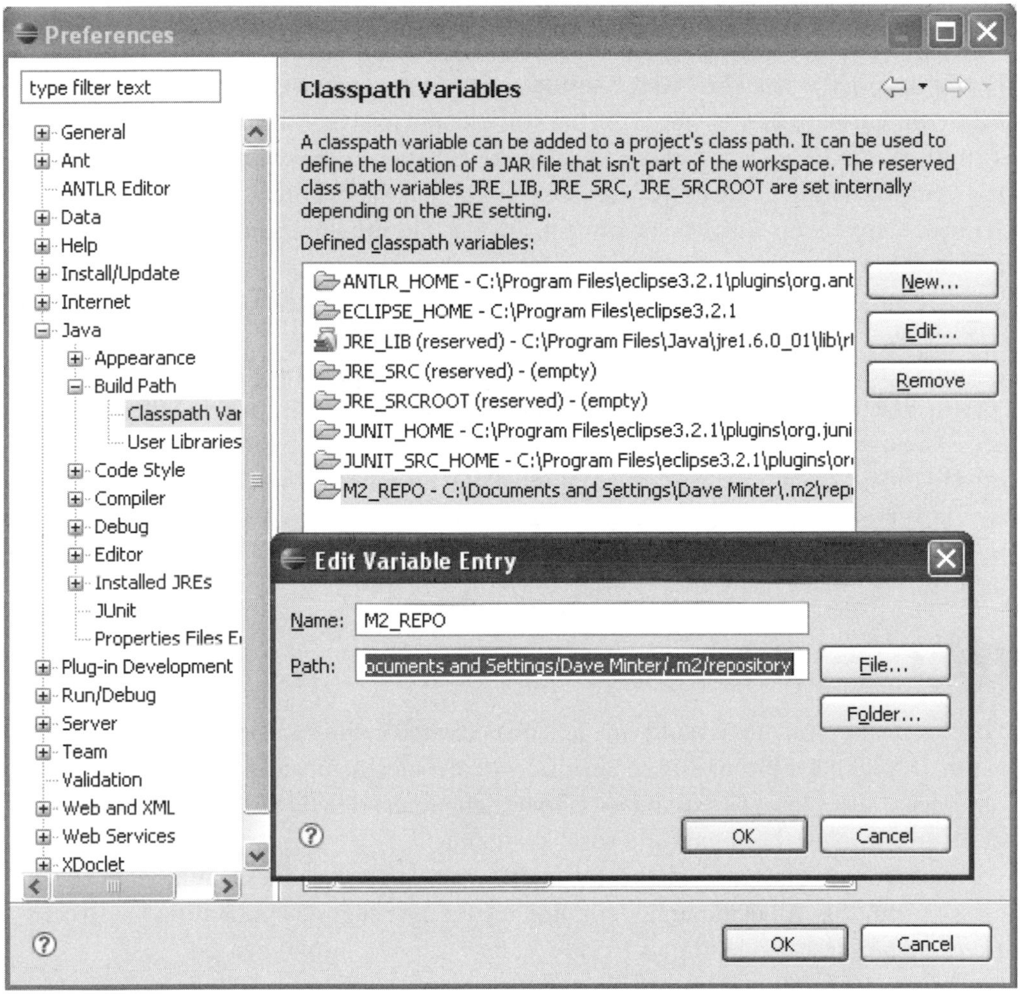

Figure 2-5. *Configuring the Maven repository classpath variable in Eclipse*

There is no need to manually add libraries to the Eclipse classpath, and indeed this should be avoided; add libraries to the `pom.xml` file and regenerate the Eclipse configuration as necessary.

Configuration Files

For the most part, the Spring framework is configured by using XML files. Some of these files will be familiar; the deployment descriptor (web.xml) of a Java EE application is something you will certainly have encountered before. Standard properties files (actually resource bundles) are used to manage error messages. Another properties file is used to configure the Log4J error-logging package.

The real meat of Spring is divided between the implementation classes discussed throughout this book and the XML files that are typically used to configure them. I discuss these configuration files as they arise, but you will find the basic discussion of configuring Spring beans in Chapter 3, and I recommend that you make sure you have a good grip on that material before trying to work on the content of other chapters.

Relative to the top-level Maven project, the Java EE configuration files are managed in the following directory:

```
timesheets-webapp\src\main\webapp\WEB-INF
```

The contents of this directory are copied to the Java EE WEB-INF directory when the WAR file is built. The rest of the configuration files (aside from the pom.xml files themselves) are retained in the \src\main\resources directory of each of the web projects. Most of the files related to the configuration of the timesheet example application are retained in the web application project, while the ones in the core project are mostly those used to illustrate the stand-alone examples of the next chapter.

Tests

When performing a Maven build, any unit tests created in the appropriate directories will be run. By making the unit tests an intrinsic part of a successful build rather than a related but independent component, the developer is encouraged to fix tests rather than letting them atrophy after the initial suite has been built.

Creating useful unit tests can be demanding, but Spring provides a number of classes to assist with this. All of the major components in the example application have corresponding unit tests, and Chapter 10 looks at how these are implemented.

The Web Application

Not all Spring applications are web applications, but most are. The example application is no exception. With Tomcat installed and the example application running, most of your interactions with it will be via the web browser.

I have chosen to build a simple but clean web interface by using HTML for the content and cascading style sheets (CSS) to control the presentation of the content. As with most of the other design decisions in this application, it allows me to concentrate on the Spring-specific concerns, but it is not the only way to go.

■**Note** The administrative username and password for the example web application are `admin` and `setec`, respectively, as indicated in the "Specification" section of this chapter. These are automatically created in the HSQL database when the application is first started, so you won't need to run any database scripts to get up and running.

Although you can certainly build Spring-based applications that use Ajax or Macromedia Flash in the browser, these presentation details do not usually make much difference to the implementation of the rest of the site and are therefore not addressed here. However, I do show some examples of remote clients to the Spring application's service layer in Chapter 9.

Conclusion

In this chapter, I have introduced you to the example application and some of the tools that you should familiarize yourself with in order to work with the examples in this book. In the next chapter, I explain the fundamental concepts of the Spring framework itself.

■ ■ ■

CHAPTER 3

The Heart of Spring: Inversion of Control

Generally, when you are writing code, your class will accumulate dependencies. Typically, you will use dozens of other classes: the primitive wrapper classes, the collection classes, and so on. Some of these will be as general as `String` or `Integer`, and others will be domain specific.

For the most part, nothing changes with inversion of control. The internal implementation details of your classes should look much the same before and after. However, if your class has a dependency on a particular external class that could reasonably have alternative implementations, or if a class represents data that you might reasonably want to change at some future date, inversion of control frameworks such as Spring allow you to supply these dependencies at a later date. Because you are providing the dependencies from outside the class instead of acquiring them directly, this form of inversion of control is also known as *dependency injection (DI)*.

Spring doesn't do any magic here—you still need to supply reference variables with which to manipulate these external dependencies—but it does move the configuration details of these dependencies from compile-time to runtime.

Benefits and Disadvantages of DI

In principle, you don't need a framework to inject dependencies into your code; you can do this from code. In practice, however, most applications built by using inversion of control use a framework of some type to carry out the dependency injection. Typically, as with Spring, these read configuration information and then use the Java reflection API or bytecode manipulation to invoke the appropriate methods on your code to inject the dependencies.

Although this behavior is not innate in the dependency injection approach, it is so widespread that it might as well be. Unfortunately, it leads directly to the one real disadvantage that containers such as Spring have over hard-coding of dependencies: that they lose some of the advantages of *static* type checking. The configuration information will not be read until runtime; therefore, any incompatible type information given in the configuration will not cause errors to be produced until runtime.

If you are worried by this sudden loss of an important advantage of Java development, I can reassure you. This is not as big a deal as you might think. When I first encountered Spring, I was very resistant to the dynamic type checking aspect of it. However, experience proved to me that it was not the awful design flaw that I at first took it for. In practice, in Spring this disadvantage is ameliorated by the tendency for the configuration information to be processed as early as possible in the life cycle of a Spring-based application. Java is a *strongly* typed language, so inappropriate casts will usually cause a conspicuous and immediate application failure. That in turn means that a reasonable minimum of testing in your development infrastructure will allow you to detect most type inconsistencies at build-time, which is very nearly as good as compile-time for most purposes. Additionally, tools such as the Spring IDE (discussed in the appendix) provide features to perform type validation during the development process.

TYPE SYSTEMS

Developers are sometimes hazy about the distinctions between static and strong typing, probably because the specific terminology is unimportant unless you are frequently migrating between languages using other approaches to typing.

A strongly typed language such as Java does not allow operations to be performed at runtime on variables of the wrong type. For example, Java does not allow an Integer reference to be assigned to a String variable. A weakly typed language would perform an implicit type conversion, allowing the assignment.

A statically typed language such as Java determines all (or as many as possible) type incompatibilities at runtime and will not compile until these are eliminated. A dynamically typed language does not perform any type checking until runtime.

There are a few other minor disadvantages to Spring as a specific framework for dependency injection. The XML-based configuration files typically used can become confusing if they are not thoughtfully maintained. Expressing relationships between Java components in XML sometimes feels inelegant. The extensive use of reflection to inject dependencies can make debugging more complex. These issues are specific to Spring's implementation, not to DI itself, but the use of Spring as an implementation more than compensates for these.

Coupling

The big win in using dependency injection is that it allows you to make your applications loosely coupled. That is to say, any one class of your implementation will tend not to have any dependencies on any other class's specific implementation.

You will still have dependencies on the type system that you're establishing in your application, of course, but loose coupling encourages the use of programming to interfaces rather than to abstract or concrete implementations.

Tight Coupling

Rather than talking in abstract terms, I will show you an example of some tightly coupled code to illustrate these concerns (see Listing 3-1).

Listing 3-1. *A Minimal Tightly Coupled Component*

```
package com.apress.coupling;

public class TightlyCoupled {
    private Transport transport = new SmtpImpl();

    public void sendMessage() {
        transport.send();
    }
}
```

This code is a little contrived in its simplicity, but it reflects a real-world scenario in which tight coupling can cause some problems. The transport mechanism to be used by this class is obviously SMTP. The implementation has been hard-coded into the class and cannot be changed except by recompilation. This leads to two major concerns: testing and reusability.

A unit test written for this class cannot readily separate the behavior of the TightlyCoupled class from the behavior of SmtpImpl class. If we encounter a bug, narrowing down its location will be more difficult. Depending on the contents of SmtpImpl, we may have to set up a mail server dedicated to the test and write code to determine whether the e-mail was transmitted successfully. Our unit test has become an integration test.

Because the TightlyCoupled implementation has the SmtpImpl implementation hard-coded, the SmtpImpl transport cannot readily be replaced it if it becomes necessary to use a different transport (for example, SOAP) for whatever content is to be transmitted. This necessarily reduces the reusability of the class in other situations.

Loose Coupling

Loosely coupled code allows the major dependencies to be supplied from external code. Again, I'll give a simple example of a class that has a loose coupling with its dependency (see Listing 3-2).

Listing 3-2. *A Minimal Loosely Coupled Component*

```
package com.apress.coupling;

public class LooselyCoupled {
    private Transport transport;

    public LooselyCoupled(final Transport transport) {
        this.transport = transport;
    }

    public void sendMessage() {
        transport.send();
    }
}
```

Again this code is somewhat contrived, but it does illustrate clearly the breaking of the dependency on the specific transport implementation. By allowing the implementation to be passed via the constructor, we allow alternative implementations to be passed in. By breaking the tight coupling, we have also removed the hindrances to the development of external tests and reusability.

For our testing, a mock object can be supplied to the constructor, allowing us to test that the appropriate method call is made without needing any of the underlying infrastructure associated with the real transport implementations.

For reusability, we can swap out the SMTP implementation for a SOAP, RMI, or any other suitable transport.

The only notable disadvantage to the loose coupling approach, as illustrated in Listing 3-2, is a slight increase in the verbosity of the resulting class implementation, mostly deriving from the demands of the JavaBean specification when adding properties to classes.

Knowing When to Stop

Not all implementation details need to be exposed to the outside world, even when creating an application to run within the Spring framework. Only dependencies that you might want to substitute in order to test the component in isolation are likely to be candidates for access in this way. Listing 3-3 shows a class with two candidate dependencies.

Listing 3-3. *A Simple Implementation with Two Dependencies*

```
package com.apress.coupling;

import java.util.SortedSet;
import java.util.TreeSet;
```

```java
public class Mailinglist {
   private SortedSet<String> addresses = new TreeSet<String>();
   private Transport transport = new SmtpImpl();

   public void addAddress(final String address) {
      addresses.add(address);
   }

   public void send() {
      for( final String address : addresses) {
         transport.send(address);
      }
   }
}
```

In Listing 3-3, our implementation contains a dependency on a specific Transport and a dependency on a specific SortedSet. It would be reasonable to assume that both of these dependencies should be provided via injection. In practice, however, I would be inclined to inject only the Transport implementation. The Transport implementation is a good candidate because of the following:

- It is likely to be a part of our own code base and thus itself a candidate for unit tests.

- It is reasonable to foresee a circumstance in which we would want to use an alternative message transport.

- It is likely that the implementation itself has a substantial set of dependencies on other classes.

- It is likely that the SmtpImpl implementation requires additional infrastructure to support it.

In my view, the SortedSet implementation is not a good candidate for several reasons:

- TreeSet is a part of the standard class library available in the JDK, and thus unlikely to be a candidate for unit tests.

- We are unlikely to use an alternative implementation of SortedSet unless we are involved in minute performance-related debugging concerns.

- TreeSet will have no dependencies beyond the JDK itself. The JDK is generally assumed to be correct unless proven otherwise and does not require its own unit tests.

Adding the specific set implementation to the API here would provide very little advantage in return for the extra complexity added to our `MailingList` class implementation.

Of course, there are possible counterarguments even for this scenario, but in the end the choice of when to make a dependency injectable resides with the developer. My advice is to choose whatever approach will make your unit tests easiest to write, and then refactor your code as it proves appropriate. Although this won't give you the correct answer every time, it will at least be easy to change your architecture without needing to substantially rework your unit tests, which will in turn reduce the frustration involved in changing APIs and will keep your code clean and the bug count low.

The Need for a Framework

The framework is not an absolute requirement of dependency injection. Taking our loosely coupled example from Listing 3-2, it is obvious that the injection of the dependencies can be carried out from conventional code.

Indeed, as Listing 3-4 shows, this is the sort of code you will have written frequently. Dependency injection is not some strange abstract new technique; it is one of the normal tools of the developer.

Listing 3-4. *Dependency Injection from Conventional Code*

```
final Transport smtp = new SmtpImpl();
final LooselyCoupled lc1 = new LooselyCoupled(smtp);
lc1.sendMessage();

final Transport soap = new SoapImpl();
final LooselyCoupled lc2 = new LooselyCoupled(soap);
lc2.sendMessage();
```

In some ways, this is one of the attractive features of dependency injection. You do not have to learn a completely new programming style in order to get the associated advantages; you just have to be a little more disciplined in selecting how and when to apply this technique.

Nonetheless, we do in practice use frameworks, so it is reasonable to ask what these offer over and above the benefits available from the kind of hard-coded approach used in Listing 3-4.

The Container

The basic container for your Spring application is a `BeanFactory`. As the name implies, this is a class that is responsible for manufacturing bean instances and then configuring their

dependencies. A Spring bean can be any Java object, although generally we will be refer-
ring to standard Java beans.

Depending on the bean definition information retained by the bean factory, the beans
it instantiates may be created on demand, or may be shared among all clients of the factory.
Table 3-1 shows the methods available on classes implementing the BeanFactory interface.

Table 3-1. *BeanFactory Methods*

Method	Description
boolean containsBean(String name)	Determines whether the factory contains a bean with the given name.
String[] getAliases(String name)	Determines the alternative names (aliases) for a bean with the given name.
Object getBean(String name)	Obtains an instance of the bean with the given name from the factory. This may be a new instance or a shared instance.
Object getBean(String name, Class requiredType)	Obtains an instance of the bean with the given name and type from the factory. This is used by the auto-wiring feature described in the "Autowiring" section of this chapter.
Class getType(String name)	Determines the type of a bean with a given name.
boolean isPrototype(String name)	Determines whether the bean definition is a proto-type. A prototype is a named set of bean definition information that can be used to abbreviate the configuration of a "real" bean definition. If a bean definition is a prototype, it cannot be instantiated with a call to getBean().
boolean isSingleton(String name)	Determines whether calls to getBean() for the named bean will return a new instance with every call, or a single shared instance (a singleton instance).
boolean isTypeMatch(String name, Class targetType)	Determines whether the named bean matches the provided type—essentially determines whether a call to getBean(String,Class) would be successful.

The implementation of the factory (how it actually goes about acquiring the instances
and configuring their dependencies) is not really our problem. As long as we can acquire
a bean factory that materializes suitable beans, we need inquire no further. The limited
set of methods available should help to illustrate the fact that a BeanFactory really is a
container; the methods provided to you are exclusively about querying the factory about
its contents and obtaining items from it. Listing 3-5 shows the instantiation, configuration, and use of a BeanFactory implementation purely from code.

Listing 3-5. *Manually Constructing a Bean Factory*

```
// Establish the factory to
// contain the bean definitions
final DefaultListableBeanFactory bf =
new DefaultListableBeanFactory();

// Register the transport implementations
bf.registerBeanDefinition("smtp",
        new RootBeanDefinition(SmtpImpl.class,true));
bf.registerBeanDefinition("soap",
        new RootBeanDefinition(SoapImpl.class,true));

// Register and configure the SMTP example as
// a bean definition
BeanDefinitionBuilder builder = null;
builder = BeanDefinitionBuilder.
   rootBeanDefinition(LooselyCoupled.class);
builder = builder.setSingleton(true);
builder = builder.addConstructorArgReference("smtp");
bf.registerBeanDefinition("looseSmtp",builder.getBeanDefinition());

// Register and configure the SOAP example as
// a bean definition
builder = BeanDefinitionBuilder.
   rootBeanDefinition(LooselyCoupled.class);
builder = builder.setSingleton(true);
builder = builder.addConstructorArgReference("soap");
bf.registerBeanDefinition("looseSoap",builder.getBeanDefinition());

// Instantiate the smtp example and invoke it
final LooselyCoupled lc1 = (LooselyCoupled)bf.getBean("looseSmtp");
lc1.sendMessage();

// Instantiate the soap example and invoke it
final LooselyCoupled lc2 = (LooselyCoupled)bf.getBean("looseSoap");
lc2.sendMessage();
```

The first question that would tend to spring to mind after reading through Listing 3-5 and comparing it to Listing 3-4 is, "Why would I *ever* want to do something so ungainly?" You wouldn't, of course. Listing 3-5 is purely an illustration of what goes on under the covers of the framework. You might use a few of these classes if you were extending part of the framework itself, but most developers will never (or at most rarely) need to touch upon BeanDefinitionBuilder and the like. I will show you how the equivalent Spring configuration would really be defined in the discussion of Listing 3-7 later in this chapter.

Listing 3-5 does illustrate some important parts of the architecture that you will be working with, however, so it is worth taking the time to understand what is involved here.

The first line of the application establishes a DefaultListableBeanFactory instance. This is a bean factory that provides no direct assistance in preparing the bean definition information. The developer must programmatically assign all the bean definition information:

```
final DefaultListableBeanFactory bf = new DefaultListableBeanFactory();
```

The next block of the implementation creates two new bean definitions for the transport implementation classes. This is metadata about the implementations, not instances of the implementations themselves. We declare that two beans should be available from the factory, we specify the implementation classes that define them, and we specify that they are both singletons (the second parameter of the RootBeanDefinition constructor). Multiple calls to the factory's getBean() method for the bean named smtp will only ever return one instance of the SmtpImpl class:

```
bf.registerBeanDefinition("smtp",
        new RootBeanDefinition(SmtpImpl.class,true));
bf.registerBeanDefinition("soap",
        new RootBeanDefinition(SoapImpl.class,true));
```

We then configure two bean definitions for one implementation class. These are configured similarly but not identically:

```
BeanDefinitionBuilder builder = null;
builder = BeanDefinitionBuilder.
    rootBeanDefinition(LooselyCoupled.class);
builder = builder.setSingleton(true);
builder = builder.addConstructorArgReference("smtp");
bf.registerBeanDefinition("looseSmtp",builder.getBeanDefinition());
```

Both are definitions for the LooselyCoupled class, both are defined as singletons, but the constructors are defined as taking different *bean definitions* for their parameters:

```
builder = BeanDefinitionBuilder.
    rootBeanDefinition(LooselyCoupled.class);
builder = builder.setSingleton(true);
builder = builder.addConstructorArgReference("soap");
bf.registerBeanDefinition("looseSoap",builder.getBeanDefinition());
```

I have chosen my wording carefully here. We have not passed anything to the constructor of the class; we have merely specified the definitions of these beans (looseSmtp and looseSoap) in terms of the named definitions of the earlier smtp and soap beans:

```
final LooselyCoupled lc1 = (LooselyCoupled)bf.getBean("looseSmtp");
lc1.sendMessage();

// ...

final LooselyCoupled lc2 = (LooselyCoupled)bf.getBean("looseSoap");
lc2.sendMessage();
```

Only when the factory has been fully populated with all of the relevant bean definitions do we use it to materialize actual objects. These are normal Java objects quite indistinguishable from the objects returned from the calls to the new operators in Listing 3-4.

XML Configuration

Although a Spring application can in principle be configured in any number of different ways, XML configuration files are by far the most common approach. Indeed, for most developers, the set of XML files used to configure the factory for a Spring project and the BeanFactory instance itself are virtually synonymous. The XML is the representation of the factory that will be available to you at runtime, so this is not a bad way of thinking of them, but do bear in mind that it is a useful approximation to the reality of the situation.

Ultimately, we need to use a language of some sort to configure our dependencies. Traditionally, this has been the Java programming language itself, occasionally resorting to properties files when the problems of tight coupling became too painful. XML files offer us a better balance of flexibility, readability, verbosity, and expressiveness.

Something to remember in particular is that there is no 1:1 correspondence between factories and XML files. It is entirely possible (and normal) to use multiple files to configure a single factory, or to use a single file to instantiate several discrete factories (though this is unusual).

Listing 3-6 represents the same configuration information that we painstakingly hardcoded in Listing 3-5 of the previous section.

Listing 3-6. *A Complete but Simple XML Spring Configuration File*

```
<?xml version="1.0" encoding="UTF-8"?>
<beans
   xmlns="http://www.springframework.org/schema/beans"
   xmlns:xsi="http://www.w3.org/2001/XMLSchema-instance"
   xsi:schemaLocation=
     "http://www.springframework.org/schema/beans
      http://www.springframework.org/schema/beans/spring-beans-2.0.xsd">

   <bean id="smtp" class="com.apress.coupling.SmtpImpl" />
```

```
    <bean id="soap" class="com.apress.coupling.SoapImpl" />

    <bean id="looseSmtp" class="com.apress.coupling.LooselyCoupled">
        <constructor-arg ref="smtp" />
    </bean>

    <bean id="looseSoap" class="com.apress.coupling.LooselyCoupled">
        <constructor-arg ref="soap" />
    </bean>
</beans>
```

This is still quite wordy, but when you discount some of the boilerplate and redundancy of the XML format itself, you can see that this is a much closer approximation to the simplicity of Listing 3-4. In fact, in some ways we have already started to see some of the power of the Spring configuration approach.

By default, XML bean definitions describe singletons (this can be overridden by use of the scope attribute on the bean element). Listing 3-4 uses the transport implementations only once, but if we did so multiple times, we would have to write a suitable singleton container for each of the implementations. Here Spring provides this out of the box.

Listing 3-7 shows how we can create a factory from the configuration file shown in Listing 3-6, and one way that the appropriate beans can be extracted from the factory and methods invoked upon them.

Listing 3-7. *Creating a Spring Bean Factory from an XML File and Pulling Beans from It*

```
final BeanFactory bf =
    new ClassPathXmlApplicationContext("exampleContext.xml");

final LooselyCoupled c1 =
    (LooselyCoupled)bf.getBean("looseSmtp");
c1.sendMessage();

final LooselyCoupled c2 =
    (LooselyCoupled)bf.getBean("looseSoap");
c2.sendMessage();
```

This extraction of the bean by name in this example is actually dependency lookup rather than dependency injection. A stand-alone application would generally extract at most one bean by dependency lookup, and this in turn would be configured with the rest of the dependencies required over the application's lifetime. A web application would usually be configured from a servlet provided as a part of the Spring library, which would carry out this lookup for us.

Autowiring

In Listing 3-5, we defined the relationships between the beans explicitly in terms of their names. There is an alternative. Some Spring bean factories are capable of something known as *autowiring*. Here a bean's dependencies are not explicitly stated. Instead, the container will automatically determine the appropriate dependencies to inject.

This sounds pretty clever, but in fact the mechanism used to determine which beans to inject into which dependency is quite straightforward. The properties available to be set on a bean can be determined by using normal Java reflection at runtime. You can choose to perform the autowiring on the basis of the property name, in which case a property called session would be populated from a bean definition also called session. You can alternatively choose to perform the autowiring on the basis of the property type—in which case a method called setFoo that took a Session property would be assigned the first bean defined as having type Session. It really is that simple. An additional mode is defined that first tries to set the dependencies by name, and then resorts to setting them by type if no suitably named bean can be found.

The code in Listing 3-8 shows a configuration of our LooselyCoupled class with the SMTP transport implementation. The LooselyCoupled class is configured to use autowiring of the constructor (see Table 3-2). There is no need to give the transport an id attribute, because the name will not be needed to inject the attribute.

Listing 3-8. *A Factory Configuration Using Autowiring*

```
<bean class="com.apress.coupling.SmtpImpl" />
<bean class="com.apress.coupling.LooselyCoupled" autowire="constructor"/>
```

Listing 3-9 shows that beans can readily be extracted from the factory by type, but the usage is necessarily less compact because a request for a bean of a particular type is not guaranteed to return a single instance. There could in principle be a dozen beans of type LooselyCoupled, all configured with different names.

Listing 3-9. *Extracting a Bean from the Factory by Type*

```
final Collection<LooselyCoupled> beans
    = (Collection<LooselyCoupled>)
        ctx.getBeansOfType(LooselyCoupled.class).values();

for( final LooselyCoupled bean : beans ) {
    bean.sendMessage();}
```

The benefit of autowiring is that it reduces the verbosity of the configuration, but I don't personally feel that this is a big enough advantage to compensate for some of the issues that arise from its use.

Table 3-2. *Permitted Values for the Autowire Attribute*

Attribute Value	Description
no	Autowiring is disabled (the default).
byName	Autowiring is carried out by locating beans that are named by using the id attribute and that have the same name as the properties to be set on the target bean.
byType	Autowiring is carried out by locating beans of the same type as the properties to be set on the target bean.
constructor	Autowiring is carried out by using beans of the same types as the constructor's parameters.
autodetect	Equivalent to byType if the target bean has a default constructor, or to constructor otherwise. byType is used when a constructor exists because constructor parameter names are not retained at runtime and therefore cannot be determined by reflection.

The problem with autowiring is that it makes the relationship between the beans and their dependencies completely implicit. This can make diagnosing configuration problems quite difficult (it is relatively easy to assign the wrong dependency without having any conspicuous entry in the configuration files to indicate this), and autowiring can seem a little too much like "magical" behavior to novice Spring developers.

The other limitation of autowiring is that you cannot configure multiple beans of the same type that are to be used for the autowiring of other beans, because the framework would then have no way to determine which bean was to be injected. Autowiring is therefore of no use for the general case. It could still be used when a single definition of the required type will be made available (as, for example, tends to be the case for the Hibernate session factory discussed in the next chapter). However, mixing autowiring and explicit wiring of beans just adds unnecessary *hidden* complexity to your configuration files.

Bean Configuration

Listing 3-6 shows several beans being declared along with their dependencies. The complexity of the XML configuration file will depend on the number of beans being set, the wiring mode being used to associate beans with each other, the number of properties being set on the various beans, whether they require constructor parameters, and so on. Listing 3-10 shows a simple bean, defined with a single parameter, a default constructor, accessible by the name ref from the factory.

Listing 3-10. *A Bean Configured with a Single Property*

```
<bean id="ref" class="com.apress.coupling.config.RefExample">
   <property name="text" value="RefExample"/>
</bean>
```

By default, beans are configured as singletons; when `ref` is used as a property of other beans, it will always be the same `RefExample` instance that is provided. The `scope` attribute can be used to change this behavior. In a stand-alone application, this will consist of the default `singleton` or can be overridden to `prototype`, where a new bean instance will be provided wherever the definition is requested.

Property Injection

The properties on the beans are set by using `PropertyEditor` implementations to convert the configuration representation of the property into the runtime value. Typically, the properties take references to other beans, primitives, wrapped primitives, or strings. Any type can be provided as a parameter to a bean property, but the support for this set of common types is particularly comprehensive.

Of these common types, the commonest will be the primitives, wrappers, and strings. For all of these types, you can configure the parameter by using a straight string representation of the value to be applied. Where necessary, the appropriate `PropertyEditor` will be invoked to type-convert the string value into the target type. This has exactly the same effect as parsing the string value by using the parsing methods of the corresponding wrapper types.

The properties are configured from XML as elements within the body of the bean element. They can be added in any order.

For a string property value, of course, no type conversion is necessary, but for all of the simple property types (as shown in Listing 3-11), the parameter's representation is simplicity itself.

Listing 3-11. *Injecting a String Property Value*

```
<property name="text" value="Hello World"/>
```

References to other bean types are just as straightforward. The bean must be declared elsewhere in the configuration, and unless you are using autowiring, should be given a name. Listing 3-12 shows the syntax for configuring references.

Listing 3-12. *Injecting a Reference Value*

```
<property name="ref" ref="ref"/>
```

Use the `ref` attribute (instead of the `value` attribute or an element body) to reference the existing bean definition.

■**Caution** A common "gotcha" when configuring Spring beans is to use the `value` attribute in place of the `ref` attribute. This is hard to spot when looking through a complex configuration file. The problem is fairly easy to diagnose after you have encountered it a few times, but is frustrating until then. The Spring error messages are quite explicit about the causes of such runtime errors, so just bear it in mind as one of the possible culprits when diagnosing context startup problems.

For the collection classes, things are a little (but only a very little) more complicated. A number of elements are provided specifically to allow you to represent collections directly in your markup. The entries in these collections can be nested, and can accept both values for type conversion and references to external beans.

As Listing 3-13 shows for a Map collection type, it is good practice to use generics to represent the type information for the elements of the collections. Here it is clear that we are mapping String key types to lists of strings as the value type.

Listing 3-13. *Appropriate Use of Java 5 Generics in Method Signatures*

```
public void setMap(final Map<String,List<String>> map) {
   this.map = map;
}
```

Listing 3-14 shows that the corresponding XML configuration of the property is readily human readable, and also illustrates that the map can contain other nested collections (in this case, a list) for the value types, as indeed it can for the keys.

Listing 3-14. *Spring Configuration of a Map Property*

```
<property name="map">
 <map>
    <entry key="Mammal">
       <list>
          <value>Cat</value>
          <value>Dog</value>
          <value>Human</value>
       </list>
    </entry>
    <entry key="Fish">
       <list>
          <value>Minnow</value>
          <value>Shark</value>
       </list>
```

```
      </entry>
  </map>
</property>
```

Listing 3-15 shows the configuration of a list type. Compare this with the configuration of the list entries for the map in Listing 3-14. There is no difference between configuring a list as a property value and a list as a map entry.

Listing 3-15. *Spring Configuration of a List Property*

```
<property name="list">
 <list>
  <value>Mauve</value>
  <value>Puce</value>
  <value>Burnt Umber</value>
  <value>Beige</value>
 </list>
</property>
```

The configuration of the set in Listing 3-16 introduces no surprises: these are XML representations of the underlying types and so they reflect the similarities between their corresponding collection types.

Listing 3-16. *Spring Configuration of a Set Property*

```
<property name="set">
 <set>
    <value>London</value>
    <value>Paris</value>
    <value>Tokyo</value>
    <value>Washington</value>
 </set>
</property>
```

Constructor Injection

Some beans will not have a default constructor; these will need to be configured via the constructor. The constructor values are provided in much the same way as the property parameters.

Listing 3-17 shows the configuration of a constructor parameter for the `LooselyCoupled` class.

Listing 3-17. *Injecting Constructor Parameter*

```
<bean id="looseSoap" class="com.apress.coupling.LooselyCoupled">
  <constructor-arg ref="soap" />
</bean>
```

The parameter here is a reference to the SOAP transport implementation. Where appropriate, you can provide a `constructor-arg` element body containing collection elements exactly as for the property elements.

The one "gotcha" with the use of constructor parameter injection is that the names of the parameters are not known at runtime, so you cannot name the parameter to be injected.

If the configuration is unambiguous (if the parameters are all of incompatible types, or if there is only one parameter), you can just list the appropriate `constructor-arg` elements. However, if there is an ambiguity in the types of parameters to the constructor—as in Listing 3-18, where the constructor takes two string parameters—you must provide an `index` attribute to each of the constructor arguments to identify. The order of the `constructor-arg` elements in the configuration file does not matter; only the `index` attribute is pertinent here.

Listing 3-18. *Injecting Ambiguously Typed Customer Parameters*

```
<bean id="userAccount" class="com.apress.coupling.UserAccount">
   <constructor-arg index="0" value="jdoe"/>
   <constructor-arg index="1" value="pa55word"/>
</bean>
```

XML Schema–Based Configuration

With Spring 2 arrives the ability to enhance the configuration information by combining implementation classes with the standard XML schema syntax. In principle, you can add as many extra tags (managed within their own namespaces) as you deem necessary by including them in the namespace declarations and schema location definitions (for XML validation).

In practice, this feature is more useful for library writers than it is for developers. I don't expect most developers to need to create their own schema extensions, so I don't cover any further in this book. However, you will almost certainly want to take advantage of a number of the extensions that are provided with the framework. Some of them add substantial extra functionality to the configuration syntax, and I cover those in later chapters.

One, however, is pertinent to the simple configuration issues, and this is the property name namespace.

The property name namespace is referenced by adding the following namespace definition to the root beans element:

```
xmlns:p="http://www.springframework.org/schema/p"
```

This allows you to use attributes from the property namespace with the :p suffix within the scope of the beans element—that is, throughout the definition.

The namespace does not have a schema definition for validation, however, because the attributes that are added within this namespace are the names of the properties for the bean that it is to apply for. That is to say, you can replace the bean definition from Listing 3-6 with the one given in Listing 3-19.

Listing 3-19. *Defining Property Values by Using the Property Namespace*

```
<bean
    id="ref"
    class="com.apress.coupling.config.RefExample"
    p:text="RefExample"/>
```

In Listing 3-19, the only property is a String value. Where a reference to another bean definition is required, you append -ref to the property name. So, for example, a setFoo(Foo) method would have an associated property attribute of p:foo-ref="foo", assuming an existing bean definition named foo for an implementation of type Foo.

The property attributes cannot be used to declare constructor parameters, and they don't actually do anything above and beyond what can already be done with property elements. They are only syntactic sugar that can be used to keep your bean definitions more compact.

An additional schema extension allows you to more flexibly manage the injection of collection types. Listing 3-20 shows the use of the util namespace to manage a group of collections as independent bean definitions and then inject them into the target bean. This can also be achieved by using provided collection-specific factory bean implementations such as ListFactoryBean, but again the use of the util namespace improves the readability of the resulting code considerably.

Listing 3-20. *Defining Collections by Using the util Namespace*

```
<bean id="pte"
    class="com.apress.coupling.config.PropertyTypeExample"
    p:text="Hello World"
    p:ref-ref="ref"
    p:list-ref="list"
    p:set-ref="set"
    p:map-ref="map"/>
```

```
<util:list id="list">
   <value>Mauve</value>
   <value>Puce</value>
   <value>Burnt Umber</value>
   <value>Beige</value>
</util:list>

<util:set id="set">
   <value>London</value>
   <value>Paris</value>
   <value>Tokyo</value>
   <value>Washington</value>
</util:set>

<util:map id="map">
   <entry key="Colours" value-ref="list"></entry>
</util:map>
```

Annotation-Based Configuration

Spring is usually driven from XML configuration files. The programmatic example in Listing 3-5 is very much the exception rather than the rule. Java 5 introduced annotations, which allow arbitrary metadata to be attached to source code and retained at runtime.

Although the Spring framework has embraced some of the other new features of Java 5, the annotations library remains quite small. This is partly because of the Spring philosophy of making its extensions noninvasive; Spring-based code should be readily portable to other frameworks and other environments. Most of the features are only tangentially related to inversion of control and dependency injection, and these are covered in their appropriate chapters. Two annotations are left for us to discuss here: the @Configurable and @Required annotations.

@Required

One of the easiest mistakes to make when wiring up a Spring configuration file is to omit one of the vital properties from a bean definition. Beans can be written to implement the InitializingBean interface, and if they are, the Spring framework will call the afterPropertiesSet method after all of the configured properties have been injected. Therefore, it is possible for the developer to explicitly check to see that all the references have been assigned legal values, but this is tedious.

Listing 3-21 shows the extent of the boilerplate that you might have to write to check that the properties had been set using this method. But that is not its only failing: the afterPropertiesSet method is really a life-cycle method to allow object initialization to occur after setters have been applied during bean initialization. Beans will often take their dependencies through property setter methods instead of via the constructor, so this method is really analogous to the purpose of the constructor. Tests for property status can therefore be a distraction from the major purpose of the method.

Listing 3-21. *Verifying Property Values After Injection by Using the afterPropertiesSet Method*

```
public void afterPropertiesSet()
   throws Exception
{
   if( set  == null )
      throw new NullPointerException("set property is null");
   if( map  == null )
      throw new NullPointerException("map property is null");
   if( list == null )
      throw new NullPointerException("list property is null");
   if( text == null )
      throw new NullPointerException("text property is null");
}
```

The @Required annotation allows a Spring developer to avoid this tedious reference checking. If the annotation is present and the factory has been configured to contain a RequiredAnnotationBeanPostProcessor bean, an error will be produced at initialization if any of the pertinent properties have not been configured.

■**Note** The required annotation checks to make sure only that the required setters of the bean have been called. It does *not* check the value that has been passed in. Specifically, the postprocessor does not cause any errors to occur if a null value is explicitly passed into the property, so sadly the type of boilerplate shown in Listing 3-21 may still be necessary.

In keeping with the principle that Spring should not intrude upon the implementation of a class where it is not wanted, the postprocessor can use alternative annotations supplied by the developer in place of Spring's own @Required annotation. This is configured by calling the setRequiredAnnotationType method and passing in the appropriate class.

@Configurable

Spring provides for configuration by using Java 5 annotations. The classes are annotated with the @Configurable annotation. This annotation can be used to specify the name of the bean to be created from the class, the autowiring approach to be used (if any), and whether dependency checks should be carried out to determine if the class can be instantiated.

Although the annotation concerned is quite straightforward, it suffers from some of the problems discussed in the earlier "Autowiring" section. Because it uses AspectJ-specific aspect-oriented programming (AOP) facilities, it also requires the configuration and use of the AspectJ code-weaving capabilities. Finally, it creates dependency-specific information in the source code, something that seems to be a move in the opposite direction to the rest of the Spring philosophy.

AOP is discussed in depth in Chapter 5, but I do not use the `@Configurable` annotation any further in this book.

Bean and BeanFactory Life Cycle

Having seen some of the ways that a bean can be configured, you should look briefly at the life cycle of the bean factory and how that affects the life cycle of the beans that reside within it.

Any bean that implements `BeanFactory` is expected to honor an ordered set of method calls to beans implementing standard interfaces. Table 3-3 enumerates the methods called during the initialization of a bean.

Table 3-3. *Methods Called on Startup*

Interface	Method	Purpose
BeanNameAware	setBeanName	Notifies the bean of its name within the factory. It is generally not recommended that a dependency be created on the bean name, but it may prove useful for logging purposes.
BeanClassLoaderAware	setBeanClassLoader	Intended for use by classes within the framework.
BeanFactoryAware	setBeanFactory	Allows beans to look up other beans by name from the factory. This is generally unnecessary because bean dependencies are typically received by injection.
ResourceLoaderAware	setResourceLoader	Permits resources to be looked up directly from the resource loader—for example, where the name to be used is calculated as a suffix to some fixed root.

Table 3-3. *Methods Called on Startup (Continued)*

Interface	Method	Purpose
ApplicationEventPublisherAware	setApplicationEventPublisher	Provides the event publisher(s) associated with the factory (typically the ApplicationContext itself). This allows some life-cycle events to be received as published events. By default, only started, closed, and web request–handled events are published by ApplicationContext, so the normal life cycle methods tend to be more useful.
MessageSourceAware	setMessageSource	Provides the message source for the factory (again, typically the ApplicationContext itself). A message source is an interface for resolving localized messages for error reporting and the like. The message source can alternatively be provided as a normal property value, as it will be a normal bean with the name messageSource.
ApplicationContextAware	setApplicationContext	Provides the application context for the factory. Again, the dependencies available from the application context are usually better obtained by receiving them as injected properties.
ServletContextAware	setServletContext	Provides the servlet context to beans configured from within a servlet, such as the web controller classes discussed in Chapter 6.
BeanPostProcessor	postProcessBeforeInitialization	Called before general bean initialization starts (that is, after the constructor has been invoked, but before any non-constructor-parameter properties have been injected). This is primarily used by Spring's own implementation classes.

Table 3-3. *Methods Called on Startup (Continued)*

Interface	Method	Purpose
InitializingBean	afterPropertiesSet	Called after all of the properties have been injected into the bean. This can be used to verify that property values are correctly assigned, to initialize bean implementation details, and to acquire resources.
BeanFactory	n/a	Any custom initialization methods defined by the specific implementation. The purpose of these methods depends entirely on the implementer of the bean factory in question.
BeanPostProcessors	postProcessAfterInitialization	Called after general bean initialization has completed (that is, after all the parameter properties have been set and the afterPropertiesSet method has been invoked).

Note that not all of the methods will be called for all bean factory types because they are not always appropriate. For example, the setServletContext method in the ServletContextAware bean will be called only if the bean factory is a WebApplicationContext implementation or otherwise hosted within a servlet.

Additional methods are called during the life cycle of a bean factory that is being discarded—for example, during the removal of a Spring-based web application. Table 3-4 enumerates these methods.

Table 3-4. *Methods Called on Shutdown*

Interface	Method	Purpose
DisposableBean	destroy	Called to allow beans to release resources obtained at startup or during execution of the bean.
BeanFactory	n/a	Any custom destroy methods defined by the specific implementation.

Despite the benefits that implementing these interfaces can offer to your application, you do need to bear in mind that adding them creates a hard dependency on the Spring API, possibly forcing you to use Spring or imitate the Spring bean life cycle in otherwise unrelated contexts.

Of course, if you have no beans implementing any of these interfaces in your implementation, you have no such hard dependency, but then you will not receive any of these life cycle events. In practice, many implementations use `InitializingBean` at least, and it is worth familiarizing yourself with the life cycle so that you are aware what life cycle management is available to you.

Application Contexts

The Spring framework provides a large number of `BeanFactory` implementations, but also defines some derived interfaces to guarantee additional features. For example, the `DefaultListableBeanFactory` that we used in Listing 3-5 implements the `ListableBeanFactory` interface, whose contract guarantees that clients can enumerate the available bean instances instead of requiring them to specify the bean names explicitly. Among these interfaces, `ApplicationContext` (which extends `BeanFactory`) and `WebApplicationContext` (which in turn extends `ApplicationContext`) are particularly important.

ApplicationContext

Implementations of `ApplicationContext` are usually the primary building block around which you will build your Spring-based application. Implementations are provided that can be initialized from files (sought on the file system or on the classpath), and because `ApplicationContext` extends a number of other useful interfaces in addition to `BeanFactory` itself, the implementations are required to provide a much richer environment for configuring injectable resources than are available from a minimal `BeanFactory` implementation. Table 3-5 lists these additional interfaces.

Table 3-5. *Interfaces Extended by the ApplicationContext Interface*

Interface	Description
`ApplicationEventPublisher`	Permits associated listener beans to be notified of events in the context's life cycle.
`HierarchicalBeanFactory`	Allows the context to be part of a hierarchy. Usually a context that is a member of a hierarchy will have access to beans only in the parent or in child contexts—not from its siblings in the hierarchy.
`ListableBeanFactory`	Allows the bean instances available from the context to be enumerated.
`MessageSource`	Provides for message strings to be obtained (and thus injected) based on identifying key and locale information. This facility is used extensively in making applications locale sensitive.

Table 3-5. *Interfaces Extended by the ApplicationContext Interface*

Interface	Description
ResourceLoader	Permits file-like resources to be obtained (and thus injected) based on an identifying path. In conjunction with the ResourcePatternResolver, this allows file resources to be specified with simple strings, greatly simplifying XML configuration files.
ResourcePatternResolver	Allows for the use of various wildcard styles (including Ant style and Regular Expression style) when specifying resource paths.

The Spring framework includes implementations that can be configured from XML files found directly on the file system or from network resources, that can be loaded from classpath-relative paths, and that can be configured programmatically. It also provides several web application–specific implementations and several abstract partial implementations used by these. You will not normally need to create your own application context implementation, but an ApplicationContext implementation (rather than other more-limited BeanFactory implementations) is the usual starting point for creating a Spring application.

WebApplicationContext

The WebApplicationContext does not expand dramatically on the contract offered by the ApplicationContext interface, but in a web application you will often have a 1:1 relationship between WebApplicationContext instances and the servlet that is servicing a particular web request.

The hierarchical capabilities of the web application context (inherited via ApplicationContext from HierarchicalBeanFactory) are used to good effect here to give the individual WebApplicationContext instances access to the parent ApplicationContext instance associated with the application as a whole, but not with any of their siblings. This approach makes the configuration information more modular with cleaner separation of concerns. You will see the application of this in Chapter 6, where a DispatcherServlet implementation initializes a WebApplicationContext instance and forwards all its incoming web requests to beans defined in the WebApplicationContext's configuration file. These beans in turn are injected with dependencies obtained from the parent ApplicationContext.

Resource Properties

As mentioned in the preceding section, ApplicationContext implementations allow for file-like resources to be injected based on path strings given in the configuration file. This capability arises from the ResourceLoader superinterface.

For a file-like resource to be injectable on a bean, the receiving property must be specified as an implementation of the org.springframework.core.io.Resource interface. The resource type to be used will be determined by looking for the prefix on the property value.

Listing 3-22 shows a variety of resources that will be resolved to appropriate types.

Listing 3-22. *A Set of Confi12gured Resources*

```
<bean id="describer" class="com.apress.coupling.ResourceConsumer">
   <property name="resources">
      <list>
         <value>classpath:config.xml</value>
         <value>file:config.xml</value>
         <value>http://example.com/config.xml</value>
         <value>ftp://config.xml</value>
         <value>config.xml</value>
      </list>
   </property>
</bean>
```

Listing 3-23 shows the implementation of the resources property setter.

Listing 3-23. *A Property Configured to Receive Resources*

```
public void setResources(final List<Resource> resources) {
   this.resources = resources;
}
```

The Resource interface provides methods allowing a file or URL object to be obtained for the resource, but an exception will be thrown if the resource is not available in the selected form. However, the interface also extends the InputStreamSource interface that allows an InputStream to be obtained from the resource. This method will fail only if the underlying resource does not exist or is inaccessible.

The first four examples given in Listing 3-22 are returned (respectively) as a resource from the classpath of the application, from the file system relative to the working directory, as a web request, and as an FTP transfer. The last value, for a named resource with no prefix, is ambiguous; the resource returned will depend on the factory that the bean is hosted within. For example, for the ClassPathXmlApplicationContext used in Listing 3-7, the configuration file would be obtained as a resource from the classpath. Other application context types may return other resource types—typically, file resource types from appropriate directory roots.

Conclusion

In this chapter, you have looked at the core classes of the Spring framework and the configuration files associated with the creation of bean factories from which your configured beans are obtained. In the next chapter, you will look at the facilities that Spring provides for accessing databases, the foundation blocks of any enterprise application.

■■■

CHAPTER 4

Data Access

In this chapter, you will look at Spring's support for databases. Spring provides libraries to help you create ordinary JDBC-based data access, but it also provides some support for several Object Relational Mapping (ORM) tools.

The examples in this chapter are both based around the data access object (DAO) pattern. This is not the only way in which you can use Spring, but is probably the commonest approach in general use at the moment.

Persistence Frameworks

In this chapter, I build the same DAO implementation upon two different persistence APIs. The first of these is JDBC, the standard database connectivity API in JSE and Java EE. In practice, almost all developers have at least a passing familiarity with the JDBC API.

My second DAO implementation is based on the Hibernate ORM framework. I have chosen to use Hibernate because it is a popular and effective tool, because Spring provides comprehensive support for it, and because it is the ORM tool that I am most familiar with. Unfortunately, Hibernate (along with the other ORM tools) is too complicated to explain in detail in this chapter. I am therefore forced to assume that you have some familiarity with Hibernate and to restrict my explanations to the limited parts of it that I happen to use in my examples.

Nonetheless, if you are not familiar with Hibernate, I would recommend that you skim through the "Hibernate" section later in this chapter to see what features you are missing. This is especially true if you are familiar with another ORM tool, as many of the techniques applied to using the Hibernate framework within Spring will be analogous to those required to use other ORM frameworks.

Speaking of which, Spring offers support for the following APIs and frameworks:

- JDBC

- Java Persistence API (JPA)

- Java Data Objects (JDO)

- Hibernate

- Common Client Interface (CCI)

- iBATIS SQL Maps

- Oracle TopLink

You may not be familiar with the relatively new JPA and JDO specifications, however. These are standard APIs, rather than specific frameworks. Indeed, Hibernate can be used as a JPA implementation, and there are a number of JDO implementations such as Java Persistent Objects (JPOX) and Orient. As with JDBC, in principle a cleanly written JPA or JDO application may be ported to a completely different implementation without affecting the application's behavior.

DAOs

Chapter 2 covered the architecture of our example program, and in this section I will quickly review those parts of it that are directly pertinent to this chapter. Figure 4-1 shows the basic relationship between the service layer, the DAO layer, and the underlying data store (typically a relational database).

Figure 4-1. *The data access architecture*

Our application is centered around the entity classes that represent the data that we will be manipulating. The database access logic to ensure that these entities are correctly represented in the database is implemented within DAO classes. These hide the specific database access mechanism from the service layer above it. We should be able to swap out one DAO implementation (for example, a Hibernate-based DAO) for any other (for example, a plain JDBC-based one) with no changes to the implementation of the service layer. In fact, the only additional changes necessary should be in the configuration of the application context to ensure that the alternative DAO is set up and injected into the appropriate service classes.

Figure 4-2 shows the entities that our DAO classes will service. They are the UserAccount and UserRole classes representing user authorizations in the application.

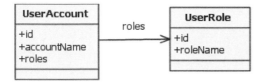

Figure 4-2. *The entities serviced by our DAO implementation*

The basic implementation of the UserAccount bean is shown in Listing 4-1.

Listing 4-1. *The UserAccount Entity Bean*

```java
package com.apress.timesheets.entity;

import java.util.*;
import javax.persistence.*;

public class UserAccount {
    private Long id;
    private String accountName;
    private Set<UserRole> roles = new HashSet<UserRole>();

    public UserAccount() {
    }

    public UserAccount(final String accountName) {
        this.accountName = accountName;
    }

    public Long getId() {
        return id;
    }

    public void setId(final Long id) {
        this.id = id;
    }

    public Set<UserRole> getRoles() {
        return roles;
    }
```

```
    public void setRoles(final Set<UserRole> roles) {
        this.roles = roles;
    }

    public String getAccountName() {
        return accountName;
    }

    public void setAccountName(String accountName) {
        this.accountName = accountName;
    }
}
```

I have chosen the UserAccount bean for our example because user account management is a common requirement for web applications. It also has the advantages of some reasonably complex associations with one other bean, the UserRole entity (implementation not shown), which make the DAO implementation sufficiently nontrivial to be used as a starting point for real-world applications.

Figure 4-3 shows the tables that will be used to represent these entities in the database. There are a pair of tables corresponding to the entities themselves, and a join table representing the relationship between the user accounts and the roles. As always, all of the examples in this chapter are provided in the Source Code/Download area of the Apress website (www.apress.com).

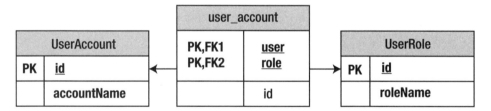

Figure 4-3. *The database tables corresponding to the UserAccount and UserRole entities*

As you will see in Chapter 10, the unit tests for the example have been written to use identical test code (aside from setup and teardown of the DAO itself) against the three DAO implementations, making it far more likely that we will have compatible versions.

The interface shown in Listing 4-2 is divided by comments into four sections: Create, Read, Update, and Delete, which form the *CRUD* mnemonic. These are the basic operations that most applications will need to perform on their data, so they will usually need to exist in some form. Your specific methods should be tailored to the requirements of your application.

Listing 4-2. *The Interface That My DAO Implementations Will Honor*

```java
package com.apress.timesheets.dao;

import java.util.List;
import com.apress.timesheets.entity.UserAccount;

public interface UserAccountDao {
    // Create methods
    public void create(UserAccount account);

    // Read methods
    public List<UserAccount> list();
    public UserAccount read(Long id);
    public UserAccount read(String accountName);

    // Update methods
    public void update(UserAccount account);

    // Delete methods
    public void delete(UserAccount account);
    public void delete(Long id);
}
```

In fact, the *You Ain't Gonna Need It (YAGNI)* principle of agile programming suggests that I may already have produced a more complicated API than is strictly required for the timesheet application, although it is still useful for the purposes of my examples. In a real application, your API should be driven by the requirements and should not necessarily reflect Listing 4-2 exactly. If one of the CRUD operations is not required by your application's use cases, there is no need to implement it.

Templates and Support Classes

Although the various data access libraries supported by Spring have quite different implementations, they do tend to have similar usage patterns. Spring takes advantage of this by providing sets of tailored support classes to aid in the building of data access logic, and specifically to aid in building DAO implementations.

When building a DAO for a supported database access mechanism, you will generally find that Spring provides helper classes to aid in your implementation. These usually include a template class and a DAO support class. Figure 4-4 shows the relevant classes supporting plain JDBC data access.

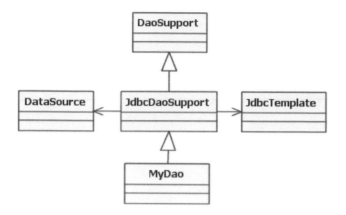

Figure 4-4. *Using the Spring helper classes for JDBC*

Table 4-1 shows the database access frameworks and the helper classes that Spring provides to support them.

Table 4-1. *Helper Classes for the Supported Database Access Mechanisms*

Framework	DAO Support Class	Template Class
CCI	CciDaoSupport	CciTemplate
Hibernate*	HibernateDaoSupport	HibernateTemplate
JDBC	JdbcDaoSupport	JdbcTemplate
Java Data Objects	JdoDaoSupport	JdoTemplate
Java Persistence API	JpaDaoSupport	JpaTemplate
iBATIS SQL Maps	SqlMapClientDaoSupport	SqlMapClientTemplate
Oracle TopLink	TopLinkDaoSupport	TopLinkTemplate

* *Two sets of Hibernate helper classes are supplied in different packages for Hibernate 2.x and Hibernate 3.x.*

There is little commonality of API between these classes. Although the DaoSupport class exists as the parent of the specific implementations, it is really there to aid in the management of the support classes' life cycles and has a distinctly minimal API. The template classes don't even share a common root class or interface.

Despite the API differences, there are strong similarities in the purpose of the two classes regardless of the particular framework that is being used. The DAO support class provides a base for your own DAO implementation class. Typically, it will manage a DataSource used to obtain connections to the database. It will also provide factory methods allowing a template implementation to be obtained. The purpose of the template is to wrap up as much of the boilerplate code associated with database access as possible, allowing you to focus purely on your novel application logic.

Plain Old JDBC

Any moderately experienced Java developer—certainly any developer experienced enough to have recognized a need for the Spring framework in their architecture—will have some basic experience with JDBC.

Developing software with Spring's support for JDBC does not require you to learn fundamentally new libraries, but it does provide a suite of helper classes that can substantially cut down on the boilerplate logic required in your implementation—particularly the various minutiae of managing connection, statement, and result set resources and ensuring that they are released reliably and in the right order.

Creating the JDBC DAO

The DAO will honor the interface defined in Listing 4-2. However, to play nicely with Spring, the DAO needs to allow the resources it will take advantage of to be injected. To this end, and for its other benefits, my implementation extends the JdbcDaoSupport class.

This implementation accepts a standard JDBC DataSource implementation as one of its properties, allowing the implementation to be configured directly from Spring.

In addition to providing this convenience, JdbcDaoSupport provides a very large suite of helper methods to allow you to carry out basic JDBC operations without the usual boilerplate logic.

For example, Listing 4-3 shows how a JDBC method from a non-Spring application might be implemented to obtain an instance of our entity class.

Listing 4-3. *A Traditional JDBC Delete Method*

```
public void traditionalDelete(final Long id) {
    Connection conn = null;
    PreparedStatement stat = null;
    try {
        conn = getDataSource().getConnection();
        stat = conn.prepareStatement(DELETE_BY_ID);
        stat.setLong(1, id);
        stat.execute();
    } catch( final SQLException e ) {
    } finally {
        try {
            if( stat != null) stat.close();
        } catch( SQLException e ) {
            log.log(Level.SEVERE,"Problem closing statement",e);
        }
    }
```

```
        try {
            if( conn != null) conn.close();
        } catch( SQLException e ) {
            log.log(Level.SEVERE,"Problem closing connection",e);
        }
    }
}
```

Compare this with Listing 4-4, which shows the implementation taking advantage of the helper classes.

Listing 4-4. *A Spring JDBC Delete Method*

```
public void delete(final Long id) {
    getTemplate().update(DELETE_BY_ID, id);
}
```

By obtaining a JdbcTemplate object from the supporting superclass, we have access to methods that encapsulate the necessary resource management logic. Calls to these methods will ensure that the connection is closed regardless of any exceptions that may be thrown.

The update method is one of the simplest methods, but it is in select (read) methods that the worst cases of duplication tend to occur. In traditional JDBC logic, it is usually necessary to iterate over a result set, building objects as we go. There is a real risk that this logic will at best be moved out into helper methods (still requiring duplication of the result-set iteration logic) but still left verbatim in a large number of methods.

The Spring framework allows the logic behind this population of the entity objects from the result set to be encapsulated in implementations of a variety of wrapper interfaces. The most useful of these is the ParameterizedRowMapper interface. The API for this mapper is shown in Listing 4-5.

Listing 4-5. *The ParameterizedRowMapper's mapRow Method*

```
public interface ParameterizedRowMapper<T>
    extends RowMapper<T>
{
    public T mapRow(ResultSet rs, int rowNum);
}
```

As you can see, the interface requires you to implement a single method, and is parameterizable with a single type-parameter, which is the type of the entity that can be populated by the mapRow() implementation. Listing 4-6 shows my implementation of this for the UserAccount entity.

Listing 4-6. *An Implementation of a RowMapper for the UserAccount Entity*

```
final ParameterizedRowMapper<UserAccount> userMapper =
    new ParameterizedRowMapper<UserAccount>() {
  public UserAccount mapRow(ResultSet rs, int rowNum)
    throws SQLException
  {
    UserAccount account = new UserAccount();
    account.setId(rs.getLong("id"));
    account.setAccountName(rs.getString("accountName"));
    return account;
  }
};
```

The implementation in Listing 4-6 receives a populated result set and creates a single instance of the entity in question. Typically, the row number is not used, although it is sometimes useful when ordered selections require an associated surrogate index.

The mapper abstracts the population of the entity from a set of columns into a single well-defined implementation. We can then use this with other helper methods from the JdbcTemplate class, as shown in Listing 4-7.

Listing 4-7. *Using a RowMapper to Materialize a List of Entities*

```
public List<UserAccount> list() {
  final List<UserAccount> list =
    getTemplate().query(SELECT_ACCOUNTS, userMapper);
  for(final UserAccount account : list) {
    populateRoles(account);
  }
  return list;
}
```

Configuring the JDBC DAO

The JdbcDaoSupport class requires a DataSource to be provided, so this must be configured first. For this example, we will use a DriverManagerDataSource, which is a simple wrapper to allow a basic DataSource implementation to be created by injecting the Connection properties directly.

Listing 4-8 shows the configuration of a data source for an in-memory HSQL database (an embedded Java database that runs within the same JVM as your application logic).

Listing 4-8. *Configuring a DriverManagerDataSource*

```
<bean id="dataSource"
  class="org.springframework.jdbc.datasource.DriverManagerDataSource"
  destroy-method="close"
  p:driverClassName="org.hsqldb.jdbcDriver"
  p:url="jdbc:hsqldb:mem:JdbcDaoTest"
  p:username="sa"
  p:password=""/>
```

Configuration for other databases would take appropriate driver class and URL parameters, and would naturally require the appropriate driver JAR to be in the classpath and the database instance to be up and running.

With a data source available, it can be injected into the DAO implementation (which inherits from JdbcDaoSupport and therefore has appropriate getters and setters for the data source property). Listing 4-9 shows the injection of the data source from Listing 4-10 into an instance of the UserAccountDao bean.

Listing 4-9. *Configuring the JDBC DAO Implementation*

```
<bean id="jdbcUserAccountDao"
  class="com.apress.timesheets.dao.jdbc.JdbcUserAccountDaoImpl"
  p:dataSource-ref="dataSource"/>
```

No further configuration of the DAO is required. It is available to be used by other beans after it has been injected into them.

Listing 4-10 shows the JDBC-based implementation being injected into a service bean to provide database access. Assuming that the userAccountDao property of the service bean takes a UserAccountDao interface type rather than the concrete implementation type as its parameter, the implementation could be swapped out for another by changing the name of the bean defined as this property's value.

Listing 4-10. *Injecting Our JDBC DAO Implementation into a Service Class*

```
<bean id="userAccountService"
  class="com.apress.timesheets.service.UserAccountServiceImpl"
  p:userAccountDao-ref="jdbcUserAccountDao"/>
```

Hibernate

The logic of the JDBC-based DAO implementation is easy to follow for any of the individual methods, but it does have its own complexity. For example, the method used to read in an Account object populates the Roles set. This operation may be entirely redundant; if the code that consumes the materialized UserAccount object does not make use of the role information, then we have made unnecessary JDBC calls. Individually this is insignificant, but collectively the performance hit can be substantial enough to matter.

In addition to performance, there are other issues of complexity. The SQL statements used to retrieve the information are somewhat redundant in their design, reflecting the similarities of the underlying tables.

Hibernate alleviates these and other problems. At the expense of some leaky abstractions of the detail of JDBC-based data access, the use of Hibernate significantly reduces the overall complexity of the application logic, making your DAO implementations shorter and easier to understand.

Hibernate Mappings

To allow Java objects to be represented as tables in a relational database, it is necessary to create a mapping between the database objects and the Java classes. When Hibernate is configured, it reads in the mapping information and uses this to build a model in memory representing these relationships.

The Hibernate mappings can be supplied in two ways: as proprietary XML files, or using Java 5 annotations.

My example application uses Java 5 annotations. I do not use the Hibernate XML mapping approach because it is considerably more verbose and less transparent than the annotations-based approach. Listing 4-11 shows the UserAccount entity from Listing 4-1 with appropriate annotations added for my Hibernate implementation.

Listing 4-11. *The UserAccount Entity Bean with Hibernate Annotations*

```
package com.apress.timesheets.entity;

import static javax.persistence.CascadeType.PERSIST;
import static javax.persistence.FetchType.LAZY;
import java.util.*;
import javax.persistence.*;

@Entity
@NamedQueries( {
    @NamedQuery(name = "getUserAccountByName",
            query = "from UserAccount where accountName = :name"),
    @NamedQuery(name = "listUserAccountByName",
            query = "from UserAccount order by accountName")
})
```

```java
public class UserAccount {
   private Long id;
   private String accountName;
   private Set<UserRole> roles = new HashSet<UserRole>();

   public UserAccount() {
   }

   public UserAccount(final String accountName) {
      this.accountName = accountName;
   }

   @Id
   @GeneratedValue
   public Long getId() {
      return id;
   }

   public void setId(final Long id) {
      this.id = id;
   }

   @ManyToMany(fetch = LAZY, cascade = PERSIST)
   @JoinTable(name = "account_role",
             joinColumns = { @JoinColumn(name = "user") },
             inverseJoinColumns = { @JoinColumn(name = "role") })
   public Set<UserRole> getRoles() {
      return roles;
   }

   public void setRoles(final Set<UserRole> roles) {
      this.roles = roles;
   }

   @Column(unique = true, nullable = false)
   public String getAccountName() {
      return accountName;
   }

   public void setAccountName(String accountName) {
      this.accountName = accountName;
   }
}
```

There are two types of annotations available to Hibernate. For the basic mapping information, Hibernate takes advantage of standard JPA annotations in the `javax.persistence` package namespace. A Hibernate entity mapped exclusively by using these annotations can be supported by other JPA-compliant ORM tools. Hibernate also offers a set of Hibernate-specific annotations that can be used to enable additional Hibernate features. Although we are using a Hibernate-specific set of Spring implementation classes, my implementation does not require any Hibernate-specific annotations.

The @Entity Annotation

The `@Entity` annotation marks the class as being an entity for persistence into the database. Optionally, the annotation can supply the default name for the table that the entity will be mapped to.

The @Id Annotation

The `@Id` annotation marks the property as representing the primary key of the entity. Although I am using a surrogate key that will be generated automatically (see `@GeneratedValue`), there is nothing to prevent you from assigning one of your business attributes as the primary key field, and if you need to use multiple attributes, additional annotations are available to support this.

The @GeneratedValue Annotation

The `@GeneratedValue` annotation is used here to indicate that the primary key (`Id`) attribute that it is attached to will be generated by Hibernate rather than being explicitly assigned. This reduces the burden on the developer quite considerably. Because I have not specified any further details, the generated value will be created in the default manner for the underlying database, allowing you to take advantage of database-specific features without creating a dependency on the specific database in your implementation. This usage does, however, require you to create an appropriate set of database objects to support Hibernate. In the case of HSQLDB, which I use in my example configuration, this entails the use of an identity type on the primary key column.

The @Column Annotation

The `@Column` annotation can be used to specify a column name (other than the default of the attribute name), or as here can be used to indicate that additional constraints should apply to the column. I have specified that the `accountName` attribute is unique, and that it should not accept a null value.

The @ManyToMany Annotation

The `@ManyToMany` annotation indicates the relationship between the two entities. Any `UserAccount` may be associated with any `UserRole` entity and vice versa. The fetch type of

LAZY indicates that a UserRole entity will not be loaded immediately (see the "Hibernate Lazy Loading" section later in this chapter). The cascade type indicates that when we save the UserAccount entity, any unsaved UserRole entities associated with it should be saved too.

The @JoinTable Annotation

The @JoinTable annotation supplements the @ManyToMany annotation. It is impossible to express a many-to-many relationship between two database entities by using a simple foreign key relationship in the relevant tables. Instead, a join table must be created to manage the relationship. Here we specify the name of the join table as account_role, and the name of the columns of the table. These will be foreign keys into the UserAccount (joinColumns) and UserRole (inverseJoinColumns) tables, respectively.

The @NamedQuery Annotation

The @NamedQueries is a container for @NamedQuery annotations, allowing us to attach more than one of them to a particular entity. @NamedQuery annotations represent standard queries against the database of objects.

Hibernate Query Language

Hibernate Query Language (HQL) is a relational language that can be used to manage the persistent Hibernate entities. It is exactly analogous to SQL, except that it manipulates objects in place of database entities. HQL queries are converted into SQL for execution, and the results of these SQL queries are then converted back into objects (although the use of caching may eliminate some or all calls into the database layer).

Creating the Hibernate DAO

A large part of the implementation of a Hibernate-based DAO is in fact the configuration information required by Hibernate to associate the tables and columns of the database representation of an entity with the classes and properties of its Java representation.

Before Java 5, this could be represented by configuring the DAO from code, or by creating a set of XML-based mapping files. The advent of Java 5's annotation features, however, allows us to include these configuration details in the implementation of the entity itself. These are the annotations that you can see in Listing 4-11.

With a correctly configured Hibernate session available, the DAO implementation then becomes a set of calls to the ORM engine. For comparison with the JdbcTemplate-based implementation that we looked at first, Listing 4-12 shows that a delete method can be created in a similarly compact form.

Listing 4-12. *A Hibernate-Based Entity Deletion Method*

```
public void delete(final UserAccount account) {
   getHibernateTemplate().delete(account);
}
```

The two deletion methods are of comparable simplicity. However, if we now take a look at the Hibernate-based account creation logic (see Listing 4-13), we start to see a substantial advantage of Hibernate over JDBC-based logic.

Listing 4-13. *Creating a User Account by Using Hibernate*

```
public void create(final UserAccount account) {
   getHibernateTemplate().persist(account);
}
```

Although Listing 4-13 is not very different from Listing 4-12, the corresponding JDBC persist method would be much more complex. Listing 4-14 shows part of a JDBC-based implementation.

Listing 4-14. *Creating a User Account by Using JDBC*

```
public void create(final UserAccount account) {
   // Make the account entity persistent
   getTemplate().update(INSERT_ACCOUNT, account.getAccountName());
   final Long accountId = getTemplate().queryForLong(SELECT_LAST_ACCOUNT_ID);
   account.setId(accountId);
   persistTransientRoles(account);
}
```

The Spring Hibernate template successfully reduces several complex operations down to a single line of code:

- It generates the primary key of the account entity.

- It ensures that the transient entity is updated with the new primary key.

- It ensures that associated entities (roles) are saved as necessary.

The underlying complexity is hidden in two places. First, Hibernate itself removes the need to create explicit code to convert result sets into entities. The annotations in the entity class contain enough information to allow this to be deduced. If you use the default annotation values where possible (for things such as the table name, the column name, and so forth), as you can when creating a build from scratch, the annotations are extremely terse. Where necessary, you can override these default behaviors at the expense of some slightly more verbose configuration information.

Second, the Spring `HibernateDaoSupport` class provides the `HibernateTemplate` implementation, which wraps up the various boilerplate bits of logic to ensure that a Hibernate session is correctly established and disposed of. (This is essential because leaking Hibernate session instances is liable to result in underlying leaks of JDBC connection instances—eventually emptying the connection pool or exhausting database resources.) The `HibernateDaoSupport` class is configured by injecting a `SessionFactory` instance.

You should be aware that it is entirely possible to use Hibernate within Spring without using the Spring template classes at all. The standard Hibernate `SessionFactory` class provides a `getCurrentSession()` method, which gives you access to a `ThreadLocal` instance of the session. Experienced Hibernate developers may well prefer to use this standard Hibernate approach to session management. Nonetheless, the Spring template gives you some useful helper methods that make Hibernate operations more succinct, and provides more consistency with Spring's helpers for other data access technologies. Regardless, the differences between the two approaches are now relatively minor, and the decision is not a fundamental one.

Configuring the Hibernate DAO

Hibernate requires a minimum set of configuration information in order to operate:

- The database connection

- The database "dialect"

- The mapping information

The database connection is provided so that Hibernate can talk to the database. The database dialect (all major databases types are covered) allows Hibernate to tailor its generated SQL to take maximum advantage of specific database features. The mapping information is used to allow Hibernate to convert objects into representations within the database and vice versa.

Hibernate represents all of this configuration information in a `Configuration` class implementation. Which implementation is used depends on how Hibernate's mappings are obtained. These are usually supplied by using XML files or by using Java 5 annotations. In the latter case, the `AnnotationConfiguration` class is used to represent them. Using the configuration object, a `SessionFactory` is constructed. This is in turn used to create a `Session` object.

The annotation configuration object is expensive to construct. It needs to read mapping data and build a corresponding model in memory. The `SessionFactory` is relatively inexpensive to construct, but is a singleton class used to produce `Session` objects. You should have only one SessionFactory in a single Hibernate application. The Session objects are extremely inexpensive to produce. You should create at least one for each thread of execution (Session objects are not thread-safe) that will be making Hibernate calls.

Configuration of the Hibernate DAO therefore requires rather more boilerplate configuration than the plain JDBC implementation, but is of similar complexity to the configuration information required to set up a stand-alone Hibernate application. Listing 4-15 shows the bean's configuration.

Listing 4-15. *Configuration of a SessionFactory*

```
<bean id="sessionFactory"
class="org.springframework.orm.hibernate3.annotation.AnnotationSessionFactoryBean"
  p:dataSource-ref="dataSource">
  <property name="annotatedClasses">
    <list>
      <value>com.apress.timesheets.entity.UserRole</value>
      <value>com.apress.timesheets.entity.UserAccount</value>
      <value>com.apress.timesheets.entity.Period</value>
      <value>com.apress.timesheets.entity.RateType</value>
      <value>com.apress.timesheets.entity.Rate</value>
      <value>com.apress.timesheets.entity.Timesheet</value>
    </list>
  </property>
  <property name="hibernateProperties">
    <props>
      <prop key="hibernate.dialect">
          org.hibernate.dialect.HSQLDialect
      </prop>
      <prop key="hibernate.show_sql">true</prop>
    </props>
  </property>
</bean>
```

Because I am using annotations, the factory bean is an AnnotationSessionFactoryBean. If I were using XML configuration files, it would be the simpler SessionFactoryBean but would require the paths to a set of XML mapping configuration files instead of the classes specified here. The dialect has been specified as HSQLDialect, indicating that the HSQL database is being used. I have also enabled a debugging option that causes the SQL used to communicate with this underlying database to be echoed to the standard output.

This session factory bean is then injected into our implementation class to populate its session factory property. The session factory is the SessionFactory instance used by the HibernateDaoHelper to acquire Hibernate Session objects, which are in turn used to manipulate the persistent object model.

The configuration of a service shown for a JDBC session factory in Listing 4-16 can be swapped for the configuration shown in Listing 4-17 without changing the behavior of the application as a whole.

Listing 4-16. *Configuration of the Hibernate DAO Implementation*

```
<bean id="hibernateUserAccountDao"
class="com.apress.timesheets.dao.hibernate.HibernateUserAccountDaoImpl"
  p:sessionFactory-ref="sessionFactory"/>
```

Listing 4-17. *Injecting Our Hibernate DAO Implementation into a Service Class*

```
<bean id="userAccountService"
  class="com.apress.timesheets.service.UserAccountServiceImpl"
  p:userAccountDao-ref="hibernateUserAccountDao"/>
```

Hibernate Lazy Loading

You will not always want all the elements of an association loaded on all occasions that the parent entity is loaded. As an extreme example, consider a product catalog. Loading the basic details of the product catalog (such as its description) does not necessarily justify loading all of the associated details of the products contained within that catalog.

Hibernate approaches this problem by allowing you to specify that associations are to be loaded lazily. When using the XML configuration files, this is the default behavior, but when using annotations (in order to comply with the JPA standard), it is not—and I have therefore specified this explicitly in my annotations.

Generally, lazy loading offers superior performance, so I would recommend turning on eager (the opposite of lazy) loading only when you have a specific performance problem and a reason to believe that lazy loading is the cause.

The problem with lazy loading is that in order to allow the associated entities to be loaded at some later point than the loading of the original entity, it becomes necessary to create proxy objects to represent the real association objects, and to keep a reference to the Hibernate session in order to retain access to the database. If for any reason the session object is closed (releasing the associated database connection) prior to the attempt to access the lazy association, an exception will be thrown—the notorious LazyInitializationException.

Understanding the cause of the problem is half the battle, however, and Spring provides several tools allowing automated management of the Hibernate session to prevent the problem from arising. The HibernateSessionFilter approach used to resolve this problem in the example application is discussed in more depth in Chapter 6.

Conclusion

This chapter has covered Spring's support for a variety of data access approaches. I have shown how loose coupling can allow an application to be made less dependent on the specifics of the database being used.

In a chapter on database access, you may have been expecting some discussion of transaction management. However, although transaction management is a feature of databases, it is not exclusively so. In the next chapter, I discuss the service layer and explain how you can use declarative transaction management to ensure that transactions are honored by all transactional resources—not just databases—without needing to encode the transaction behavior into your DAO implementations.

CHAPTER 5

■ ■ ■

The Service Layer, Transaction Management, and AOP

The service layer of an application represents the suite of operations that can be performed with that application. This layer is often broken down into several business domains. The service layer typically serves several purposes:

- Exposing the functionality of the application to the outside world

- Grouping together logically related functionality

- Implementing business logic

- Providing the boundary for transactional operations

For example, the timesheet application exposes a number of methods to the presentation layer, and all operations on the underlying model are performed through this API. In principle, we could provide additional remote method invocation (RMI) or SOAP interfaces to the service layer, allowing different types of client applications to communicate with the same system. You will look at these issues in more detail in Chapter 9.

The timesheet application groups together the facilities of the service layer into those concerned with manipulating users and those concerned with manipulating timesheets. The specific boundary of separation is a matter of convenience to the developers; there is no rule for deciding the matter. In practice, it will usually be clear what groups of functionality go together naturally.

In some very simple applications, the DAO layer and the service layer may have a one-to-one correlation, in which case it may be appropriate to have a single implementation of both. However, in most systems—and the example application is no exception—the service layer should be given its own implementation, as shown in Figure 5-1.

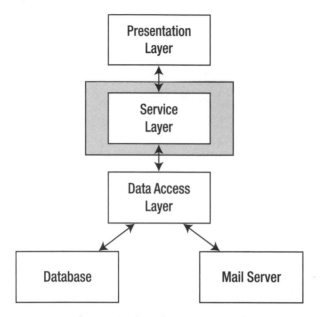

Figure 5-1. *The service layer's position in the architecture*

In addition to grouping functionality for use by higher layers, the service layer will typically group the functionality of lower layers into individual methods. Whereas the DAO classes will provide methods concerned with a single type of data source such as the database or a mail service (again as illustrated in Figure 5-1), the service layer can access multiple DAO classes in order to carry out operations across these underlying implementations. A typical example is updating the database and sending an e-mail in a single method call.

The service layer can group together access to multiple data sources—including different types of data such as e-mail and relational databases, but also including different physical repositories of data, such as relational databases hosted on different servers. Because the service layer is the point at which these different resources are grouped, it is also the point at which transactional concerns apply.

The easiest way to implement transactional requirements in Spring is by using the support for aspect-oriented programming (AOP). I discuss the various ways this can be applied to enforce transactions within the service layer later in this chapter, and I also show how AOP can be used to solve other problems that occur when creating a service layer.

Implementing Services in Spring

The actual implementation of a service in Spring is something of an anticlimax. The *service* is defined as an interface laying out the methods that will be required by external components.

The interface in Listing 5-1 defines a set of services concerned with manipulating the timesheets in the system. Using this API, we can create, read, update, and delete the timesheets and the other entities that they are composed of. This is the layer at which security must be applied if we are to expose the service to external components.

Listing 5-1. *The Timesheet Service Interface*

```
public interface TimesheetService {
    List<Timesheet> listTimesheets(UserAccount account);
    Timesheet findTimesheet(Long id);
    void createTimesheet(Timesheet timesheet);
    void updateTimesheet(Timesheet timesheet);
    void deleteTimesheet(Timesheet timesheet);
    List<RateType> getRateTypeList();
    Period findPeriod(Long id);
    Period createPeriod(
        Timesheet timesheet,
        Calendar startTime,
        Calendar endTime,
        String note,
        BigDecimal rate,
        String rateId);
    void deletePeriod(Timesheet timesheet,Period period);
}
```

The implementation of the API may use DAO implementations to perform its functions. Listing 5-2 shows the DAO properties for our implementation of the timesheet service. The service uses a database-oriented DAO to access the timesheet data and a simple mail transport protocol (SMTP)–oriented service to send e-mails.

Listing 5-2. *Part of the Corresponding Timesheet Service Implementation*

```
@Transactional
public class TimesheetServiceImpl implements TimesheetService {
    private TimesheetDao timesheetDao;
    private EmailDao emailDao;

    // ... service methods omitted ...

    public void updateTimesheet(final Timesheet timesheet) {
        timesheetDao.update(timesheet);
        emailDao.sendTimesheetUpdate(timesheet);
    }
```

```
    @Required
    public void setEmailDao(EmailDao emailDao) {
        this.emailDao = emailDao;
    }

    @Required
    public void setTimesheetDao(final TimesheetDao timesheetDao) {
        this.timesheetDao = timesheetDao;
    }
}
```

The updateTimesheet service method shown in Listing 5-2 demonstrates the fundamental difference between the service layer and the data access layer. The method draws on two quite distinct DAO mechanisms in order to embody some business logic. In this case, when a timesheet is updated, its details should be sent by e-mail to the administrative user.

The service layer does not necessarily restrict itself to aggregating data access functionality. Services can embody any functionality at the business level. Although in practice the service methods often do correspond to data access mechanisms, they can also perform calculations, and sort and collate information provided to them.

Transactions

Because the service layer is the point at which multiple data sources are often bound together, this is also the point at which we will usually want to mark transactional boundaries.

Consider the updateTimesheet method in Listing 5-2. Here we perform two quite distinct operations: updating a timesheet in the database and sending an e-mail to the administrative user. Although the implementations are completely distinct, we potentially have a problem: if one of the methods fails for some reason, we cannot permit the other to proceed.

If the DAO method to update the timesheet fails, we are in the clear; any exception thrown by the DAO will propagate up to us and prevent the e-mail method from commencing. The reverse is not true, however. If the attempt to queue the e-mail fails (if the SMTP server is temporarily unavailable, for example), we will not find this out until after the database update has completed. Reversing the order of the method invocations just reverses the order of the problem and solves nothing.

The solution of course is to make the method transactional, and in practice this is the behavior we want for all of the methods in the timesheet service. Invoking any method should begin a transaction. If the method call completes successfully, we will want to commit the transaction, but if the method throws an exception, we will want to roll back the transaction.

In principle, the transactionality of the methods could be implemented by explicitly writing all of the methods with appropriate `try` and `catch` blocks, and accessing the transaction manager in order to begin, commit, and roll back the transaction as appropriate. In practice, this would be quite a laborious operation; the boilerplate code highlighted in Listing 5-3 would need to be applied to any transactional method.

Listing 5-3. *Manually Managing a Transaction*

```
public void updateTimesheet(final Timesheet timesheet) {
    try {
        transactionManager.begin();
        timesheetDao.update(timesheet);
        emailDao.sendTimesheetUpdate(timesheet);
        transactionManager.commit();
    } catch( final RuntimeException e ) {
        transactionManager.rollback();
        throw e;
    }
}
```

Spring allows us to avoid all of this boilerplate code by using declarative transaction management. We use an annotation and/or a configuration file to state which methods of which classes should be treated as transactional.

Transactions Using Annotations

When annotations are available, we annotate the implementation classes that are to be transactional by using the `org.springframework.transaction.annotation.Transactional` annotation. This is the `@Transactional` annotation seen at the top of Listing 5-2.

Strictly speaking, my earlier statement was wrong: we do not want *all* of the methods in our implementation to be transactional. The set methods for the properties cannot fail, because they merely assign a value to a private field, so making them transactional holds no benefit. On the other hand, the overhead associated with invoking them in a transactional mode is likely to be quite low. In our implementation, we ignore the minor overhead and wrap these methods in a redundant transaction anyway.

If we did have methods that would incur significant overhead in a transactional mode, or for which transactionality was actively undesirable, we could avoid the problem by annotating the individual methods instead of the class as a whole as being transactional. An example of the alternative approach of individual method annotations is shown in Listing 5-4.

Listing 5-4. *A Service Method Individually Annotated As Transactional*

```
@Transactional
public void updateTimesheet(final Timesheet timesheet) {
    timesheetDao.update(timesheet);
    emailDao.sendTimesheetUpdate(timesheet);
}
```

The configuration file entry that enables the use of annotations is really quite remarkably simple. You must declare a transaction manager bean. This is what Spring will use to begin, commit, and roll back your transactions. In a full Java EE environment, you should use the JtaTransactionManager, as shown in Listing 5-5. This will orchestrate transactions for all the relevant transactional resources running within the container, regardless of whether they are running within Spring.

Listing 5-5. *Configuration for JTA Transactions*

```
<bean id="txManager"
class="org.springframework.transaction.jta.JtaTransactionManager"/>
```

In an environment where JTA transactions are not available (for example, when running within Tomcat), you will want to configure the DataSourceTransactionManager shown in Listing 5-6. This will manage transactions for any class that uses the DataSourceUtils helper class to manage transactions, which is the case for the JdbcTemplate class used by the JdbcDaoSupport helper class.

Listing 5-6. *Configuration for Stand-Alone Transactions*

```
<bean id="txManager"
class="org.springframework.jdbc.datasource.DataSourceTransactionManager">
    <property name="dataSource" ref="dataSource"/>
</bean>
```

Finally, for a Hibernate application in which you are unable to use JTA transactions, you will need to configure a HibernateTransactionManager bean so that the appropriate session methods are called to flush pending persistence operations out to the database before committing the transaction. Listing 5-7 shows the configuration of a transaction manager for use with Hibernate.

Listing 5-7. *Configuration for Stand-Alone Transactions with Hibernate*

```
<bean id="txManager"
class="org.springframework.orm.hibernate3.HibernateTransactionManager">
  <property name="sessionFactory" ref="sessionFactory"/>
</bean>
```

Having selected and configured a suitable transaction manager bean, all you need to do to take advantage of the transactional annotations is to add the declaration shown in Listing 5-8 to your configuration file.

Listing 5-8. *Configuring Annotation-Based Transactions*

```
<tx:annotation-driven transaction-manager="txManager"/>
```

This uses XML namespaces and the Spring 2 support for XML schemas as a shorthand for the configuration of beans that generate and substitute a proxy class for your service implementation as it is injected into dependent classes such as the controller. Figure 5-2 shows where this proxy fits into the hierarchy of configured beans.

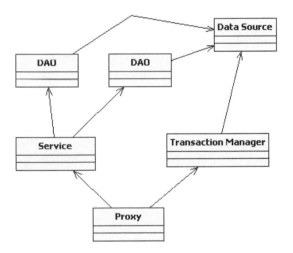

Figure 5-2. *Managing transactions*

Calls to the generated proxy implementation of the service will create the transaction through the transaction manager before invoking the service method. If the method completes without error, the proxy commits the transaction. If a runtime exception is thrown, the proxy rolls back the transaction (both through the transaction manager). It thus provides the functionality illustrated in Figure 5-3.

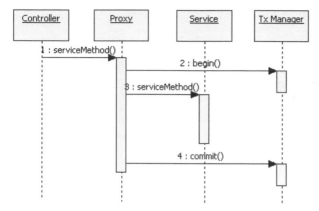

Figure 5-3. *The proxy intercepting a service call*

The proxy class is generated at runtime rather than being directly configured as with most of the Spring beans you have used so far. Although the bean is not something you will normally interact with directly, it does become visible under certain circumstances. First, you will encounter it when working with your classes under an interactive debugger. Method calls that would otherwise call directly into your service implementation will first disappear into the runtime proxy.

The other place you will encounter these generated proxy classes is when looking through the stack trace of thrown exceptions. Listing 5-9 shows some excerpts from a stack trace generated when an error occurs in the timesheet service implementation's transactional createTimesheet method. If no other classes were involved, the onSubmit method would call directly into the createTimesheet method, but because there are, the proxy object is clearly visible along with some additional lines.

Listing 5-9. *Abbreviated Excerpts from a Stack Trace Showing the Proxy Class*

```
com.apress...TimesheetServiceImpl.createTimesheet(...)
...
$Proxy64.createTimesheet(...)
com.apress...TimesheetCreateController.onSubmit(...)
...
```

Note that you can end up with multiple AOP proxies around the same target class in some circumstances, so you may see entries similar to Listing 5-9 appearing multiple times within the same call stack.

The additional elided lines between the proxied createTimesheet method and our createTimesheet implementation in Listing 5-9 are merely method calls in the reflection API used by the proxy to invoke the service.

You may have noted that I have described the transaction as rolling back for *unchecked* exceptions only. Checked exceptions will not automatically cause a rollback, but the annotation can be parameterized to require this.

■**Caution** The exception does not have to leave the boundary of the service class itself for the transaction logic to apply. A service method that throws a runtime exception will cause a rollback even if the calling method was within the same service class and caught and quashed the transaction.

There are other details of the transaction that can be configured, such as its isolation level and a fixed time-out period after which the transaction will be deemed to have failed. Table 5-1 shows the various properties that can be used to configure these details.

Table 5-1. *Properties of the @Transactional Annotation*

Parameter	Type	Description
isolation	Isolation (enum)	The transaction isolation level. This will be the default of the underlying data store unless specified explicitly. Changing this value can have significant performance implications.
noRollbackFor	Class<? extends Throwable>[]	The list of exceptions that would otherwise cause a rollback (that is, unchecked exceptions that should force a commit). An example declaration might be @Throwable(noRollbackFor= {MyRuntimeException.class}).
noRollbackForClassName	Array of strings	Performs the same function as the noRollbackFor property but specifies the class name as a String instead of providing an instance of the Class object. This is more verbose and more error prone, so it holds little value and I do not recommend using it.
propagation	Propagation (enum)	The transaction propagation type, which defines the circumstances under which a new transaction should be created if one does not already exist as the method is invoked. The default propagation depends on the transaction manager being used, but is typically to create a new transaction if one has not yet been established.
readOnly	boolean	Flags that the transaction is to be opened in read-only mode, which will sometimes allow for some performance benefits.

Table 5-1. *Properties of the @Transactional Annotation (Continued)*

Parameter	Type	Description
rollbackFor	Class<? extends Throwable>[]	The list of exceptions that will cause a rollback but would not otherwise (for example, checked exceptions that should force a rollback).
rollbackForClassName	String[]	Performs the same function as the rollbackFor property but specifies the class name as a String instead of providing an instance of the Class object. This is more verbose and more error prone, so it holds little value and I do not recommend using it.
timeout	int	A transactional method that does not complete after the specified number of seconds will be rolled back automatically. A value of −1 represents no time-out. The default will depend on the underlying transaction manager.

* *Enumerations are defined in the org.springframework.transaction.annotation package.*

These parameters give us fine-grained control over the transactional behavior. Although the annotations can be applied to interfaces, interface methods, classes, or class methods, you should apply them to the concrete implementations only. Annotations are not inherited, so if you annotate interfaces, the behavior will depend on the precise type of proxy being used. Annotation of concrete implementations (classes) only is recommended because the behavior is then unambiguous.

Transactions Using XML Mappings

If you are not able to use Java 5 enhancements in your application, you can configure beans to achieve the same effect without annotations. Listing 5-10 shows the XML-based configuration, which is equivalent to the single line of configuration (shown in Listing 5-8) that was necessary to declare the use of annotation-based transactions.

Listing 5-10. *Declarative XML Configuration of the Transactions*

```
<tx:advice id="txAdvice" transaction-manager="txManager">
  <tx:attributes>
    <tx:method name="*"/>
  </tx:attributes>
</tx:advice>
```

```
<aop:config>
  <aop:pointcut
    id="timesheetServiceOperations"
expression="execution(* com.apress.timesheets.service.*Service*.*(..))"
  />
  <aop:advisor advice-ref="txAdvice"
    pointcut-ref="timesheetServiceOperations"/>
</aop:config>
```

The declaration of the transaction manager remains the same and is not shown in Listing 5-10. Although this is more verbose than the annotation-based equivalent, the actual configuration details are comparable.

The aop:config section of the configuration file specifies the classes that will be subjected to transactionality (see the following "Aspect-Oriented Programming" section for the specifics of this configuration). The tx:advice section specifies the methods within these classes that will be made transactional. For this reason, the properties of the tx:method element explained in Table 5-2 correspond almost exactly with the parameters of the @Transaction annotation.

Table 5-2. *Properties of the tx:method Element*

Property	Default	Description
name	-	The name of the method to be made transactional. Wildcards can be used.
isolation	DEFAULT	The isolation level to apply during the transaction. Legal values are DEFAULT, READ_COMMITTED, READ_UNCOMMITTED, REPEATABLE_READ, or SERIALIZABLE. DEFAULT uses the default isolation of the underlying data store.
no-rollback-for	-	The fully qualified names of unchecked exceptions that will not cause rollbacks to occur.
propagation	REQUIRED	The transaction propagation type, which defines the circumstances under which a new transaction should be created if one does not already exist as the method is invoked. Legal values are MANDATORY, NESTED, NEVER, NOT_SUPPORTED, REQUIRED, REQUIRES_NEW, or SUPPORTS. The default of REQUIRED specifies that a transaction will be created if one does not already exist.
timeout	-1	A transactional method that does not complete after the specified number of seconds will be rolled back automatically. A value of -1 represents no time-out.
read-only	false	When true, this indicates that the transaction is to be opened in read-only mode, which will sometimes allow for some performance benefits. Legal values are true and false.
rollback-for	-	The fully qualified names of checked exceptions that will cause rollbacks to occur.

Regardless of the method used—XML based or annotation based—the underlying implementation of this behavior is applied by using Spring's support for aspect-oriented programming combined with its support for XML schema extensions.

Aspect-Oriented Programming (AOP)

Aspect-oriented programming (AOP) is a technique that allows for implementation of generic behavior that does not fit well into the object-oriented model. Managing transactions is a good example of this sort of problem; we could build a set of classes to integrate into our object model to manage transactions, but the resulting implementation would be specific to our system.

Logging, auditing, and security can also present problems of this sort. For example, an auditing system may need to keep track of the users invoking certain methods on the data access objects. However, the user information may not be directly available at these points in the implementation, and altering the application so that the credentials are passed around the system appropriately will tie the application inextricably to the auditing implementation and complicate the design. Problems of this type that cut across various parts of the object model are described as *cross-cutting concerns*.

Databases have the notion of triggers to allow related functionality to be invoked when particular events occur in the relational model. Similarly, aspects allow related functionality to be invoked when particular events occur in the object model.

AOP comes with a substantial body of terminology. This chapter does not attempt to explore AOP in full detail, but I will briefly cover the terminology related to the examples you will look at:

Cross-cutting concern: A problem that applies to parts of the object model that are not conveniently related, or that are not related in an object-oriented manner. For example, a problem that applies to method return values *in general*, rather than to the methods of a single class, is not an object-oriented problem as such.

Pointcut: A rule for matching the parts of the object model that the functionality will be applied to. This is analogous to the rule defining when a database trigger would apply.

Aspect: A package of functionality providing the cross-cutting requirements. A set of triggers for auditing database access would be analogous to an AOP aspect for auditing.

Advice: The implementation of functionality that will be applied. This is analogous to the implementation of a database trigger.

Note that my analogies with database triggers are not intended to imply that AOP applies only to data access. On the contrary, aspects can be applied anywhere in the object model that can be identified with a pointcut. AOP can be used to audit application performance as readily as it can be used to audit user access to particular data entities.

Schema Extensions and Annotation-Based Transactions

The transaction management that you looked at in the section "Transactions Using Annotations" could hardly have been simpler. The addition of this entry, shown in Listing 5-11, in the application context creates all of the appropriate AOP objects and uses the annotations on the relevant classes to manage transactionality.

Listing 5-11. *The Single-Line Annotation Configuration*

```
<tx:annotation-driven transaction-manager="txManager"/>
```

This configuration can be so terse because of the provision in Spring for facilities to allow custom extensions to the configuration schema. The `tx:` prefix on elements indicates that a body of code registered with the environment using the standard XML namespace extension facilities will be invoked and that the rest of the configuration information required is extracted from annotations at runtime.

This book does not attempt to cover the implementation of these namespace extension facilities because most beginner Spring developers will be consumers rather than authors of the extensions—and as Listing 5-11 illustrates, they tend to make the configuration so terse as to need no explanation! The namespace extensions can, for the most part, be taken as mere configuration file entries. You should be aware that they are backed by an implementation, but then this is equally true for the conventional configuration elements of the default namespace such as the `<bean>` element.

Next you will look briefly at the relationship between the schema-based (rather than annotation-based) use of the transaction schema extension. You will then look at a simple use of the Spring AOP support to implement a security aspect. Finally, you will see some of Spring's support for other ways of creating and managing aspects.

Schema-Based Transaction Declaration

Revisiting the schema-based declaration of the transactions from Listing 5-10, you can start to see some of the AOP terminology. The first part of the listing declares and configures an advice implementation, as shown in Listing 5-12.

Listing 5-12. *Declaring a Transaction Manager Advice*

```
<tx:advice id="txAdvice" transaction-manager="txManager">
   <tx:attributes>
      <tx:method name="*"/>
   </tx:attributes>
</tx:advice>
```

The attributes are configuring the advice bean that will be created by use of the
`tx:advice` element. Then the configuration details in Listing 5-12 declare a pointcut
describing the service classes and their methods and map it to the advice created by the
configuration entry of Listing 5-13.

Listing 5-13. *Configuring a Pointcut for the Timesheet Service Advisor*

```
<aop:config>
   <aop:pointcut
      id="timesheetServiceOperations"
expression="execution(* com.apress.timesheets.service.*Service*.*(..))"
   />
   <aop:advisor
      advice-ref="txAdvice"
      pointcut-ref="timesheetServiceOperations"/>
</aop:config>
```

The specific beans created by these configuration entries are hidden from us, but this
does not particularly matter because the enhanced XML syntax allows us to express all of
our requirements directly through the configuration file.

A Custom Aspect Implementation

You will now look at the implementation of a mechanism to secure calls to the service
layer based on the user who is currently logged in to the application. This is a classic cross-
cutting concern.

I have chosen two methods from our service layer interface of Listing 5-1 to secure, and
their signatures are shown in Listing 5-14.

Listing 5-14. *Methods to Secure*

```
List<Timesheet> listTimesheets(UserAccount account);
Timesheet findTimesheet(Long id);
```

Between them, these two methods allow me to illustrate some of the most useful applications of AOP. Before the call to `listTimesheets`, we want to check whether the account
details provided match those of the current user. We therefore need to intercept both the
method and its return parameter. After the call to `findTimesheet`, we want to determine
whether the timesheet returned belongs to the current user, so the aspect must be invoked
after the method call and must have access to the return value of the method.

■**Note** The specifics of how we acquire the authentication information for the currently logged-in user is taken as a given in this chapter. The specifics are covered in Chapter 7, but the techniques described here apply regardless of how the user credentials are retrieved.

The advice implementation class implements two methods, each parameterized for the value that will be intercepted: the user account parameter for the listTimesheets method and the return value of findTimesheet. Listing 5-15 shows these method signatures and the name of the class that implements them. (The full implementation of these methods is given in Listing 5-25, where the alternative use of annotations is explained.)

Listing 5-15. *The Advice Implementation Class and Methods*

```
public class TimesheetSecurityAdvice {
    public void list(final UserAccount account) {
        // ...
    }

    public void findTimesheet(final Timesheet timesheet) {
        // ...
    }
}
```

This advice class is configured as a normal Spring bean, as shown in Listing 5-16, and can therefore be injected with any other beans useful to the aspect. For example, in principle we might want to conduct a limited database query via a DAO bean to determine the user's access to the timesheet instead of relying on the service to retrieve the identified timesheet and then verify the access rights after the fact. However, for the sake of this example, we use the less-efficient method, and so no additional properties are required.

Listing 5-16. *Declaring the Bean Implementing the Advice*

```
<bean id="securityAdvice"
 class="com.apress.timesheets.TimesheetSecurityAdvice"/>
```

The behavior of the advice is specified by using the aop:config element, which in turn contains aop:pointcut and aop:aspect elements (in that order). Listing 5-17 shows the pointcut to describe the listTimesheet method.

Listing 5-17. *The Ordering of the aop:config Element*

```
<aop:config>
  <aop:pointcut .../>
  ...
  <aop:aspect .../>
  ...
</aop:config>
```

Pointcut definitions can be shared between multiple aspects, or can be declared as an attribute of the aspect definition itself. Typically, a pointcut is defined by using a wildcard. In Listing 5-18 we are specifying method names beginning with *list* and having any return value in the `com.apress.timesheets.service` package, where the class name begins with `TimesheetService` and the method may take zero or more parameters (note the use of the double-period syntax to indicate this last requirement). The `and args(account)` part of the declaration names the first parameter. This name is then used by the aspect to identify which parameter of the service method should be mapped to the parameter of the aspect method.

Listing 5-18. *The Pointcut Identifying the Service's listTimesheets Method*

```
<aop:pointcut id="listTimesheets"
expression="execution(* com.apress.timesheets.service.TimesheetService*.list*(..)) ➥
and args(account)" />
```

Having declared the pointcut that our aspect will use to identify the service's `listTimesheet` method, we then declare the relationship between the aspect method and the pointcut by using the `aop:aspect` element (referencing the aspect implementation bean) and its component elements. In Listing 5-19 we use the `aop:before` element to indicate that the aspect implementation method must be invoked before the call to the service method. We also supply the name of the aspect implementation method as the parameter to the method attribute, the name of the arguments to be provided to the aspect (the name defined in the pointcut of Listing 5-18) as the parameter to the `arg-names` attribute, and we reference the pointcut to be used as the parameter to the `pointcut-ref` attribute.

The pointcut declaration intercepting the `findTimesheet` method, shown in Listing 5-19, is specified similarly to that for the `listTimesheets` method but omits the parameter names because we are concerned only with the (unnamed) return value of the method.

Listing 5-19. *Relating the Aspect Implementation Details to the Pointcut Declaration*

```
<aop:aspect ref="securityAdvice">
   <aop:before method="list"
      arg-names="account"
      pointcut-ref="listTimesheets"/>
   ...
</aop:aspect>
```

Similarly, we relate the pointcut describing the service layer's findTimesheet method to its aspect implementation in Listing 5-20.

Listing 5-20. *The Pointcut for the findTimesheet Method*

```
<aop:pointcut id="findTimesheet"
expression=
"execution(* com.apress.timesheets.service.TimesheetService*.findTimesheet(..))"/>
```

In Listing 5-21 we use the aop:after-returning element to indicate that the service method should be invoked and only then will the aspect implementation be invoked. The method name is specified as before, but we also specify the parameter name corresponding to the value returned from the service method by using the returning attribute. The aspect is associated with its pointcut as before, by using the pointcut-ref attribute.

Listing 5-21. *Declaring the Aspect for findTimesheet*

```
<aop:after-returning
   method="findTimesheet"
   returning="timesheet"
   pointcut-ref="findTimesheet"/>
```

Collating these individual excerpts from the aop:config element, we get the full definition used to relate the aspect implementation to the pointcuts defining where it applies. This is shown in Listing 5-22.

Listing 5-22. *The Complete Aspect Definition*

```
<aop:config>
   <aop:pointcut id="listTimesheets"
expression="execution(* com.apress.timesheets.service.TimesheetService*.list*(..)) ➥
and args(account)"/>
   <aop:pointcut id="findTimesheet"
```

```
expression=
"execution(* com.apress.timesheets.service.TimesheetService*.findTimesheet(..))"/>
    <aop:aspect ref="securityAdvice">
        <aop:before method="list"
            arg-names="account"
            pointcut-ref="listTimesheets"/>

        <aop:after-returning
            method="findTimesheet"
            returning="timesheet"
            pointcut-ref="findTimesheet"/>
    </aop:aspect>
</aop:config>
```

Having seen how the implementations whose signatures were outlined in Listing 5-14 are mapped to the pointcuts determining when and how they are invoked, we will now take a look at their pleasingly simple implementation.

The first method is to be invoked when a call is made to the listTimesheets service method. The single parameter of that method will be mapped to the first parameter of this method (shown in Listing 5-23). If for any reason the current user does not match the user details supplied to this method (if, for example, the user has edited a form submission to specify a username other than his own), an exception will be thrown. This exception will prevent the call to the service from commencing unless the current user is an administrative user, who would be presumed to have permission to access any user's timesheets.

Listing 5-23. *Checking Whether the User Is Allowed Access to the Requested List*

```
public void list(final UserAccount account) {
    if( usersMatch(account) || isAdministrator()) {
        return;
    }

    final UserAccount currentUser = PrincipalHelper.getUser();
    throw new TimesheetSecurityException(
            "Access violation while attempting to list resources",
            currentUser);
}
```

The next method will be checking the return value of the service layer's findTimesheet method after it has been called. Spring's AOP components will make the method call and then invoke our method after the fact, supplying the returned value as the parameter to this method as dictated by our configuration.

■**Caution** Strictly speaking, this is a less-secure operation than the previous one. Because we have already retrieved the data, it is conceivable that we could somehow leak it "up" to the invoking method, perhaps as part of the exception details (although this is not the case in the specific implementation we have here). I have used the approach here purely as an illustration of the technique.

We extract the owning user from the timesheet object supplied and check whether the current user matches (or is an administrator) as before, as shown in Listing 5-24.

Listing 5-24. *Checking Whether the User Is Permitted Access to the Returned Timesheet*

```
public void findTimesheet(final Timesheet timesheet) {
    final UserAccount account = timesheet.getConsultant();
    if( usersMatch(account) || isAdministrator()) {
        return;
    }

    final UserAccount currentUser = PrincipalHelper.getUser();
    throw new TimesheetSecurityException(
            "Access violation while attempting to list resources",
            currentUser);
}
```

In both of the implementations, I have used the approach of throwing an exception to indicate that the requirements were not met regardless of whether the original method succeeded or failed. This allows the specific security event to be communicated to higher layers without needing to cater for special security-oriented return values in the API of the service layer.

In this section, you have looked at only a couple of the types of advice that can be declared (before and after-returning). The other mechanisms available are after-throwing for intercepting exceptions, after (which runs regardless of how the method completes—the after-returning method won't be invoked if the service method throws an exception of its own accord), and around, which allows you to take full control of the method life cycle, even preventing the service method from being invoked without needing to throw an exception.

Further Support for AOP in Spring

In the previous section, you looked at a single mechanism for implementing aspects in Spring. In this section, I will briefly mention other ways of implementing aspects by using the AspectJ annotation-based syntax and by creating custom Advice and Pointcut implementation classes.

Using @AspectJ Annotations

Spring provides support for the annotations of a third-party library, AspectJ. AspectJ annotations allow you to express the pointcut definitions, the advices' relationships with the pointcuts, and the aspect implementation all within the class implementation files. The major advantage of this technique is that this configuration information can be picked up purely by adding the `<aop:aspectj-autoproxy/>` element to the configuration file. Conversely, this can be a disadvantage if the user expects to have more visibility on the configuration and it's hidden away in an implementation file.

Listing 5-25 shows the implementation of our timesheet security advice class with suitable annotations to apply the same rules as were specified in Listing 5-22. The initial set of five private methods in Listing 5-25 are provided purely as places to define the pointcuts.

Listing 5-25. *Applying the Aspect Configuration by Using AspectJ Annotations*

```
@Aspect
public class TimesheetSecurityAdvice {
    @Pointcut("args(account,..)")
    private void accountParameterOperation(UserAccount account) {}

    @Pointcut("execution(com.apress.timesheets.entity.Timesheet *(..))")
    private void timesheetReturningOperation() {}

    @Pointcut("execution(*
com.apress.timesheets.service.TimesheetService.*(..))")
    private void accountServiceOperation() {}

    @Pointcut("accountServiceOperation() && timesheetReturningOperation()")
    private void findTimesheetOperation() {}

    @Pointcut("accountServiceOperation() && accountParameterOperation(account)")
    private void accountTimesheetOperation(UserAccount account) {}

    @Before("accountTimesheetOperation(account)")
    public void list(final UserAccount account) {
        validateCurrentUser();

        if (usersMatch(account) || isAdministrator()) {
            return;
        }
```

```java
      final UserAccount currentUser = PrincipalHelper.getUser();
      throw new TimesheetSecurityException(
            "Access violation while attempting to list resources", currentUser);
  }


  @AfterReturning(pointcut="findTimesheetOperation()",returning = "timesheet")
  public void findTimesheet(final Timesheet timesheet) {
     validateCurrentUser();

     final UserAccount account = timesheet.getConsultant();
     if (usersMatch(account) || isAdministrator()) {
        return;
     }

     final UserAccount currentUser = PrincipalHelper.getUser();
     throw new TimesheetSecurityException(
            "Access violation while attempting to list resources", currentUser);
  }

  private boolean usersMatch(final UserAccount target)
          throws TimesheetSecurityException {
     final UserAccount currentUser = PrincipalHelper.getUser();
     return target.getId().equals(currentUser.getId());
  }

  private void validateCurrentUser() throws TimesheetSecurityException {
     final UserAccount currentUser = PrincipalHelper.getUser();
     if (currentUser == null) {
        throw new TimesheetSecurityException("No user logged in", null);
     }
  }

  private boolean isAdministrator() {
     final UserAccount currentUser = PrincipalHelper.getUser();
     for (final UserRole role : currentUser.getRoles()) {
        if (UserRole.ROLE_ADMINISTRATOR.equals(role.getRoleName())) {
           return true;
        }
     }
     return false;
  }
}
```

The first method, `accountParameterOperation`, defines a pointcut that will apply to any method in any class that takes at least one parameter. The type of parameter is defined by the parameter list of the annotated method as being a `UserAccount` reference. The name of the parameter in the pointcut annotation must correspond to the name of the parameter in the method definition, and can be made available to advice logic by using this same name.

The second method, `timesheetReturningOperation`, defines a pointcut that will apply to any method in any class that returns a `Timesheet` reference.

The third method, `accountServiceOperation`, defines a pointcut that will apply to any method that implements the `TimesheetService` interface.

In order to apply our two advice methods, we need to combine these pointcuts to form more-restrictive pointcuts. We can do this by using the names of the methods defining the pointcuts combined with the && operator (equivalent to the and keyword in Listing 5-22). The last two private methods therefore define combinations of the first three operations.

The method `findTimesheetOperation` therefore defines a pointcut that will apply to any method of a `TimesheetService`-implementing class that returns a `Timesheet` reference. Given the methods available in the interface, this means that the pointcut will apply to the `findTimesheet` implementation.

The method `accountTimesheetOperation` defines a pointcut that will apply to any method of a `TimesheetService`-implementing class that takes a `UserAccount` reference as its first parameter. This will mean that the pointcut applies to the `listTimesheets` implementation.

The advice definitions are applied by using the `@Before` and `@AfterReturning` annotations. As you would expect, these determine that the annotated method should be applied to the pointcut-defined methods before and after invocation, respectively, and there are `@AfterThrowing`, `@After`, and `@Around` annotations available to support advice applying to the other phases of the method life cycle.

The methods use the pointcut-defining methods to identify the methods to which they will be applied. It is possible to omit the `@Pointcut` annotations entirely. Listing 5-26 shows the `@Before` annotation with the pointcut definition included explicitly.

Listing 5-26. *A Pointcut Declaration Within the Advice Annotation*

```
@Before("execution(* com.apress.timesheets.service.TimesheetService.*(..)) "
    +" && args(account,..)")
public void list(final UserAccount account) {
...
}
```

It is possible to move the pointcut annotations into a separate class from the aspect implementation, and Listing 5-27 shows a suitable pointcut definition class.

Listing 5-27. *The Annotated Advice Implementation Class*

```
@Aspect
public class TimesheetSecurityPointcuts {
    @Pointcut("args(account,..)")
    public void accountParameterOperation(UserAccount account) {}

    @Pointcut("execution(com.apress.timesheets.entity.Timesheet *(..))")
    public void timesheetReturningOperation() {}

    @Pointcut("execution(*
com.apress.timesheets.service.TimesheetService.*(..))")
    public void accountServiceOperation() {}

    @Pointcut("accountServiceOperation() && timesheetReturningOperation()")
    public void findTimesheetOperation() {}

    @Pointcut("accountServiceOperation() && accountParameterOperation(account)")
    public void accountTimesheetOperation(UserAccount account) {}
}
```

An advantage of taking this approach is that the pointcut definitions become independent of the aspects. They can be used to apply other aspects. They also reduce the "clutter" of the aspect implementation class.

The disadvantage of this approach is that the corresponding method name when used in advice annotations must be fully qualified. Listing 5-28 shows the resulting change to the @Before and @AfterReturning annotations from Listing 5-25 when the pointcut methods have been moved into the external class of Listing 5-27.

Listing 5-28. *The Fully Qualified References to the Pointcut Names in an External Class*

```
@Before("com.apress.timesheets.TimesheetSecurityPointcuts ➥
.accountTimesheetOperation(account)")
public void list(final UserAccount account) {
...
}

@AfterReturning(pointcut=
    "com.apress.timesheets.TimesheetSecurityPointcuts.findTimesheetOperation()",
    returning="timesheet")
public void findTimesheet(final Timesheet timesheet) {
...
}
```

The advice annotations have become almost as unwieldy as the explicit example of Listing 5-26. Unless you need to apply the pointcuts to invoke multiple advice implementations, or unless the advice implementations are extremely complicated, you will probably find it easiest to include the pointcut and advice annotations in the same class.

Using AspectJ

The AspectJ annotations originate in the AspectJ library, created independently of the Spring project. AspectJ itself provides a preprocessing tool, allowing aspect information to be created by using extra keywords in the source code, and retained in the class files at compile time. This information can then be used with an AspectJ library, using a technique referred to as *code weaving*, to generate suitable proxy classes from the extra metadata.

Spring supports a subset of the features offered by AspectJ itself, but it is possible to use the AspectJ libraries in conjunction with AspectJ-generated code to take advantage of the full AspectJ feature set. The use of AspectJ in this manner lies outside the scope of this book, but you can find additional information on this subject on the Spring website, and on the AspectJ page of the Eclipse project website: `http://www.eclipse.org/aspectj/`.

Explicit Implementations with Spring

In the previous sections, we have used a declarative approach to the management of our pointcuts and advice objects. In this last section, you will take a look at how advice objects can be created in code, and how pointcut objects can be defined that result in their invocation.

The use of explicit implementations to manage these processes gives us complete control over the criteria by which our advice methods are applied, but we will still rely greatly upon the Spring Framework libraries to make the necessary configuration and invocations, so the additional effort necessary to create these implementations is actually quite small.

Using the ProxyBeanFactory

The first technique you will look at is the use of the `ProxyBeanFactory` object to apply an interceptor implementation. The `ProxyBeanFactory` generates a proxy in place of the specified classes. When a method is invoked on the proxy, it will create a `MethodInvocation` object representing the parameters of the method call. This is then passed to a configured `Advice` class. The `Advice` class carries out any processing necessary before the method call, and can use `try/catch/finally` notation to determine the actions to take during the life cycle of the method call, and indeed can omit the call entirely if this is deemed necessary.

Listing 5-29 shows the `Advice` class that we will provide to the `ProxyBeanFactory`. This checks the parameters of the method being called, applies the "before" advice to its parameter if appropriate, makes the method call, and then applies the "after" advice to its return value if appropriate.

Listing 5-29. *The Implementation of a Method Interceptor Advice*

```java
public class TimesheetInterceptor implements MethodInterceptor {
    private final TimesheetSecurityAdvice advice =
        new TimesheetSecurityAdvice();

    public Object invoke(final MethodInvocation invocation) throws Throwable {
        final Object[] args = invocation.getArguments();
        if( (args.length >= 1) && (args[0] instanceof UserAccount)) {
            advice.list((UserAccount)args[0]);
        }

        final Object retVal = invocation.proceed();

        if( retVal instanceof Timesheet ) {
            advice.findTimesheet((Timesheet)retVal);
        }

        return retVal;
    }
}
```

The implementation in Listing 5-29 is straightforward. Its complexity lies in the proxy factory bean's implementation, but this is a library class, so all you have to do is configure it. Listing 5-30 shows how we configure it to apply the advice of Listing 5-29 to the TimesheetService bean implementation.

Listing 5-30. *The Configuration of a Proxy Factory Bean with the Interceptor*

```xml
<bean id="timesheetService"
    class="org.springframework.aop.framework.ProxyFactoryBean">
    <property name="proxyInterfaces">
        <value>
            com.apress.timesheets.service.TimesheetService
        </value>
    </property>
    <property name="interceptorNames">
        <list>
            <value>timesheetInterceptor</value>
        </list>
    </property>
    <property name="target" ref="timesheetServiceRaw"/>
</bean>
```

```
<bean id="timesheetInterceptor"
   class="com.apress.timesheets.customaop.TimesheetInterceptor"/>
```

The original `TimesheetService` implementation bean will be renamed to `timesheetServiceRaw` and referenced from the line shown in bold in Listing 5-30. This provides the proxy with the underlying method implementations that advice objects will have access to. The other properties of the proxy factory specify the service interface that the proxy object must implement, and the name of the interceptor bean that will be invoked. It is possible to configure the proxy factory to use the CGLIB code-generation library in place of standard JDK proxy objects if the bean to be proxied does not implement any suitable interfaces.

Using the DefaultPointcutAdvisor and a Pointcut

The `ProxyFactoryBean` is a good solution, but allows us only a very crude level of interception—at the class level—where the annotations and declarative XML approaches provided much finer control. The advice invocation also leaves something to be desired as we effectively need to implement the complete life cycle logic when we may be interested in only one particular phase.

Admittedly, this is not a particularly difficult, but it can reduce the clarity of the implementation slightly. We can instead create `Advice` and `Pointcut` objects independently, and then tie them together by using a `DefaultPointcutAdvisor` object.

Listing 5-31 shows the implementation of a before advice, and Listing 5-32 the implementation of an after returning advice. Rather than repeat the implementation logic of the advice used in the earlier examples, I have delegated the advice operation details to a `TimesheetSecurityAdvice` object retained as a field within the class. This is for the purposes of this example only. Normally, you would either implement the advice logic explicitly, or inject the delegate as a bean property.

Listing 5-31. *The Implementation of a Before Advice*

```
public class TimesheetBeforeAdvice implements MethodBeforeAdvice {
   private final TimesheetSecurityAdvice advice
      = new TimesheetSecurityAdvice();

   public void before(final Method method, final Object[] args,
      final Object target) throws Throwable
   {
      advice.list((UserAccount)args[0]);
   }
}
```

Listing 5-32. *The Implementation of an After Returning Advice*

```
public class TimesheetAfterReturningAdvice implements AfterReturningAdvice {
   private final TimesheetSecurityAdvice advice = new TimesheetSecurityAdvice();

   public void afterReturning(final Object retVal, final Method
      method, final Object[] args, final Object target) throws Throwable
   {
      advice.findTimesheet((Timesheet)retVal);
   }
}
```

Corresponding advice interfaces exist for the other phases of the method life cycle: `AfterThrowingAdvice` and `AfterAdvice` (with `MethodInterceptor` corresponding to the around advice).

Pointcuts are defined as implementations of the `Pointcut` interface. Two distinct types of pointcuts are available: static pointcuts and dynamic pointcuts.

Static pointcuts are used in advance to determine the methods to which advice will be applied based purely on the method and class signatures. Runtime information such as parameter values (rather than parameter types) cannot be used in a static pointcut. A static pointcut is typically created by extending the `StaticMethodMatcherPointcut` interface, as shown in Listing 5-33.

Listing 5-33. *The Implementation of a Static Pointcut*

```
public class TimesheetStaticPointcutImpl extends StaticMethodMatcherPointcut {
   public boolean matches(final Method method, final Class type) {
      if( !TimesheetService.class.isAssignableFrom(type)) {
         return false;
      }

      if( method.getParameterTypes().length == 0 ) {
         return false;
      }

      if(!UserAccount.class.isAssignableFrom(method.getParameterTypes()[0])) {
         return false;
      }

      return true;
   }
}
```

The matches method of the pointcut implementation will be called for candidate methods to determine whether the pointcut applies to them. The proxy will then be generated to make the appropriate method calls. The matches method here specifies that advice associated with this pointcut will be applied to methods when (according to the if conditions) the target class is a TimesheetService implementation, the method takes at least one parameter, and the first parameter of the method is a UserAccount reference. This is exactly equivalent to the pointcut defined declaratively in Listing 5-26.

With a pointcut and advice defined, we combine them into an advisor that will apply the pointcut to corresponding methods. The advisor is detected by the Spring bean factory when it is loaded and used to generate appropriate proxy implementations. The advisor configuration is shown in Listing 5-34.

Listing 5-34. *Configuring an Advisor for the Before Advice and Static Pointcut*

```
<bean id="timesheetBeforeAdvice"
    class="org.springframework.aop.support.DefaultPointcutAdvisor">
    <property name="advice">
        <bean class="com.apress.timesheets.customaop.TimesheetBeforeAdvice"/>
    </property>
    <property name="pointcut" ref="staticPointcut"/>
</bean>

<bean id="staticPointcut"
    class="com.apress.timesheets.customaop.TimesheetStaticPointcutImpl"/>
```

Listing 5-35 defines a similar static pointcut that will apply to methods in the TimesheetService class that return a Timesheet reference, thus matching the pointcut used by the AfterReturning advice of earlier examples.

Listing 5-35. *An Alternative Static Pointcut Implementation*

```
public class TimesheetReturningStaticPointcutImpl
    extends StaticMethodMatcherPointcut
{
    public boolean matches(final Method method, final Class type) {
        if( !TimesheetService.class.isAssignableFrom(type)) {
            return false;
        }

        if(!Timesheet.class.isAssignableFrom(method.getReturnType())) {
            return false;
        }
```

```
      return true;
   }
}
```

This is again configured as a DefaultPointcutAdvisor bean in Listing 5-36 to apply the advice to methods identified by the pointcut.

Listing 5-36. *Configuring the After Returning Advice with a Static Pointcut*

```
<bean id="timesheetAfterReturningAdvice"
   class="org.springframework.aop.support.DefaultPointcutAdvisor">
   <property name="advice">
      <bean
class="com.apress.timesheets.customaop.TimesheetAfterReturningAdvice"/>
   </property>
   <property name="pointcut" ref="returningPointcut"/>
</bean>

<bean id="returningPointcut"
   class="com.apress.timesheets.customaop.TimesheetReturningStaticPointcutImpl"/>
```

Pointcuts do not have to be statically defined. They can be defined dynamically, so that the decision of whether to invoke the method is made immediately prior to the call itself. *Dynamic pointcuts* therefore have information about the current state of the application (including ThreadLocal contents) and the parameters to be passed to the method.

Listing 5-37 defines a pointcut that will be used to avoid calling the advice logic if the current user is an administrator. The class implements the same matches method as was used in Listing 5-35 for static pointcuts. This allows the framework to avoid generating proxies for inappropriate types. A second (abstract) matches method is then implemented to determine at runtime whether the advice should be applied.

Listing 5-37. *Implementing a Dynamic Pointcut*

```
public class TimesheetDynamicPointcutImpl
   extends DynamicMethodMatcherPointcut
{
   @Override
   public boolean matches(final Method method, final Class type) {
      if( !TimesheetService.class.isAssignableFrom(type)) {
         return false;
      }
```

```
      if(!Timesheet.class.isAssignableFrom(method.getReturnType())) {
         return false;
      }

      return true;
   }


   public boolean matches(final Method method, final Class type,
      final Object[] args)
   {
      for( final UserRole role : PrincipalHelper.getUser().getRoles() ) {
         if("ROLE_ADMINISTRATOR".equals(role.getRoleName())) {
            return false;
         }
      }

      return true;
   }
}
```

Listing 5-38 shows that the dynamic pointcut can be applied to exactly the same advice logic shown in Listing 5-32 that was configured with a static pointcut in Listing 5-36.

Listing 5-38. *Configuring the After Returning Advice with a Dynamic Pointcut*

```
<bean id="timesheetAfterReturningAdvice"
   class="org.springframework.aop.support.DefaultPointcutAdvisor">
   <property name="advice">
      <bean
class="com.apress.timesheets.customaop.TimesheetAfterReturningAdvice"/>
   </property>
   <property name="pointcut" ref="dynamicPointcut"/>
</bean>

<bean id="dynamicPointcut"
   class="com.apress.timesheets.customaop.TimesheetDynamicPointcutImpl"/>
```

The example implementation source code provided at the Source Code/Download area of the Apress website (www.apress.com) includes copious output-logging logic that I have omitted for the sake of brevity. If you configure the use of the dynamic pointcut, you will see that the TimesheetAfterReturningAdvice logic is invoked only when a nonadministrative user carries out operations that cause the findTimesheet method to be invoked.

Conclusion

In this chapter, you have looked at the development of the service layer containing business logic. You have seen how the methods of the service layer can be made transactional by using AOP. You also have also seen how AOP classes can be created to enforce security guarantees upon the service layer without influencing its design.

In the next chapter, we will finally build our presentation layer—the web application—upon the foundation provided by the service layer created in this chapter.

■ ■ ■

CHAPTER 6

Web Applications

In the preceding chapter, you looked at the issues around building the service layer for our application. In this chapter, we start to build the presentation layer of our application as a web application.

The Model View Controller Pattern

The standard architectural model for building a web application now is the Model View Controller (MVC) pattern, shown in Figure 6-1. I will present this briefly before embarking on a discussion of the specific implementations that are available to you when building a Spring application.

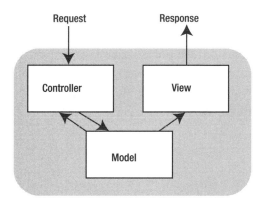

Figure 6-1. *The Model View Controller pattern*

The *model* is the domain-specific representation of the data that is involved in your application. Our entity beans and the service layer form the model in a Spring application; your presentation layer is merely used to manipulate the data in the model.

The *view* is a representation of the data in the model. This is not to say that there is no other data in the view—it may well contain transitory data and implementation data—but that the main purpose of the view is to accurately represent the data in the model and reflect changes to that data.

The *controller* updates the model in reaction to events received from the user, and causes the appropriate view for the model to be displayed or updated.

It is entirely possible to build an MVC application by using ordinary Java EE components. For example, you could build the model by using JDBC and beans (or even use `ResultSet` objects directly). You can build the views from JSPs and servlets, and the controllers from servlets.

Although it is possible to build an MVC application by using traditional Java EE technologies, it is not an edifying experience. None of these components establishes a clean boundary of responsibility, so the distinction between controller and view, for example, is often lost in large applications with the corresponding increase in code complexity and loss of clarity. Instead, Spring provides its own MVC frameworks: Spring MVC and Spring Web Flow (the two are closely related).

Managing Contexts

The web application will need to draw Spring beans from a context. This means that the context must be available to filters, servlets, JSPs, and any other objects that will be encountered during the processing of a request.

Context Loader Listener

The context loader listener is a standard Java listener implementation, and as such it is ideally situated to maintain state information during the life cycle of the web application that it is attached to. The context loader listener must be declared in your web application's deployment descriptor file (`web.xml`), as shown in Listing 6-1.

Listing 6-1. *Declaring a Context Loader Listener*

```
<listener>
  <listener-class>
     org.springframework.web.context.ContextLoaderListener
  </listener-class>
</listener>
```

By default, this will read an XML bean configuration file from `WEB-INF/applicationContext.xml` and maintain the beans declared here until the web application is shut down.

This default location can be overridden by using a `context-param` entry in `web.xml`, as shown in Listing 6-2.

Listing 6-2. *Overriding the Default Context Configuration File*

```
<context-param>
  <param-name>contextConfigLocation</param-name>
  <param-value>classpath:applicationContext.xml</param-value>
</context-param>
```

Here I instruct the listener to load the configuration file from the root of the classpath instead of the WEB-INF directory. ContextLoaderListener uses a property editor to parse the parameter values, so the normal syntax for specifying resource types (for example, the classpath: prefix) can be used as if this were a standard bean definition. You can specify multiple configuration files by providing a comma-separated list of resources for the parameters' values.

Context Loader Servlet

Listeners were added in version 2.3 of the Servlet API. If you are working with an older application server, you must use ContextLoaderServlet instead. There is an ambiguity in version 2.3 about the order in which servlets and filters should be initialized; if your web server does not initialize listeners before servlets, you will need to use the context loader servlet instead of the context loader listener configuration. Listing 6-3 shows the configuration of the context loader servlet in the deployment descriptor.

Listing 6-3. *Configuring the Context Loader Servlet*

```
<servlet>
  <servlet-name>context</servlet-name>
    <servlet-class>
      org.springframework.web.context.ContextLoaderServlet
    </servlet-class>
  <load-on-startup>1</load-on-startup>
</servlet>
```

The context loader servlet performs exactly the same job as the context loader listener, but you will need to provide a little more information. By default, servlets can start up in any order—and if not explicitly requested, the application server is able to use *lazy loading* to initialize them on demand. Because the context loader servlet needs to be initialized in order to initialize the Spring beans defined by it, you must provide an explicit load-on-startup parameter for the context loader servlet. If a nonzero value is specified here, the application will guarantee that the servlet is started up when the application server is started up.

Furthermore, any other servlets using Spring beans have a dependency on this servlet and must therefore be started later. The load-on-startup parameter also dictates the initialization order: the lower the value specified, the earlier in the initialization sequence the servlet will be loaded. You will therefore need to give the context loader servlet a `load-on-startup` value of 1, as shown in Listing 6-3. Any other servlets using Spring technologies must be given a higher `load-on-startup` value.

The context loader servlet uses the same default configuration file as the listener, and can use the same `context-param` entry to override this default.

Other Contexts

Other daughter contexts may well be managed by other components. For example, when using a Spring MVC dispatcher servlet, it will create its own private application context. The application context managed by the context loader listener or servlet is the only context that is visible to all other contexts. Other contexts are not necessarily visible to each other, and beans created in these contexts are not necessarily visible to beans created in the main application context.

Spring MVC

The Spring MVC framework is a powerful environment within which to create clean, decoupled web applications. There is excellent support for simple tasks such as handling form submission and rendering content in multiple output formats. The key components of the framework are controller classes to make decisions and invoke business logic, command beans to represent form and request parameters, and view resolvers to render the contents of the command beans and reference data supplied by the controllers.

Dispatchers

Because Spring MVC runs as a standard Java EE web application, the entry point to the framework is a Java EE servlet. This servlet dispatches incoming web requests to a URL mapping bean, which in turn determines which Spring controller will handle the request. Listing 6-4 shows the configuration of a suitable dispatcher servlet.

Listing 6-4. *Configuring the Dispatcher Servlet*

```
<servlet>
  <servlet-name>timesheet</servlet-name>
  <servlet-class>
    org.springframework.web.servlet.DispatcherServlet
  </servlet-class>
```

```
<init-param>
  <param-name>contextConfigLocation</param-name>
  <param-value>classpath:timesheet-servlet.xml</param-value>
</init-param>
</servlet>
```

The dispatcher servlet is given a name, which will be used to correlate it with the URL or URLs that it will service for the application server. `DispatcherServlet` is responsible for making calls into Spring beans to process the request. Typically, you will configure a single dispatcher to service all requests, but you can configure multiple dispatchers if necessary. You would typically do this to simplify the configuration of multiple Spring MVC applications within a single Java EE web application.

The dispatcher servlet has a context configuration file associated with it. The beans defined in the context are not visible to contexts associated with other dispatchers. By default, the configuration file is the servlet name (as specified in the `servlet-name` element of the deployment descriptor) suffixed with `-servlet.xml`, but this can be overridden by an initialization parameter, as shown in Listing 6-4.

Listing 6-5 shows the mapping of the servlet to its path within the web application's context.

Listing 6-5. *Configuring the Servlet Path*

```
<servlet-mapping>
  <servlet-name>timesheet</servlet-name>
  <url-pattern>/</url-pattern>
</servlet-mapping>
```

The timesheet application would probably be deployed to a context of `/timesheet`. The servlet mapping indicates that this servlet should correspond to paths in the root of this context. We would therefore invoke our servlet by requesting a path with the form `http://example.com/timesheet/`.

Any path below this one that does not already have an existing mapping will be translated into a call to the dispatcher servlet. Therefore, this path is also a call into our dispatcher: `http://example.com/timesheet/admin`.

To determine exactly what behavior should be available on these paths, we need to create a mapping between paths and controllers.

Mappings

`DispatcherServlet` loads `HandlerMapping` by autowiring (type-based selection of the appropriate bean) from its own context file. The mapping converts all incoming URLs into invocations of the appropriate controller, so there cannot be two different handler mappings.

For most purposes, the SimpleUrlHandlerMapping class shown in Listing 6-6 will be appropriate when building a web application.

Listing 6-6. *Mapping Dispatcher URLs to Controller Classes*

```
<bean class=
"org.springframework.web.servlet.handler.SimpleUrlHandlerMapping">
  <property name="mappings">
   <map>
    <entry key="/login" value-ref="loginHandler"/>
    <entry key="/accessDenied" value-ref="accessDeniedHandler"/>
    <entry key="/admin" value-ref="adminUserListController"/>
    <entry key="/admin/list" value-ref="adminUserListController"/>
    <entry key="/admin/view/**" value-ref="adminUserViewController"/>
   </map>
  </property>
  <property name="defaultHandler" ref="defaultHandler"/>
</bean>
```

All the paths are relative to the mapping of the dispatcher servlet that is using the handler mapping. In our example, the dispatcher is mapped to the root of its application context, and the web application is deployed to the /timesheet application context. In Listing 6-6, the first entry therefore corresponds to a URL of http://example.com/timesheet/login, and any requests (typically GET and POST requests) will be handed to this controller for processing.

A default handler can be specified that will be used to handle URLs that are the responsibility of this dispatcher but don't match any of the explicit mappings. This will usually be the "home page" of the functionality represented by the dispatcher.

The simple handler mapping also allows you to specify wildcards, allowing multiple paths with the same prefix to be passed to the same controller without tedious enumeration of the pathnames.

Wildcards are represented by using the AntPathMatcher helper class, and allow the following distinctions to be made:

   ? matches any single character.

   * matches any series of characters or no character.

   ** matches zero or more directories in a path.

Our mapping for admin/view/** therefore matches any path starting with admin/view/ regardless of any additional / delimiters that might appear within it. This process can be overridden by injecting a custom implementation of the PathMatcher interface if AntPathMatcher is insufficient.

Controllers

The controller is the core of the presentation logic for Spring MVC. An incoming request—for example, a GET request resulting from pointing a browser at a mapped URL—will be received by the dispatcher servlet. A suitable controller will be identified from the URL handler mapping component, and the life cycle of the controller will then be invoked. At its simplest, the life cycle can consist of passing the incoming request directly to a view for rendering. Listing 6-7 shows an example of this type of minimal controller.

Listing 6-7. *Configuring a View Controller for a Single Page*

```
<bean id="defaultHandler" class=
"org.springframework.web.servlet.mvc.ParameterizableViewController">
   <property name="viewName" value="home"/>
</bean>
```

The controller in Listing 6-7 identifies the view to be used as "home" and passes the request on to a view resolver component for rendering (discussed later in this chapter). For the purpose of rendering a single page in response to a web request, this is obviously quite complicated, but the framework's advantages become apparent when we start to demand more of our controllers. The SimpleFormController can be overridden to do the following:

- Provide reference data to the view for rendering.

- Validate incoming request parameters.

- Assign (and type-convert) incoming request parameters to attributes of a command object representing the form to be rendered. (This is known as *binding* the request parameters to the command object.)

- Bind incoming form submissions to the command object.

- Validate the command object upon form submission.

- Forward to the original view if validation of the command object fails.

- Populate the request with error objects representing the points of failure in validation.

- Provide localized messages associated with the validation errors.

All of this is available from standard Spring objects that receive all of their dependencies by injection and are therefore quite simple to unit-test.

The timesheet application's user administration page includes a simple form controller that lists the users known to the application. The configuration of this controller is shown in Listing 6-8.

Listing 6-8. *Configuring a Simple Form Controller*

```
<bean id="adminUserListController" class=
"com.apress.timesheets.mvc.UserListController">
    <property name="commandClass"
        value="com.apress.timesheets.mvc.UserListForm"/>
    <property name="commandName" value="userListForm"/>
    <property name="formView" value="admin/listUser"/>
    <property name="successView" value="admin/listUser"/>
    <property name="userAccountService" ref="userAccountService"/>
</bean>
```

Although the controller configured in Listing 6-8 is a very simple component, the configuration snippet is quite typical. This is a normal Spring bean configured by injection. The first four properties are standard SimpleFormController properties—only the last is a custom field, the UserAccountService bean used to obtain a list of users. The standard properties are (respectively) the class of the command object that will be used to hold incoming form submissions, the attribute name that this object will be assigned when it is placed in the request object, the view that will be displayed when the controller is first invoked (and when form submissions fail validation), and the view that a form submission will be forwarded to if it is processed successfully.

Listing 6-9 shows the ease with which we can create this simple controller. We override the referenceData() method. This is invoked on receipt of the web request in order to provide reference data to the rendering view. In our case, we extract the list of users from the service layer (provided by injection as usual), and return this as a map from the overridden reference data method. The contents of the map will then by added to the request by the controller, and the request will be forwarded to the appropriate view. In the next section, we look at how the views are configured.

Listing 6-9. *The Implementation of the User List Controller*

```
public class UserListController
    extends SimpleFormController
{
    private UserAccountService userAccountService;

    @Override
    protected Map referenceData(final HttpServletRequest request)
        throws Exception
```

```
{
    final Map<String,List<UserAccount>> refData =
        new HashMap<String,List<UserAccount>>();
    refData.put("users", userAccountService.listUsers());
    return refData;
}

public UserAccountService getUserAccountService() {
    return userAccountService;
}

public void setUserAccountService(
    final UserAccountService userAccountService)
{
    this.userAccountService = userAccountService;
}
}
```

Views and Resolvers

When I speak of a *view*, I am typically talking about a JSP, but this is not unnecessary jargon. The actual mechanism used is pluggable. The view configured to be the form view in Listing 6-8 is not a specific file, but an instruction to the controller to find the rendering mechanism identified as admin/listUser.

The mechanism used to identify the rendering mechanism is a view resolver, and when all your views will be processed by the same mechanism, the UrlBasedViewResolver is the simplest approach.

Listing 6-10 is the definition of a resolver that will be used to convert the views specified in the controllers into corresponding JSPs.

Listing 6-10. *Configuring a View Resolver*

```
<bean id="viewResolver"
class="org.springframework.web.servlet.view.UrlBasedViewResolver">
    <property name="prefix" value="/WEB-INF/jsp/"/>
    <property name="suffix" value=".jsp"/>
    <property name="viewClass"
value="org.springframework.web.servlet.view.JstlView"/>
</bean>
```

This configuration is pretty much self-explanatory. The resolver class is declared (autowiring is used to identify the view resolver, so actually the id attribute is redundant here). The view name is prefixed with /WEB-INF/jsp/, and then suffixed with .jsp, and the JstlView class is then used to render the file in question. As you'll have anticipated, this takes the resulting path (/WEB-INF/jsp/admin/listUser.jsp) and forwards the incoming request as a servlet invocation of this JSP page.

It is good practice when using a UrlBasedViewResolver with JSPs to place the files in question under the WEB-INF hierarchy so that they cannot be viewed directly by clients browsing the site (files under WEB-INF cannot be accessed by external requests).

The body of the page used to render the resulting forwarded request is then shown in Listing 6-11.

Listing 6-11. *The JSP Used to Render the admin/listUser View*

```
<body>
    <h1>Administration</h1>
    <div id="commands">
        <h2>Commands</h2>
        <a href="${ctx}/">Home</a>
        <a href="${ctx}/admin/create?_flowId=createUser-flow">
            Add New User
        </a>
    </div>
    <div id="userList">
        <h2>Users</h2>
        <c:forEach var="user" items="${users}">
            <div id="user">
                <a href="${ctx}/admin/view/${user.accountName}">
                    ${user.accountName}
                </a>
            </div>
        </c:forEach>
    </div>
</body>
```

The users attribute (a list of UserAccount objects) was added to the request attribute via the reference data in Listing 6-9. Expression language and the standard tag library are then used to iterate over these objects, rendering a set of links to the appropriate functionality to view the account details in question.

Validation

When forms are submitted, we usually want to make sure that their content makes sense in the context of the code that will process the form. There are essentially two ways to validate a form: we can write browser-side JavaScript logic to check that the form has the correct values in it, or we can write server-side logic to check the contents of the request.

The JavaScript approach is pretty much optional. It has the advantage of relieving the server of some of the burden of form submissions, and it is quick, but it presents no hard guarantees. The user may have disabled JavaScript validation, and malicious or ingenious users may submit forms without using a browser implementation at all. The server-side approach is therefore essential, and Spring allows us to carry out convenient validation in several places.

The first opportunity for validation is the binding of the incoming HTTP request data to the form bean's fields. Generally, this will be carried out automatically; the default PropertyEditor classes will be used to convert incoming request data (by definition submitted as HTTP strings) into appropriate object values. If a form field containing non-numeric characters is submitted for a field that will be bound to an Integer form property, the error will be caught, and the form will be re-presented to the user.

The validation may also take place through custom logic in the controller. Suitable versions of the onBind or onBindAndValidate methods (those providing a BindException parameter) can be overridden for custom error handling. If the custom logic populates the provided BindException object with error information, the framework treats the form as invalid and re-presents the form to the user.

However, the validation usually takes place in either the onSubmit method's implementation body (again, a version accepting a BindException object is overridden) or in an external validator-implementing bean provided to the form.

Listing 6-12 shows the validator implementation. The interface requires us to override only two methods. The first allows the framework to determine whether the validator should be applied to the form bean in question. The second carries out the validation logic.

Listing 6-12. *A Validator Implementation*

```
public class PeriodCreateValidator implements Validator {
   public boolean supports(final Class type) {
      return PeriodCreateForm.class.equals(type);
   }

   public void validate(final Object command, final Errors errors) {
      final PeriodCreateForm form = (PeriodCreateForm)command;
      if(form.getNote() == null || "".equals(form.getNote().trim())) {
         errors.rejectValue("note", "create.period.note");
      }
```

```
        if(!form.getStartTime().before(form.getEndTime())) {
          errors.rejectValue("startTime", "create.period.startTime.swapped");
          errors.rejectValue("endTime", "create.period.endTime.swapped");
        }
      }
    }
```

The mechanism by which the framework is notified of the problems encountered with the submitted data is standard for all these approaches. An Errors interface-implementing object (BindException implements Errors) is passed to the validation logic, and methods are called on the Errors object. The form can be rejected as a whole, or individual named fields can be rejected. For example, the code errors.rejectValue("note", ...); rejects the note field of the form being validated, whereas errors.reject(...); rejects the entire form as being invalid without specifying any particular field.

The error is normally expressed as an error code that will be used to obtain a suitable message to the user from a resource bundle. For convenience during development, a default message parameter can also be provided for display if the code cannot be found in the resource bundles.

The onSubmit method may use the errors encountered during processing to present a custom validation failure page instead of the form page. Therefore, populating the Errors object does not automatically cause the framework to re-present the default form page. As a convenience, however, the original form page (with the Errors object) can be displayed by calling the showForm method, as shown in Listing 6-13.

Listing 6-13. *Using showForm to Re-present the Form Page*

```
@Override
protected ModelAndView onSubmit(
    final Object command,
    final BindException errors) throws Exception
{
  // ...
  if( errors.hasErrors()) {
    return showForm(request,response,errors);
  } else {
    return new ModelAndView(getSuccessView(),referenceData);
  }
}
```

Exception Handling

Validation is the case of "expected" errors being handled, but we also need to take account of the unusual and unanticipated error. As in normal processing, we handle these by using exceptions, but we do not usually want the user to see the unfriendly stack trace and server error messages that will appear if we allow an exception to bubble all the way to the application server's own error-handling logic.

Spring MVC allows us instead to specify the views (normal Spring MVC views) that should be presented to the user when exceptions occur. We can declare a default exception handler view, but we can also map particular families of exceptions to particular views to handle them.

Listing 6-14 shows the configuration of a suitable mapping. The dispatcher will automatically invoke the resolver named `exceptionResolver` when an uncaught exception is thrown from a controller to determine the view to be shown. Our example application uses this feature to allow an appropriate error message to be shown when the user has attempted to access timesheet details that do not belong to him.

Listing 6-14. *Configuring Exception Resolution*

```
<bean id="exceptionResolver"
class="org.springframework.web.servlet.handler.SimpleMappingExceptionResolver">
    <property name="exceptionMappings">
        <props>
            <prop key="java.lang.Exception">errors/error</prop>
            <prop key="com.apress.timesheets.TimesheetSecurityException">
                errors/access
            </prop>
        </props>
    </property>
    <property name="defaultErrorView" value="errors/error"/>
</bean>
```

The underlying ownership-checking code throws an unchecked `TimesheetSecurity` exception, and no attempt is made to catch this in the controller, so it is caught and rendered by the errors/access view. The thrown exception is passed to the view as a request attribute named `exception`. Listing 6-15 shows a simple view. Where the views are implemented as JSPs, they do *not* need to be declared with the page attribute `isErrorPage` set to `true`.

Listing 6-15. *An Exception-Handling View Implementation*

```
<h1>Access Violation</h1>
<p>An attempt was made to access timesheet data belonging to another user.</p>
<p>The exception message was: ${exception}</p>
<p>The user account was: ${exception.account.accountName}</p>
```

Spring Web Flow

Spring Web Flow allows you to model the behavior of a web application in terms of the flow through a set of states. These correspond well with the user journeys that are often used to define the behavior of a website. In the previous section, we considered a simple controller to list the current users of the application. In this section, we will create a Spring web flow to govern the creation of new users. This is a relatively simple user journey, but it will allow us to exercise the important parts of Web Flow. Figure 6-2 shows a state diagram for the user journey.

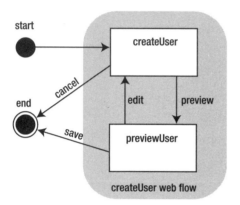

Figure 6-2. *The state diagram for this journey*

The Web Flow component is not a replacement for all of the Spring MVC components. On the contrary, Web Flow is based around the Spring MVC classes, and so you can readily combine existing Spring MVC stuff with your web flow and pass control to and fro. You would normally configure a single Web Flow controller as shown in Listing 6-16, and this then manages all of your user journeys using Web Flow.

Listing 6-16. *The URL Mapping for the Web Flow Controller*

```
<entry key="/admin/*" value-ref="flowController"/>
```

The controller is then configured as a flow controller bean, as shown in Listing 6-17.

Listing 6-17. *Configuring the Flow Controller Bean*

```
<bean name="flowController"
    class="org.springframework.webflow.executor.mvc.FlowController">
    <property name="flowExecutor" ref="flowExecutor"/>
</bean>
```

The flow controller is injected with a flow executor. This is a component that knows how to initialize and load the flow information from the flow registry (see Listing 6-18).

Listing 6-18. *Configuring the Flow Executor*

```
<flow:executor id="flowExecutor" registry-ref="flowRegistry"/>
```

These beans are configured by using a custom schema and are normally mapped to the flow: namespace prefix. The appropriate XML namespace entries are shown in bold in Listing 6-19.

Listing 6-19. *Importing the Schema Namespace*

```
<beans
  xmlns="http://www.springframework.org/schema/beans"
  xmlns:xsi="http://www.w3.org/2001/XMLSchema-instance"
  xmlns:flow="http://www.springframework.org/schema/webflow-config"
  xsi:schemaLocation="
    http://www.springframework.org/schema/beans
    http://www.springframework.org/schema/beans/spring-beans-2.0.xsd
    http://www.springframework.org/schema/webflow-config
http://www.springframework.org/schema/webflow-config/spring-webflow-config-1.0.xsd">
```

The flow registry allows you to specify a set of flow configuration files, as shown in Listing 6-20. These are where the actual user journeys are defined.

Listing 6-20. *The Flow Configuration Files*

```
<flow:registry id="flowRegistry">
  <flow:location path="classpath:**-flow.xml"/>
</flow:registry>
```

Note that the flow registry will use the filename of the flow configuration file to determine the flow name that will be used to identify it. In the example application, the web flow declaration for the flow to create a new user is in the file createUser-flow.xml on the classpath, so its flowId is therefore createUser-flow.

The flow configuration files use the same schema namespace as was used to declare the registry and executor, but as you are declaring them in an external configuration file, you would not normally need to include the general Spring schema options. Listing 6-21 shows you the typical schema definition.

Listing 6-21. *Schema Definition for a Web Flow Configuration File*

```
<flow
    xmlns="http://www.springframework.org/schema/webflow"
    xmlns:xsi="http://www.w3.org/2001/XMLSchema-instance"
    xsi:schemaLocation="http://www.springframework.org/schema/webflow
http://www.springframework.org/schema/webflow/spring-webflow-1.0.xsd">
```

Your flow configuration must list all of the states in the model, explicitly identifying the starting state and any finishing states (your flow must have a starting state, but it doesn't absolutely have to have a finishing state). You will also list the events that cause the model to transition between states.

Listing 6-22 shows the set of states corresponding with the state diagram shown in Figure 6-2. These also name the views that will be used to render the flow when it is in a given state. The views are rendered by using the normal view resolver mechanism of Spring MVC. The end state can pass control to another view, forward control to another controller (identified by its URL as usual), or use a browser redirect to transfer control to another controller, as shown here.

Listing 6-22. *The States Declared in Our Web Flow Configuration*

```
<start-state idref="createUser"/>

<view-state id="createUser" view="admin/createUser">
   <transition on="preview" to="previewUser"/>
   <transition on="cancel" to="listUsers"/>
</view-state>

<view-state id="previewUser" view="admin/previewUser">
   <transition on="edit" to="createUser"/>
   <transition on="save" to="listUsers"/>
</view-state>

<end-state id="listUsers" view="externalRedirect:/admin"/>
```

Spring Web Flow uses action beans to invoke the appropriate business logic as you move through the user journey. An *action* is literally any class that implements the Action interface.

Actions can be invoked at the following points in a web flow:

- When the flow starts

- When the flow enters a state

- When the flow is about to transition to another state (or to itself!)

- When the flow is about to exit a state

- When the flow is about to render the view of a state (useful for a reference data population)

- When the flow ends

Listing 6-23 shows the interface that action classes must implement.

Listing 6-23. *The Action Interface*

```
public interface Action {
    Event execute(RequestContext context) throws Exception;
}
```

RequestContext represents the current state of the web flow and the data associated with it. It's somewhat analogous to the HttpRequest and HttpResponse objects that are made available to a lot of Spring MVC form methods, and indeed you can put objects into the servlet request context by manipulating the RequestContext object.

Instead of directly implementing the Action interface to provide all of your functionality, you would accept a lot of the default functionality from the FormAction class, overriding it only to provide calls into the service layer. The FormAction serves a very similar purpose to the various form controller classes that provide much of the boilerplate functionality in Spring MVC. Listing 6-24 shows our CreateUserAction bean, which does exactly this.

Listing 6-24. *The Configuration of the CreateUserAction Bean*

```
<bean id="createUserAction"
class="com.apress.timesheets.mvc.webflow.CreateUserAction">
 <property name="formObjectName" value="command"/>
 <property name="formObjectClass"
     value="com.apress.timesheets.mvc.webflow.CreateUserForm"/>
 <property name="userAccountService" ref="userAccountService"/>
</bean>
```

The implementation of this bean is shown in Listing 6-25. Aside from the injection of the service layer dependency, there is a single business method here (although others could be added to provide form validation).

Listing 6-25. *The Implementation of the CreateUserAction Bean*

```
public class CreateUserAction extends FormAction {
    private UserAccountService userAccountService;

    public Event save(final RequestContext ctx) throws Exception {
        Logger.getLogger(CreateUserAction.class).
            info("save(ctx) called");
        final CreateUserForm form = (CreateUserForm)getFormObject(ctx);
        final UserAccount account =
            new UserAccount(form.getUsername());
        userAccountService.createUser(account);
        return success();
    }

    public UserAccountService getUserAccountService() {
        return userAccountService;
    }

    public void setUserAccountService(
        final UserAccountService userAccountService)
    {
        this.userAccountService = userAccountService;
    }
}
```

When the save method is called, it will return an event object to indicate the action that will be taken. Typically, we expect this to raise a "success" event (as here) but during validation or in other circumstances when the process might fail, we can raise other events as appropriate.

Although we have declared the bean, we have not yet declared how this save method will be invoked (there is no automatic correlation between the transition names and the method names). We need to add the method calls to the web flow declarations. Listing 6-26 shows a web flow with the appropriate action methods added.

Listing 6-26. *The Web Flow Declaration with the Calls into the Action*

```
<start-state idref="createUser"/>

<view-state id="createUser" view="admin/createUser">
    <render-actions>
        <action bean="createUserAction" method="setupForm"/>
    </render-actions>
```

```
      <transition on="preview" to="previewUser">
         <action bean="createUserAction" method="bindAndValidate"/>
      </transition>
      <transition on="cancel" to="listUsers"/>
  </view-state>

  <view-state id="previewUser" view="admin/previewUser">
      <transition on="edit" to="createUser"/>
      <transition on="save" to="listUsers">
         <action bean="createUserAction" method="save"/>
      </transition>
  </view-state>

  <end-state id="listUsers" view="externalRedirect:/admin"/>
```

As you can see, although we've written only a single method (other than the resource accessors), there are several calls into the action. These are all provided by the base `ActionForm` class. We use the `setupForm` method to create the command object (the form bean), and then this is placed in the session for future use. (It is possible to use Spring Web Flow without the use of a session, but it's far less convenient to do so.) The `bindAndValidate` method is called when the form is submitted during the transition to the preview state. This copies the submitted fields into the command object. Finally, when the preview state is submitted (transitioning to the end state and thus back to the list of users), our save method is called, persisting the information into the database.

Listing 6-27 shows the form that is used to render the `createUser` view.

Listing 6-27. *The Form Elements from createUser.jsp*

```
<form:form>
  <form:errors cssClass="errors" path="username"/>
  <label>Username: <form:input path="username"/></label>
  <input type="submit" name="_eventId_cancel" value="Cancel"/>
  <input type="submit" name="_eventId_preview" value="Preview User"/>
</form:form>
```

This allows the user to specify the name of the user to be created, and to click either a Cancel button taking them back out of the workflow to the list of users or a Preview button taking them to the next state of the workflow. The specific event to raise when processing a request or submission is indicated by the `_eventId` parameter. In the preceding form, the two events that we can raise are provided in the names of the Submit buttons, which raise the cancel and preview events, respectively, causing the transitions shown in Listing 6-26 to be invoked (the on attribute of the transition element identifies the event that causes the transition to occur). If we were raising the event with a GET request to the web flow, we could provide these as normal parameter values (for example, /admin/create?_eventId=preview).

The original link into the web flow was specified in Listing 6-11 in a similar form to this, where rather than an _eventId parameter, a _flowId parameter is specified to indicate which web flow the controller should initiate.

Listing 6-28 shows the form that is used to render the preview page; this is essentially the same as Listing 6-27 aside from the changes to the button names and the appropriate event ID names used to invoke the appropriate state transitions.

Listing 6-28. *The Form Elements from previewUser.jsp*

```
<form:form>
    <form:errors cssClass="errors" path="username"/>
    <label>Username: ${command.username}</label>
    <form:hidden path="username"/>
    <input type="submit" name="_eventId_edit" value="Cancel"/>
    <input type="submit" name="_eventId_save" value="Save User"/>
</form:form>
```

The custom tags used to render parts of these forms are discussed in more detail in the "Tag Libraries" section later in this chapter.

Forms and Binding

In Spring MVC and Spring Web Flow, forms are handled by converting their string representations to and from the properties of a POJO. This POJO is referred to as the *command object*. The fields of the command object are populated by the controller when a form is submitted. When the form is initially rendered, a command object may be populated by the controller from the incoming request parameters and supplied to the page; this is the behavior when you set the bindOnNewForm attribute in AbstractFormController and its derived classes.

The same form bean may be used by multiple controllers, or by multiple steps in a single controller—as, for example, with classes derived from AbstractWizardFormController. If the controller is permitted to use the HttpSession object, maintaining the content of the command object between actions is relatively simple. However, session objects come with their own problems. If you intend to operate without the session, you must ensure that any fields of the command object that are not currently editable or visible in the forms are rendered as hidden HTML form fields so that they are available to reconstruct the command object upon form submission.

In addition to the problem of maintaining the content of a command object for controllers spanning multiple form submissions, there is the problem of managing collections of objects. The collection classes are not well suited to the representation of fields in the command object because they have no associated type information at runtime. Even if using Java generics, a List<String> will be converted to a plain List at runtime by a process known as *erasure*. This means that there is no information available to Spring's `PropertyEditors` to determine the type that associated form fields should be converted to. Your alternatives are to add additional "manual" binding of these properties upon form submission, or to use Java array types where a collection class might otherwise have been more suitable.

Views

Earlier in this chapter, you saw how a view resolver could be used by Spring MVC and Spring Web Flow to convert Spring MVC view names into the concrete implementation of a JSP.

Your application is not restricted to using JSPs, however. Spring supports a wide range of view technologies, and it uses the same basic mechanism for all of them: you configure a view resolver for the appropriate output format, and establish how view names are mapped to their output.

Velocity and FreeMarker

Velocity and FreeMarker are templating languages with similar behavior and syntaxes. In some ways they are like JSPs, but unlike JSPs they are interpreted dynamically rather than being compiled by the application server into class files.

A common beginners' error with JSPs is to try to include lots of application logic in the page, when it really belongs in a servlet or some other controller class. Velocity and FreeMarker intentionally restrict the amount of logic that can easily be included in the page to those operations that are concerned with the presentation of the data supplied to it. In both cases, the syntax has a lot in common with the Java EE expression language used to dynamically incorporate content into JSPs.

Velocity templates are defined in files. Our first step when configuring velocity is therefore to define the location from which the files will be loaded. Listing 6-29 shows the configuration of Spring's `VelocityConfigurer` to define the appropriate path. The velocity configurer is one of a set of wrapper and helper classes used to make the Velocity libraries more IOC friendly.

Listing 6-29. *Configuring the Template Path*

```
<bean id="velocityConfig"
class="org.springframework.web.servlet.view.velocity.VelocityConfigurer">
  <property name="resourceLoaderPath" value="/WEB-INF/velocity/"/>
</bean>
```

With the configurer defined, we specify a Velocity view resolver, as shown in Listing 6-30. This is conspicuously similar to the configuration of the JSP view resolver in Listing 6-10.

The only notable difference is that we have enabled caching to avoid the need to reload the files each time a template is used.

Listing 6-30. *Configuring the Velocity View Resolver*

```
<bean id="viewResolver" class=
"org.springframework.web.servlet.view.velocity.VelocityViewResolver">
  <property name="cache" value="true"/>
  <property name="prefix" value=""/>
  <property name="suffix" value=".vm"/>
</bean>
```

The configuration for FreeMarker is virtually identical to that of Velocity. Listing 6-31 shows the configuration of FreeMarker's template files.

Listing 6-31. *Configuring the FreeMarker Path*

```
<bean id="freemarkerConfig"
class="org.springframework.web.servlet.view.freemarker.FreeMarkerConfigurer">
  <property name="templateLoaderPath" value="/WEB-INF/freemarker/"/>
</bean>
```

Listing 6-32 shows the corresponding configuration of the FreeMarker view resolver.

Listing 6-32. *Configuring the FreeMarker View Resolver*

```
<bean id="viewResolver"
class="org.springframework.web.servlet.view.freemarker.FreeMarkerViewResolver">
  <property name="cache" value="true"/>
  <property name="prefix" value=""/>
  <property name="suffix" value=".ftl"/>
</bean>
```

Programmatically Generated Output

Sometimes the output of your application will not be intended for presentation as HTML, but will instead be generated as a PDF, a Microsoft Word document, or an XML file. In these cases, we need to resort to code to generate the contents of the view. In fact, we need to define our own view type.

Spring views are just classes that implement the View interface, shown in Listing 6-33.

Listing 6-33. *The Spring View Interface*

```
public interface View {
    public String getContentType();
    void render(Map model,
                HttpServletRequest request,
                HttpServletResponse response) throws Exception;
}
```

When a controller needs to render a page, the view resolver calls the getContentType() method to determine the *content type: value* to return in the HTTP request, and then calls the render method, passing in the request and response headers. The implementation class can then do anything a servlet implementation would be able to do to put information into the response object.

Unless you are generating output in some particularly obscure format, you would normally override one of the standard Spring abstract view implementations provided for this purpose. There are implementations for PDF files, Microsoft Office documents, XML and XSLT output, as well as the JSP, Velocity, and FreeMarker implementations that we've already discussed.

Special View Names

In general, we expect the incoming request to be passed to the controller, processed, and then passed directly to a view to be rendered either in the original form view (if an error has occurred) or in a success view of some type (if the submitted data has been processed without error). Sometimes, however, we want to pass the incoming request to some other controller to allow further processing. Spring MVC provides two special view prefixes to support this.

The simplest of the two mechanisms to use is forwarding. Listing 6-34 shows the use of the forward: prefix to allow this.

Listing 6-34. *Using the forward: Prefix in a View Name*

```
return new ModelAndView("forward:/home",model);
```

The servlet request is forwarded to the named controller, with the request and response objects from the forwarding controller. The request can be populated with a model object exactly as if it were being forwarded to any normal view. The receiving controller will pass through all the normal life cycle phases, so it does not need to be written to be aware that it may receive forwarded requests.

The second and more-complicated of the mechanisms is the redirect: prefix shown in Listing 6-35.

Listing 6-35. *Using the redirect: Prefix in a View Name*

```
return new ModelAndView("redirect:/home",model);
```

Here the view actually causes a browser redirect response to be generated and sent back to the client's browser. The browser will then reload the path specified in the view name after the `redirect:` prefix. Model objects and any nonstring attribute objects in the request will be converted to `GET` string parameters. This mechanism is usually used to provide the browser with a new view immediately following a `POST` form submission, so that browser reloads will not cause the `POST` form data to be sent multiple times.

Tag Libraries

There is nothing to stop you from creating the HTML in your page views from scratch, or using HTML authoring tools, but Spring provides a set of custom tag libraries allowing you to generate some of the form and other page contents more conveniently.

The major tag libraries are a generic library for page content that is usually prefixed with *spring* and an additional form-specific tag that is therefore usually prefixed with *form*.

When a form has failed validation, the errors information associated with the validation failure will be placed into the request context. Accessing the appropriate error information for the field or form in question can be fiddly; the tags make this simple. Repopulating (or initializing) a form's field values with data from the request can be tedious; again, the custom tags simplify this. Finally, the radio and check box fields are awkward to use correctly in any application (because the values they represent are submitted only when they are selected); the use of tags simplifies the handling of this also.

Listing 6-36 shows the appropriate `taglib` declaration for a JSP view implementation that will be using the Spring custom tags. This is the declaration used in the implementation of the view shown in Listing 6-27, where a custom form tag is used.

Listing 6-36. *Making the Spring Tag Library Available Within the Page Context*

```
<%@taglib prefix="spring" uri="http://www.springframework.org/tags"%>
<%@taglib prefix="form" uri="http://www.springframework.org/tags/form"%>
```

The custom form tags are parameterized for all of the properties that are available to the corresponding well-formed HTML form elements. (When standard attribute names cannot be used in the custom tag because of Java naming conflicts, suitable renamed versions are provided—for example, `cssClass` in place of `class`.) The properties all take sensible default values, so that as Listing 6-27 shows, a form defined by using Spring's custom tags can be at least as terse as a plain HTML equivalent, and is usually more so.

In Listing 6-27, for example, the form element is declared by using the *form:form* custom tag. This needs no additional parameters because by default the form will be submitted by using POST, the path for submission will be the same as the original form request path, the command object's name will be command, and the default form encoding will be used—all of which is the desired behavior.

Table 6-1 shows the standard form tags. As you can see, these generally correspond closely to the form field types.

Table 6-1. *The Spring Form Tags*

Tag	Description
form	Renders the enclosing form element.
input	Renders text input elements, equivalent to a form input type of text.
password	Renders password input elements, equivalent to a form input type of password.
hidden	Renders hidden form fields.
select	Renders form select boxes and is used in conjunction with the option and options tags.
option	Used to render a single select option.
options	Used to render a set of option elements. The values and labels for the options will normally be drawn from the reference data supplied by the controller.
radiobutton	Used to render a radio input element, equivalent to a form input type of radio. An additional specially named hidden field is rendered to ensure that the binding logic can determine whether the state has changed (otherwise impossible, because an unchecked radio element's value is never submitted).
checkbox	Used to render a check box input element, equivalent to a form input type of checkbox. As with radiobutton, a specially named hidden field is rendered to ensure that state changes are always detectable.
textarea	Renders a text area element.
errors	Renders any error messages generated during validation of the form or of the named field (if any).
label	Renders a label element for a named field.

The two special cases in the table are the errors and options custom tags. The former is used to render error messages resulting from validation failures of the submitted form. The latter is used to allow the options used in standard select elements to be rendered with a single tag, without resorting to additional tag libraries or scriptlets. Table 6-2 shows the additional generic Spring custom tags that are available for use throughout the page.

Table 6-2. *The Spring Generic Tags*

Tag	Description
htmlEscape	Determines whether HTML values rendered by using the Spring tags will be escaped, effectively setting the appropriate default state for the htmlEscape property of all the other Spring tags.
escapeBody	Escapes on the server-side any HTML appearing within the tag's body. For example, ampersands will be rendered as & instead of &, which would otherwise corrupt the browser rendering of the page.
message	Displays a message with the specified code. This permits page text to be appropriately localized.
theme	Retrieves a "theme" message with the specified code. This allows for different presentation formats to be controlled from properties files.
hasBindErrors	Makes an errors instance available if errors were encountered in binding.
nestedPath	Allows a "current" path to be specified, which the bind tag's path will be considered to be relative to. For example, if nestedPath is set to timesheet and a bind tag within its body has a path set to consultant, the latter is equivalent to the unnested form timesheet.consultant.
bind	Makes a BindStatus instance available for the specified path.
transform	Within the bind tag's body, this converts the specified variable to a string by using the appropriate PropertyEditor instance.

You will generally make far more use of the form tags than of the generic tags—except for the use of the message tag, which is essential for building properly localized and internationalized applications.

Corresponding "macro" tags exist for rendering content when using the Velocity and FreeMarker templating languages.

Filters

Java EE filters provide the opportunity to intercept incoming requests and perform operations on them before the request is passed to the appropriate servlet for processing.

Figure 6-3 shows where filters fit into the request life cycle—right at the beginning. They are uniquely placed to alter the state of the request before it proceeds any further. They are a Java EE feature, rather than a Spring-specific one, but Spring takes full advantage of them.

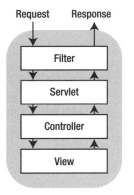

Figure 6-3. *The filter's place in the request life cycle*

Hibernate

The use of Hibernate in a web application creates an associated problem that filters are ideally suited to address. Beans loaded by Hibernate create a problem for developers who wish to use them in presentation logic—typically, while rendering JSP page views. The problem arises from Hibernate's use of lazy loading. A lazily loaded entity association can be accessed only when the entity is associated with the session, yet we do not necessarily want to taint our presentation logic with explicit references to DAO-level implementation details.

Consider the example of Listing 6-37.

Listing 6-37. *Accessing a Lazy Association in a JSP*

```
<p>Consultant: ${timesheet.consultant.accountName}</p>
```

If the timesheet's association with the Consultant entity has not yet been materialized from the database and the entity is not currently associated with the Hibernate session, the entity will throw a LazyInitializationException and the page rendering will fail.

One option would be to reassociate the entity with the session, but this creates a dependency on Hibernate in the JSP and clutters it with logic that is only very indirectly related to the rendering of page content.

Spring provides a filter to address this problem. The filter keeps track of the Hibernate session object throughout the request life cycle: after a session is requested by the support DAOs, it is retained until the request cycle has completed, thus making it available to page-rendering logic such as that in Listing 6-30 without any additional coding.

Listing 6-38 shows the filter being declared in the deployment descriptor and associated with all URLs for the web application's context path.

Listing 6-38. *Declaring the Spring OpenSessionInViewFilter*

```
<filter>
   <filter-name>hibernateFilter</filter-name>
   <filter-class>
org.springframework.orm.hibernate3.support.OpenSessionInViewFilter
   </filter-class>
</filter>

<filter-mapping>
   <filter-name>hibernateFilter</filter-name>
   <url-pattern>/*</url-pattern>
</filter-mapping>
```

Delegated Filters

Although Spring can take advantage of a filter, the reverse is not necessarily true. The deployment descriptor does support a limited flavor of dependency injection—configuration parameters can be supplied to a filter—but references to other beans cannot be supplied in this way.

In circumstances where you want the benefits of the filter's privileged place in the request-handling life cycle, but don't want to lose the advantages of Spring configuration files, you can use Spring's delegating filter proxy class. This class is a standard Java EE filter, but it passes all the incoming requests to a named Spring bean to handle. Your bean is configured in the normal way in the Spring application context. It must implement the Filter interface, and aside from the advantages of configuration, it will behave exactly as if it were declared in the deployment descriptor itself. Listing 6-39 shows the use of a delegating filter proxy to configure the Spring Security (Acegi) request filter.

Listing 6-39. *Configuring a Delegating Filter Proxy*

```
<filter>
   <description>Acegi Request Filter</description>
   <filter-name>acegi-request-filter</filter-name>
   <filter-class>
      org.springframework.web.filter.DelegatingFilterProxy
   </filter-class>
   <init-param>
      <param-name>targetBeanName</param-name>
      <param-value>acegiRequestFilter</param-value>
   </init-param>
</filter>
```

```
<filter-mapping>
    <filter-name>acegi-request-filter</filter-name>
    <url-pattern>/*</url-pattern>
</filter-mapping>
```

Localization and Internationalization

Spring makes localization of content particularly easy. Java already provides a lot of this functionality in its use of resource bundles, which allow locale-specific files to be loaded automatically.

Listing 6-40 shows the configuration of a message source that can be used by Spring to obtain content from a standard Java resource bundle. The message source is used by the message, errors, and theme page tags, making the inclusion of locale-specific content a matter of replacing inline text with appropriate custom tags.

Listing 6-40. *Configuring a Resource Bundle–Based Message Source*

```
<bean id="messageSource"
class="org.springframework.context.support.ResourceBundleMessageSource">
    <property name="basename" value="messages"/>
</bean>
```

In Spring, the process of selecting the appropriate locale to use when resolving content is usually carried out by using a LocaleResolver bean implementation. Table 6-3 lists the basic provided resolvers available to you.

Table 6-3. *The Basic Spring Locale Resolver Classes*

Resolver Name	Description
AcceptHeaderLocaleResolver	Uses the headers sent by the user's browser to determine their locale. Cannot be changed from server-side code because the browser settings are outside our control.
CookieLocaleResolver	Persists a cookie onto the user's browser to store a custom locale. If no cookie is supplied, the resolver can default to a specified locale or can take the default locale from the browser request.
SessionLocaleResolver	Persists the locale information in the user's session. Again, the resolver defaults to either a configured locale or the locale in the browser's header request.
FixedLocaleResolver	A single locale is used regardless of other settings. This locale can be explicitly configured or otherwise will default to the JVM's default locale (usually this will in turn default to the hosting operating system's locale settings).

As long as you are using a resource bundle message source to supply the content used throughout the site, you will not need to make any additional configuration changes to support localization and internationalization (i10n and i18n) concerns.

FixedLocaleResolver makes sense only when the all the users of a particular instance of an installed application are from the same location; otherwise, you should use CookieLocaleResolver or SessionLocaleResolver and allow users to override the default taken from their browser headers. AcceptHeaderLocaleResolver looks like an attractive option initially. However, because you cannot override the default option, you can end up with situations where users in a foreign locale using a locally installed browser cannot access a site in their native language—so this is not recommended.

Conclusion

In this chapter, I have given you a tour of Spring MVC and Spring Web Flow, building a small part of the example application with them (see the source code available from the Source Code/Download area of the Apress website, www.apress.com, for plenty more examples).

In the next chapter, you will look at the Spring Security framework (also known as Acegi Security) and see how this uses filters to achieve URL-based security, and how it allows you to enforce authorization and authentication concerns throughout your web application.

CHAPTER 7

■ ■ ■

Security

The Acegi security system was originally created independently of the core Spring development effort but from the beginning was designed with the Spring environment in mind. The project was so successful that it has now been adopted wholesale as the standard for security in the Spring framework, and is therefore now known interchangeably as *Spring Security* or *Acegi Security*.

Security as a whole breaks down into three areas of concern:

Authentication determines that a user is who he claims to be.

Authorization determines what the user is allowed to do if he is indeed that person.

Channel security ensures that nobody can eavesdrop on the conversation.

Managing security in an application is not a simple problem to solve at the best of times, but is made particularly difficult in practice because of the broad range of existing solutions to security and the frequent need to manage security across multiple platforms. The existing Java Authentication and Authorization Service (JAAS) API attempts to alleviate this, but in some ways presents its own problems. JAAS is a notoriously difficult API to work with, and often security is managed directly through other APIs such as the Lightweight Directory Access Protocol (LDAP) or through custom database implementations rather than using the higher-level JAAS approach.

Spring Security does offer its own (database-backed) security approach, but is also unusually accommodating of alternative implementations. It provides a simple mechanism to allow you to integrate with existing nonstandard code, as well as a number of implementations to connect to common authentication mechanisms such as LDAP.

Figure 7-1 shows the typical components in a configured Acegi-secured web application. This looks pretty daunting, but these classes divide neatly into the filters (required for managing web security) and the components that provide access to the authentication and authorization data.

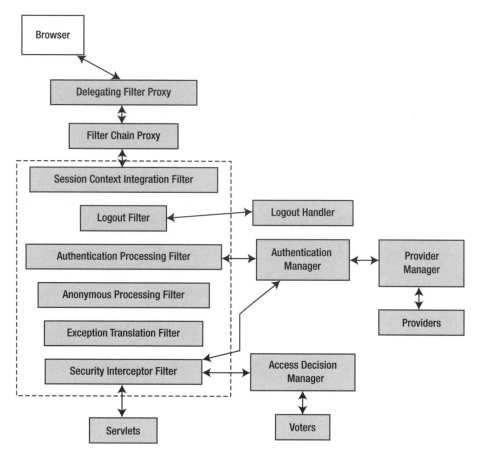

Figure 7-1. *Acegi security components*

Securing the Web Components

When securing a web application, our primary concern should be to prevent access to the application as a whole and then to open up access for specific groups of users to specific components.

This "deny by default" rule reduces the impact of errors of omission when configuring the security of a system. In our example web application, the application as a whole is off-limits to all users unless they log in. Furthermore, there are parts of the application that are off-limits to all logged-in users unless they are administrators. The configuration examples in this chapter illustrate these three parts of the application: anonymous, user, and administrator accessible.

Naturally, we do not want to embed security-related code into all of our service classes, DAOs, controller classes, and so forth. We want to set up our rules quite independently so that we will not have to change the implementation details if the access rules change.

For our web application, the first mechanism we are concerned with is restricting access to particular URLs to the various groups of users. Consider the following group of URLs, for example:

- http://example.com/timesheets/login

- http://example.com/timesheets/home

- http://example.com/timesheets/admin

All users must have access to the login page. Otherwise, nobody could establish credentials with the site. All logged-in users should have access to their home pages, but anonymous users must not. And only logged-in administrator users should have access to the administrator pages.

In principle, we could apply these security rules in the controller classes, but then we would have to implement them in every controller, and could not reuse controller classes in contexts where different security rules applied. Similarly, we could apply the security rules to the servlets, but a web application may have multiple servlets, and there is a good chance that we will want to incorporate some servlets that are unaware of the Spring environment into an application, yet we would like these to be secured by the same rules.

Fortunately, Java EE provides an ideal tool for managing security in web requests: the filter. Filters have the ideal life cycle; they allow us to intercept incoming web requests, permit them to proceed or prevent them from proceeding, and to do the same to outgoing web requests, manipulating responses and forcing redirects and forwards to other pages.

Filters

The one area in which filters are somewhat less than ideal is in their configuration. Filters are configured in the web.xml file, and as such have no special access to the Spring configuration context. Fortunately, Spring provides a solution: a DelegatingFilterProxy filter is configured in the Java EE deployment context file, and this in turn passes all the requests to a filter (literally implementing the Java EE standard javax.servlet.Filter interface) configured as a bean within the Spring application context.

Acegi provides a large number of filters to implement web security, allowing the desirable behavior to be applied by picking and choosing from the available filters. In principle, there could be as many DelegatingFilterProxy and associated Acegi filter beans as necessary, but this would divide the configuration confusingly between the Spring and Java EE configuration files. Instead, the Spring filter bean used is usually the FilterChainProxy. This is simultaneously a filter, a Spring bean, and a container for other filter beans—chaining them together and applying them in turn. Figure 7-2 shows the relationship between the filters and their respective configuration files.

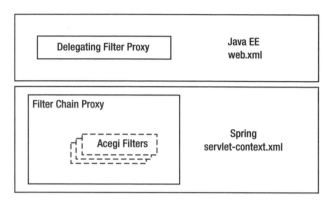

Figure 7-2. *Configuring the Acegi filters*

Listing 7-1 shows an excerpt from the Java EE deployment descriptor showing the configuration of the `DelegatingFilterProxy` filter. You should be aware that the equivalent `FilterToBeanProxy` class may instead be used, but the differences are insignificant.

Listing 7-1. *Declaring the Delegating Filter in the Deployment Descriptor*

```
<filter>
   <description>Acegi Request Filter</description>
   <filter-name>acegi-request-filter</filter-name>
   <filter-class>
      org.springframework.web.filter.DelegatingFilterProxy
   </filter-class>
   <init-param>
      <param-name>targetBeanName</param-name>
      <param-value>acegiRequestFilter</param-value>
   </init-param>
</filter>

<filter-mapping>
   <filter-name>acegi-request-filter</filter-name>
   <url-pattern>/*</url-pattern>
</filter-mapping>
```

The target bean name provided to the `DelegatingFilterProxy` indicates the name of the bean from the application context to be used (note that you cannot use beans configured for specific `DispatcherServlet` instances). In practice, this will be the name of the configured `FilterChainProxy` bean.

Listing 7-2 shows the configuration of the filter chain proxy, and this is where the meat of the configuration starts. This class originates with the Acegi project (as you can see from the package name) and is primarily a point from which to invoke other filter beans.

Listing 7-2. *Configuring the Filter Chain*

```
<bean id="acegiRequestFilter"
   class="org.acegisecurity.util.FilterChainProxy">
   <property name="filterInvocationDefinitionSource">
      <value>
CONVERT_URL_TO_LOWERCASE_BEFORE_COMPARISON
PATTERN_TYPE_APACHE_ANT
/login*=anonymousProcessingFilter
/accessdenied*=anonymousProcessingFilter
/**=httpSessionContextIntegrationFilter,logoutFilter,authenticationProcessingFilter ➥
,anonymousProcessingFilter,exceptionTranslationFilter,securityInterceptorFilter
      </value>
   </property>
</bean>
```

The filterInvocationDefinitionSource property indicates which filters should be invoked for which URLs. The first two lines declare how URLs should be matched; they will be converted to lowercase, and Ant style patterns will then be used to determine which filter to invoke.

■**Caution** If you omit the PATTERN_TYPE_APACHE_ANT declaration, regular expressions will be used—but these are Jakarta ORO regular expressions, not the standard regular expressions introduced in Java 1.4. This arises from the lack of regular expressions in Java 1.3 combined with the prevalence of Java 1.3–based application servers. Jakarta ORO was used to fill the gap, but there are significant incompatibilities between the two libraries, particularly in areas such as support for Unicode expressions. See http://jakarta.apache.org/oro/ for the specifics of the ORO syntax.

The configuration then specifies URL patterns followed by lists of filters that will be applied to these URLs. Note that this indicates nothing about what permissions are required to access the various URLs—only about what filters will be applied. The security is enforced by these chained filters, which have their own individual configuration details. The ordering of the paths is extremely important: the first match found will be used to select the set of filters to apply to the request, so you must define the finest-grained URL patterns first and the coarsest last (otherwise, the wrong filters will be applied, and you may not be correctly securing the path, or may be incorrectly securing an insecure path).

In this configuration, we can see that with two exceptions, all URL requests pass through a series of six chained filters. We will examine these out of order.

Listing 7-3 shows the authentication-processing filter.

Listing 7-3. *The Authentication-Processing Filter*

```
<bean id="authenticationProcessingFilter"
    class="org.acegisecurity.ui.webapp.AuthenticationProcessingFilter">
    <property name="authenticationManager"
        ref="authenticationManager" />
    <property name="authenticationFailureUrl" value="/login" />
    <property name="defaultTargetUrl" value="/home" />
    <property name="alwaysUseDefaultTargetUrl" value="false" />
    <property name="filterProcessesUrl"
        value="/j_acegi_security_check" />
</bean>
```

This filter looks for unauthenticated requests—that is, requests by users who have not yet logged in. If a user has not yet authenticated, the request will be redirected to the URL specified by the authenticationFailureUrl property: /login (URLs will always be relative to the web application context). Now we see the reason for the first of the exceptions to the general rules for filtering requests: the /login URL itself cannot be passed to the authentication-processing filter because this would set up a recursive filter. All users must be able to access /login regardless of whether they have authenticated.

When the user logs in, she will be taken to the path specified by defaultTargetUrl, which is the /home path. If she were trying to access another URL before she was redirected to the login page for authentication, she would instead be sent there because the alwaysUseDefaultTargetUrl property is set to false. If it were set to true, she would always arrive at the home page after login regardless of which page she originally tried to access. The behavior as configured here allows bookmarked, secure URLs to work properly, however, so in general this is the preferred configuration.

Finally, the path to which the login form must be submitted is specified (that is, the action parameter for the form). The parameters submitted by the form must be the Servlet standard j_username and j_password. When the form is submitted, the user is authenticated by using the authentication manager provided to the filter. The details of this mechanism are discussed later in the chapter, but the results of the authentication attempt (including details of role memberships) are retained in the thread context (see the section "Security Context" later in this chapter for discussion of the thread context).

When a request passes through the anonymous processing filter, as configured in Listing 7-4, an alternative "dummy" set of authentication-request information is stored in the thread context. The "key" shown here is analogous to the password entered in a real request, but allows various different sorts of anonymous users to be maintained independently. In practice, the value used does not usually matter as long as it corresponds to the value used in the anonymous authentication provider (described in the following "Providers" section).

Listing 7-4. *The Anonymous Processing Filter*

```
<bean id="anonymousProcessingFilter" class=
"org.acegisecurity.providers.anonymous.AnonymousProcessingFilter">
    <property name="key" value="timesheetAnonymous" />
    <property name="userAttribute" value="anonymous,ROLE_ANONYMOUS" />
</bean>
```

The security interceptor filter receives the request after the thread context has been populated with the authentication information. This filter is used to determine what access will be permitted to the application on the basis of the authentication achieved by the earlier filters.

The authentication information and the request being made are adjudicated by a set of decision voters. Because multiple resources can be used to determine access, we need to establish how to determine success. Listing 7-5 shows our example configured with two voters. These will decide access on the basis of the user's role and authentication status. If none of the authentication providers participate in the decision-making process, the allowIfAllAbstainDecisions property indicates that requests should by default be rejected.

Listing 7-5. *Configuring the Security Interceptor Filter*

```
<bean id="securityInterceptorFilter"
    class="org.acegisecurity.intercept.web.FilterSecurityInterceptor">
    <property name="authenticationManager"
        ref="authenticationManager" />
    <property name="accessDecisionManager">
        <bean class="org.acegisecurity.vote.AffirmativeBased">
            <property name="allowIfAllAbstainDecisions" value="false"/>
            <property name="decisionVoters">
                <list>
                    <bean class="org.acegisecurity.vote.RoleVoter"/>
                    <bean class="org.acegisecurity.vote.AuthenticatedVoter"/>
                </list>
            </property>
        </bean>
    </property>
```

```
    <property name="objectDefinitionSource">
      <value>
        CONVERT_URL_TO_LOWERCASE_BEFORE_COMPARISON
        PATTERN_TYPE_APACHE_ANT
        /login=ROLE_ANONYMOUS,ROLE_USER,ROLE_ADMINISTRATOR
        /accessdenied=ROLE_ANONYMOUS,ROLE_USER,ROLE_ADMINISTRATOR
        /**=ROLE_USER,ROLE_ADMINISTRATOR
        /admin**=ROLE_ADMINISTRATOR
      </value>
    </property>
</bean>
```

The objectDefinitionSource property is specified in a very similar manner to the FilterChainProxy configuration shown in Listing 7-2, but here it defines what roles are required to access which URLs, rather than which filters will be applied. The anonymous role is (and must be) sufficient to access the login and to access denied pages, with other users also permitted access to them. Other URLs require more-specific roles.

Listing 7-6 shows the exception-translation filter. Unlike the other filters encountered so far, this handles the request on its way back up the chain of filters.

Listing 7-6. *The Exception-Translation Filter*

```
<bean id="exceptionTranslationFilter"
    class="org.acegisecurity.ui.ExceptionTranslationFilter">
    <property name="authenticationEntryPoint">
        <bean class=
"org.acegisecurity.ui.webapp.AuthenticationProcessingFilterEntryPoint">
            <property name="loginFormUrl" value="/login" />
            <property name="forceHttps" value="false" />
        </bean>
    </property>
    <property name="accessDeniedHandler">
        <bean class="org.acegisecurity.ui.AccessDeniedHandlerImpl">
            <property name="errorPage" value="/accessDenied" />
        </bean>
    </property>
</bean>
```

The filter handles two situations. First, the filter handles the case where the user was not successfully authenticated. If the user's authentication attempt failed, the user will be redirected to the login page (with a secure connection established if the forceHttps flag is set). Second, the filter handles the case where the user was authenticated, but not authorized to access the URL that he requested. In this case, the user will be redirected to an appropriate path (typically, as here, an Access Denied page).

Note that this filter does not carry out any of the authorization or authentication process itself. The filter is purely concerned with handling the aftermath of failure to achieve either of these.

Finally, Listing 7-7 shows the configuration of the session context integration filter that handles the outbound request immediately before it completes its passage through the filters.

Listing 7-7. *The Session Context Integration Filter*

```
<bean id="httpSessionContextIntegrationFilter"
class="org.acegisecurity.context.HttpSessionContextIntegrationFilter"/>
```

Despite this filter's position in *first* place in the chain, it is also the *last* filter to have access to the request object. This filter places the authentication and authorization information into the session context for future use. Other approaches are possible, but this is the simplest mechanism available to avoid the necessity of making the user log in for every URL. When an incoming request is received after a successful authentication, the authentication information will be reestablished for the thread for access by the other filters.

Providers

The section on filters has covered the life cycle of the request in terms of the constraints that are placed on it, but does not explain how the authentication itself is carried out.

The component that needs to carry out authentication is the FilterSecurityInterceptor. When an unauthenticated request is received by this filter, it must try to authenticate (log in) the user. If authentication succeeds, the filter must determine the roles to assign to that user. It does so by consulting the authentication manager.

The authentication manager receives the credentials (typically the username and password) provided by the user and uses these to determine the authentication status of the principal (to log the user in) and the authorizations granted to the principal (to determine the user's roles).

■**Note** The *principal* is an identity used for security purposes. Security terminology avoids terms such as *account* or *username* because the principal may identify a particular system, a user, a process, or any other logical entity to which authorization and authentication may be applied. For most purposes in this chapter, however, you can think of the principal as being synonymous with *user account*.

The ProviderManager class whose configuration is shown in Listing 7-8 allows multiple Provider classes to be used to acquire the authentication information. In our example application, this is used to acquire authentication by using a DAO to retrieve user privileges from a database, or if this fails, to assign an "anonymous" authentication privilege to the user.

Listing 7-8. *Configuring the Authentication Manager with Providers*

```
<bean id="authenticationManager"
   class="org.acegisecurity.providers.ProviderManager">
   <property name="providers">
      <list>
         <ref local="daoAuthentication" />
         <ref local="anonymousAuthentication" />
      </list>
   </property>
</bean>
```

Listing 7-9 shows the configuration of this anonymous authentication provider. The provider will "log in" as the anonymous user (with username anonymous and the role ROLE_ANONYMOUS as configured in Listing 7-4) any request that has passed through the anonymous processing filter with a key matching the value configured here.

Listing 7-9. *Configuring the Anonymous Authentication Provider*

```
<bean id="anonymousAuthentication" class=
"org.acegisecurity.providers.anonymous.AnonymousAuthenticationProvider"
>
   <property name="key" value="timesheetAnonymous" />
</bean>
```

The anonymous user is not essential—we have the capacity to exclude URLs from our filters entirely, which has much the same effect—but it is often simpler to write code that manipulates users than to write code that assumes the existence of a user but takes special actions when no user exists. For example, when logging access to a website, we may want to track user information. The use of an anonymous user allows us to write code that assumes a user even when none "really" exists, reducing the amount of conditional logic required. On the other hand, this adds some additional memory overhead to the request (and potentially to the session), which may offset these advantages if you are expecting very heavy user loads.

One of the most useful providers available to us is the DaoAuthenticationProvider class. This allows us to implement a DAO class and use this to determine the user's permissions. Despite the name, this class does not need to be part of our DAO layer, architecturally speaking. In Listing 7-10, the implementation class is actually configured as a member of our service layer (and thus subject to the AOP-applied transactional constraints configured in Chapter 5).

Listing 7-10. *The DAO Authentication Provider*

```
<bean id="daoAuthentication"
   class="org.acegisecurity.providers.dao.DaoAuthenticationProvider">
   <property name="passwordEncoder" ref="passwordEncoder" />
   <property name="userDetailsService" ref="acegiUserDetailsService" />
</bean>

<bean id="passwordEncoder"
   class="org.acegisecurity.providers.encoding.Md5PasswordEncoder">
   <property name="encodeHashAsBase64" value="true" />
</bean>
```

For a class to be used by the DaoAuthenticationProvider, it need only implement the interface shown in Listing 7-11. This will be passed the username for which a UserDetails object must be retrieved.

Listing 7-11. *The UserDetailsService Interface*

```
public interface UserDetailsService {
   UserDetails loadUserByUsername(String username)
      throws UsernameNotFoundException,
            DataAccessException;
}
```

Listing 7-12 shows the interface that this UserDetails object must implement.

Listing 7-12. *The UserDetails Interface*

```
public interface UserDetails
   extends Serializable
{
   GrantedAuthority[] getAuthorities();
   String getPassword();
   String getUsername();
   boolean isAccountNonExpired();
   boolean isAccountNonLocked();
   boolean isCredentialsNonExpired();
   boolean isEnabled();
}
```

The UserDetails interface does not correspond particularly well with the UserAccount object that we discussed in Chapter 4 for maintaining the login information. For example, the getAuthorities() method for retrieving authorization information returns the GrantedAuthority objects defined by the interface shown in Listing 7-13 instead of our set of UserRole objects.

Listing 7-13. *The GrantedAuthority Interface*

```
public interface GrantedAuthority
    extends Serializable
{
    String getAuthority();
}
```

Despite this disparity, the fact that these objects are represented as interfaces in Acegi means that we can readily create suitable wrapper or delegating classes to correlate the Acegi security objects with our proprietary implementations.

Listing 7-14 shows a part of the implementation I have used to illustrate this convenient aspect of Acegi. An additional entity type has been created that delegates the retrieval of GrantedAuthority objects and the username property to the UserAccount entities. A transient AcegiGrantedAuthority class has also been created to wrap the UserRole entities.

Listing 7-14. *Part of Our Implementation of the UserDetails Interface*

```
private UserAccount userAccount;

public GrantedAuthority[] getAuthorities() {
    final Set<UserRole> roles = userAccount.getRoles();
    return AcegiGrantedAuthority.getAuthorities(roles);
}

public String getUsername() {
    return userAccount.getAccountName();
}
```

Of course, in a project that contains Acegi from the outset, you would typically create your user and role entities to implement these Acegi interfaces from the beginning, but you are not obliged to do this, so Acegi can readily be retrofitted to legacy designs.

Other Providers

You will not always need to provide your own DAO implementation to carry out authentication. There are additional providers that allow you to connect to standard authentication and authorization resources, and there are additional filter implementations to collect the necessary credentials. Your Acegi-enabled application therefore has drop-in replacements for the following mechanisms:

- Central Authentication Services (CAS)

- Java Authentication and Authorization Services (JAAS)

- Lightweight Directory Access Protocol (LDAP)

- Remote Client Protocol (RCP)

- SiteMinder

- X.509

You are unlikely to encounter a security mechanism that is not covered by one of these methods and for which the `UserDetailsService` is insufficient.

Channel Security

So far, we have checked who is connecting to the application (authentication) and which parts of the application those users are allowed to access (authorization). However, we have not yet ensured that their conversation with the application cannot be overheard, so we will now address the problem of securing the channel of communication from eavesdroppers.

The larger part of the problem has already been solved for us. Java EE defines a mechanism by which exchanges with a web application can be secured when using the Secure Sockets Layer (SSL) encryption protocol. Channel security is traded off against other considerations such as user convenience and application performance; as always, you will have some subjective decisions to make.

■**Note** The steps required to configure SSL support vary widely between web application server platforms. I do not attempt to cover them in this book. You should consult your vendor's website for specifics. Instructions for configuring the Tomcat 5.5 application server that I used while writing this book are available at http://tomcat.apache.org/tomcat-5.5-doc/ssl-howto.html.

If you want your entire application to be secured from eavesdroppers, you need do nothing more than ensure that your application server accepts connections only on the secure port. However, the use of encryption comes with some performance disadvantages.

Encrypting and decrypting communications makes significant demands of the processor, and the use of an encrypted channel prevents you from being able to cache secured pages.

In practice, it is more typical to secure only particularly sensitive information from eavesdroppers. On an e-commerce website, this would probably include the username and password, any credit card details, and perhaps the user's other personal account details. On the timesheet application, we will secure the login process, preventing a hypothetical eavesdropper from obtaining the user's credentials and using them to falsely authenticate with the application at a subsequent date.

Channel security can be enforced by using yet another processing filter. Typically, you would add this to the filter chain for all URLs being processed by the application. Listing 7-15 shows the addition of the channel filter to the filter chain established in Listing 7-2.

Listing 7-15. *The Amended Filter Invocation Definition Source*

```
<property name="filterInvocationDefinitionSource">
   <value>
      CONVERT_URL_TO_LOWERCASE_BEFORE_COMPARISON
      PATTERN_TYPE_APACHE_ANT
      /css/**=channelProcessingFilter,anonymousProcessingFilter
      /login*=channelProcessingFilter,anonymousProcessingFilter
      /accessdenied*=channelProcessingFilter,anonymousProcessingFilter
      /**=channelProcessingFilter,httpSessionContextIntegration,...
   </value>
</property>
```

Listing 7-16 shows the definition of the channel-processing filter.

Listing 7-16. *Defining the Channel-Processing Filter*

```
<bean id="channelProcessingFilter"
   class="org.acegisecurity.securechannel.ChannelProcessingFilter">
   <property name="channelDecisionManager"
      ref="channelDecisionManager"/>
   <property name="filterInvocationDefinitionSource">
      <value>
         CONVERT_URL_TO_LOWERCASE_BEFORE_COMPARISON
         PATTERN_TYPE_APACHE_ANT
         /login**=REQUIRES_SECURE_CHANNEL
         /j_acegi_security_check=REQUIRES_SECURE_CHANNEL
         /secure/**=REQUIRES_SECURE_CHANNEL
         /**=REQUIRES_INSECURE_CHANNEL
      </value>
   </property>
</bean>
```

The filter declares the paths that must be secured from eavesdroppers and delegates to the channel decision manager to determine whether these rules are in force. The syntax for the filterInvocationDefinitionSource property, which is used to specify the channel security level required for the various paths, is similar to that required to specify the filter chain to apply to paths in Listing 7-2 and the roles required to access the paths in Listing 7-5.

The definitions in Listing 7-16 define the channel security level that is *required*. It is not possible for a channel to be simultaneously secure and insecure, so you must not specify both REQUIRES_SECURE_CHANNEL and REQUIRES_INSECURE_CHANNEL for any path. Specifying REQUIRES_INSECURE_CHANNEL will actively redirect an incoming *secure* request to the *insecure* port. If instead you are prepared to let the user dictate the level of security to be applied to a particular path, you should ensure that neither of the channel security processors is specified for the path in question.

Listing 7-17 shows the configuration of the channel decision manager.

Listing 7-17. *The Channel Decision Manager Used to Determine the Channel Security in Use*

```
<bean id="channelDecisionManager"
    class="org.acegisecurity.securechannel.ChannelDecisionManagerImpl">
    <property name="channelProcessors">
        <list>
            <ref bean="secureChannelProcessor" />
            <ref bean="insecureChannelProcessor" />
        </list>
    </property>
</bean>
```

The beans configured here correlate with the keys mapped to the paths in the channel-processing filter of Listing 7-16. For example, everything below the /login path requires the use of a secure channel. When an incoming request comes in, the filter delegates to the channel decision manager, passing it the REQUIRES_SECURE_CHANNEL key and the request details. The channel decision manager polls the channel processors until the channel processor corresponding to this key is located. If the channel processor rejects the request as not having the appropriate channel security, the processor will issue a redirect to the appropriate secure resource (typically this involves redirecting from a plain-text port to an SSL port).

Listing 7-18 shows the bean definitions for the two channel processors used here.

Listing 7-18. *The Bean Definitions for the Channel Processors*

```
<bean id="secureChannelProcessor"
    class="org.acegisecurity.securechannel.SecureChannelProcessor"/>

<bean id="insecureChannelProcessor"
    class="org.acegisecurity.securechannel.InsecureChannelProcessor"/>
```

Both of these implementations use a default `PortMapper` implementation that assumes that you are running your server on port 80 with SSL on port 443, or that you are running your server on port 8080 with SSL on port 8443 (the two most common configurations). If these assumptions are not true, you will need to configure a new `PortMapperImpl` bean with an appropriate `portMappings` property map and inject this into both channel processors to override the default behavior.

Making Security Decisions

Not all of the application's security can be enforced with filters. Sometimes we need to make decisions about what content to present to the user that can be determined only as the data is being acquired or as the page is being rendered. In this section, you'll look at how the application logic can be informed by the security information available through Acegi.

Security Tag Library

On a secure website, some pages will be accessible to only certain classes of users. Other pages will be generally visible, but with certain content hidden from view according to the user roles. For example, a link to the admin functionality should not be visible to the standard user, but the developer will not want to create two distinct implementations of the page just to manage this sort of trivial discrepancy.

The Acegi library therefore provides a JSP tag library allowing certain bodies of content to be restricted according to the user's access roles. Listing 7-19 shows the page declaration to import the appropriate tag library.

Listing 7-19. *Including the Acegi Tag Library into a JSP*

```
<%@taglib prefix="authz" uri="http://acegisecurity.org/authz" %>
```

Applying the constraint is then a matter of including the appropriate tags around the restricted content. An example is shown in Listing 7-20 that restricts the display of the Administrative Menu paragraph to users with the administrator role.

Listing 7-20. *Restricting Page Content to Administrative Users*

```
<authz:authorize ifAllGranted="ROLE_ADMINISTRATOR">
   <p>Administration Menu</p>
</authz:authorize>
```

Additional tags are available to give you direct access to the authentication object established by the filters, and to manage access control lists (access control lists are outside the scope of this chapter).

Security Context

While reading the explanation of filters, you may have been puzzled by the term *thread context* and may have expected the authentication information to be stored within the request context.

Storing the authentication information within the request context makes perfect sense for a web application when you are concerned with restricting access to URLs and otherwise carrying out web-oriented security operations, but there is more to security than preventing access to URLs. You may wish to write code that is aware of the specifics of the user currently accessing the database.

In our example application, a typical example of this requirement is the need to ensure that a specific user does not access other users' timesheets. The URL concerns cannot help us: all users access the timesheet application by the same means, so we need to ensure that a user who manages to get a request for another user's timesheet past the filters cannot actually access the data in question.

The simplest way to prevent this access is to check the authenticated user's name against the request for the data. To do so, we need to access the information in layers of the software that should not have access to a servlet request object. These layers should work equally well in a stand-alone Swing application that carries out its authentication by using a dialog box.

The authentication and authorization information is therefore stored in a thread-local variable that is accessible through a static method on the SecurityContextHolder class. A call to this getContext() method allows the authentication object established elsewhere to be retrieved, as shown in Listing 7-21.

Listing 7-21. *Retrieving Authentication Information from SecurityContextHolder*

```
public static UserAccount getUser() {
    final SecurityContext sc = SecurityContextHolder.getContext();
    final Authentication auth = sc.getAuthentication();
    if( auth == null ) return null;
    final AcegiUserDetails acegiAccount =
        (AcegiUserDetails)auth.getPrincipal();
    if( acegiAccount == null ) return null;
    final UserAccount account = acegiAccount.getUserAccount();
    return account;
}
```

The authentication object allows access to the principal representing the user, from which the username, authorities (authorizations) and other basic details can be retrieved. In Listing 7-21, the UserAccount principal is retrieved from the authentication object.

An alternative approach, which uses aspect-oriented programming to enforce security constraints of this type without directly tainting the service logic with security concerns, has already been covered in Chapter 5. However, I did not explain at that point the basis on which the security details were obtained. If you revisit Chapter 5 at this point, you will see that the implementation of an AOP advice in Listing 5-23 uses the static method of Listing 7-21 to obtain the details of the current principal.

Securing the Service Layer

Having secured the web tier against inappropriate access, it would be good to be able to enforce a similar level of security in the service layer. There are service layer methods that should never be invoked by ordinary or anonymous users. For example, the operation to delete a user from the database would typically be constrained to administrative users. Similarly, the ability to load a spreadsheet should be denied to anonymous users.

One way to achieve protection of the service layer would be to hard-code lots of checks of the authorization information available from SecurityContextHolder. However, this would create an unnecessary dependency—precisely what we're trying to avoid in our use of Spring in the first place.

A superior solution exists: we can apply an AOP advice to our service layer to enforce security. If you are using the XML configuration of AOP, you can add a suitable pointcut and advice. In fact, you have already seen this approach in use in Chapter 5 where we used this very example as an illustration of applying aspects!

Method-level role-based security can be applied even more simply by using annotations. By applying the org.acegisecurity.annotations.Secured annotation to your service class methods and then applying an advice to the methods so marked, you can indicate the roles that are required to invoke them. (This is similar to the enforcing of transactionality by using @Transaction annotations as discussed in Chapter 5.) Listing 7-22 shows how the user account service interface can be annotated to enforce role-based security.

Listing 7-22. *Annotating the Security Roles Required by Service Methods*

```
public interface UserAccountService {
  @Secured({"ROLE_ADMINISTRATOR","ROLE_USER"})
  UserAccount findUser(String username);

  @Secured({"ROLE_ADMINISTRATOR"})
  void createUser(UserAccount account);
```

```
@Secured({"ROLE_ADMINISTRATOR"})
void deleteUser(UserAccount account);

@Secured({"ROLE_ADMINISTRATOR"})
void updateUser(UserAccount account);

@Secured({"ROLE_ADMINISTRATOR","ROLE_USER"})
List<UserAccount> listUsers();
}
```

Listing 7-23 shows the advice configuration needed to support the use of the @Secured annotation used in Listing 7-22.

Listing 7-23. *Configuring the @Secured Annotation–Based Method Security*

```
<bean id="attributes"
  class="org.acegisecurity.annotation.SecurityAnnotationAttributes"/>

<bean id="objectDefinitionSource"
  class="org.acegisecurity.intercept.method.MethodDefinitionAttributes">
  <property name="attributes" ref="attributes"/>
</bean>

<bean id="securityAnnotationInterceptor" class=
"org.acegisecurity.intercept.method.aopalliance.MethodSecurityInterceptor">
  <property name="authenticationManager" ref="authenticationManager"/>
  <property name="accessDecisionManager" ref="accessDecisionManager"/>
  <property name="objectDefinitionSource" ref="objectDefinitionSource"/>
</bean>
```

The attributes bean allows classes to be checked for Acegi security annotations. The object definition source bean stores the detected annotation information, and the security annotation interceptor bean then intercepts the methods so annotated and applies the appropriate security level for the role requirements detected.

Note that the interceptor of Listing 7-23 requires independent access to an access decision manager. Rather than duplicate the configuration used in the security interceptor filter of Listing 7-5, we would create a bean definition for it as shown in Listing 7-24, and reference this bean from both the security interceptor filter and the security annotation interceptor's accessDecisionManager property.

Listing 7-24. *Defining the Access Decision Manager As a Stand-Alone Bean*

```
<bean id="accessDecisionManager"
    class="org.acegisecurity.vote.AffirmativeBased">
    <property name="allowIfAllAbstainDecisions" value="false" />
    <property name="decisionVoters">
      <list>
        <bean class="org.acegisecurity.vote.RoleVoter"/>
        <bean class="org.acegisecurity.vote.AuthenticatedVoter"/>
      </list>
    </property>
</bean>
```

Conclusion

In this chapter, you have seen how the Spring Security framework allows access control to be injected into a web application. You have seen how paths can be protected, how user information can be acquired from the security framework, and how the service layer can be protected independently of the URLs that are used to invoke it.

In the next chapter, you will take a look at how e-mail can be created in response to events within the application. You will also learn about the creation of MIME messages containing rich content.

CHAPTER 8

■ ■ ■

Sending E-mail

Notifying the user of changes in the application environment is a common requirement for applications of all types, but is especially useful in web applications when processes may need to happen asynchronously and you cannot necessarily demand the user's attention for the duration of the operation. Sometimes the notification will be generated as the result of a completely different user's action, and that is the situation I have chosen to model in the timesheet application: the administrative user will be notified when a user updates a timesheet.

For the sake of simplicity my example assumes that the administrator will be notified of updates *only*, and that the only information needed is the account name of the user making the change. However, this example covers all of the basic techniques that are required for more-sophisticated solutions: populating the message dynamically with information from the application, formatting it, and sending it.

By using a DAO implementation honoring an interface, we allow the specific mechanism used for e-mail to be changed without affecting the rest of the application. I take advantage of this throughout this chapter in order to substitute three implementations of the DAO by using different formatting mechanisms.

Listing 8-1 shows the interface that these DAOs must implement. The sole method takes a timesheet entity as its parameter, and it is from this that data will be drawn to populate the e-mail content with the user account details.

Listing 8-1. *Our Basic E-mail DAO Interface*

```
public interface EmailDao {
    void sendTimesheetUpdate(Timesheet timesheet);
}
```

You looked at the usage of the e-mail DAO very briefly in Chapter 5, when we were considering the use of the service layer to group related calls to various DAOs. Listing 8-2 shows the injection of the e-mail DAO implementation into the service class that will use it.

Listing 8-2. *The Timesheet Service Bean Configuration*

```
<bean id="timesheetService"
   class="com.apress.timesheets.service.TimesheetServiceImpl">
   <property name="timesheetDao" ref="timesheetDao"/>
   <property name="emailDao" ref="simpleEmailDao"/>
</bean>
```

Because the service layer is the common point of contact to the business functionality of our application, we can be confident that any user operation to update the timesheet must pass through the service layer, and so invoke the mechanism to send e-mail as appropriate.

Using the Mail Sender

Spring provides two interfaces for sending e-mail. The first and simplest of these is the MailSender shown in Listing 8-3. This accepts an instance of the SimpleMailMessage class (which is itself, in turn, an implementation of the Spring MailMessage class). With a suitable implementation of the interface available, sending a message is a matter of constructing a SimpleMailMessage object to represent the e-mail and calling the send method. The method accepting an array of SimpleMailMessage objects allows for mail to be sent in batches.

Listing 8-3. *The Spring MailSender Interface*

```
public interface MailSender {
   void send(SimpleMailMessage simpleMessage)
      throws MailException;
   void send(SimpleMailMessage[] simpleMessages)
      throws MailException;
}
```

The MailSender implementation is appropriate for pure text-based e-mail with no attachments, but for sending e-mail containing HTML markup or attachments, an implementation of the more-sophisticated JavaMailSender is required. Implementations allow for Multipurpose Internet Mail Extensions (MIME) messages to be created that represent the standards for sending e-mails composed of multiple discrete files—typically the e-mail text, any inline images, and any attachments associated with the e-mail.

■**Note** MIME is essentially a mechanism for encoding binary files into text for transmission over mediums that do not understand binary data. In the early days of e-mail transmissions, not all mail servers would correctly handle binary files and so the encoding was necessary. Although the mechanism is no longer necessary for this specific reason, MIME has become the accepted standard and must therefore be used for sending binary data by e-mail. The standard has also been adopted in other circumstances, and related parts of the standard are used for other purposes, notably for identifying file types. As a result, the acronym does not automatically indicate any connection with e-mail when used in other contexts.

The interface is shown in Listing 8-4 and is mostly concerned with the manipulation of MIME messages. However, it extends MailSender, so as a matter of convenience you can use a JavaMailSender implementation in any context where you need a MailSender implementation.

Listing 8-4. *The Spring JavaMailSender Interface*

```
public interface JavaMailSender extends MailSender {
   MimeMessage createMimeMessage();
   MimeMessage createMimeMessage(InputStream contentStream)
      throws MailException;
   void send(MimeMessage mimeMessage)
      throws MailException;
   void send(MimeMessage[] mimeMessages)
      throws MailException;
   void send(MimeMessagePreparator mimeMessagePreparator)
      throws MailException;
   void send(MimeMessagePreparator[] mimeMessagePreparators)
      throws MailException;
}
```

All of the examples in this chapter use the JavaMailSenderImpl implementation of the JavaMailSender interface. Listing 8-5 shows the configuration of this bean in the application context configuration file.

Listing 8-5. *Configuring a JavaMailSender Bean Implementation*

```
<bean id="mailSender"
   class="org.springframework.mail.javamail.JavaMailSenderImpl">
   <property name="host" value="smtp.example.com"/>
</bean>
```

You will need to amend the host value (highlighted in bold in Listing 8-5) to the domain name of your own SMTP mail gateway. You cannot send e-mail by using the examples in this chapter without access to a mail gateway. Setting up your own gateway is beyond the scope of this book.

Sending Plain Text

As a matter of convenience for this and the other examples in this chapter, I have created a base class for the DAO implementations that accept the property values that are common between all three. This class is shown in Listing 8-6.

Listing 8-6. *An Abstract Base Class for the MailDAO Implementations*

```
abstract public class AbstractMailDaoImpl implements EmailDao {
   protected String fromAddress;
   protected String rcptAddress;
   protected String subject;

   @Required
   public void setFromAddress(String fromAddress) {
      this.fromAddress = fromAddress;
   }

   @Required
   public void setRcptAddress(String rcptAddress) {
      this.rcptAddress = rcptAddress;
   }

   @Required
   public void setSubject(String subject) {
      this.subject = subject;
   }

   abstract public void sendTimesheetUpdate(Timesheet timesheet);
}
```

Listing 8-7 shows a concrete implementation of the DAO derived from this class. Via the parent, we have access to the properties specifying the basic addressing information: the sender and the recipient. We also have access to the subject of the message. From the timesheet entity passed in by the service, we draw the account name of the user who carried out the update operation that the notification relates to.

The logic of the `sendTimesheetUpdate()` method is then implemented as you would expect: we create a `SimpleMailMessage` object to represent the e-mail to be sent, populate the address information and the subject, create a string for the text of the e-mail and populate that, and call the `MailSender`'s send method passing in the composed message object. The Spring implementation takes care of the handshaking with the remote mail server. If for any reason this fails (if the server is offline, our Internet connection is down, or the server rejects the message for any other reason), a Spring `MailException` will be thrown, allowing us to report or recover from the problem.

Listing 8-7. *An Implementation of a Simple Mail DAO*

```
public class SimpleMailDaoImpl extends AbstractMailDaoImpl {
   private static final Logger log =
      Logger.getLogger(SimpleMailDaoImpl.class);
   private MailSender mailSender;

   public void sendTimesheetUpdate(final Timesheet timesheet) {
      try {
         final SimpleMailMessage message = new SimpleMailMessage();
         message.setTo(rcptAddress);
         message.setFrom(fromAddress);
         message.setSubject(subject);
         message.setText("A timesheet has been updated by user: "
                  + timesheet.getConsultant().getAccountName());
         mailSender.send(message);
      } catch (MailException e) {
         log.error("Failed to send timesheet update message", e);
         throw e;
      }
   }

   @Required
   public void setMailSender(MailSender mailSender) {
      this.mailSender = mailSender;
   }
}
```

Listing 8-8 shows the configuration of this implementation; we have defined an abstract configuration bean that specifies the common properties of the beans to be configured, and then configured our specific implementation with this as its parent.

Listing 8-8. *The Configuration of Our Simple Mail DAO*

```
<bean id="abstractEmailDao" abstract="true">
    <property name="fromAddress" value="timesheets@example.com"/>
    <property name="rcptAddress" value="admin@example.com"/>
    <property name="mailSender" ref="mailSender"/>
    <property name="subject" value="Timesheet Update Message"/>
</bean>

<bean id="simpleEmailDao"
    class="com.apress.timesheets.mail.SimpleMailDaoImpl"
    parent="abstractEmailDao"/>
```

Because our bean does not require any additional configuration details beyond those common to the other implementations in this chapter, it does not require any other properties to be specified; they are all "inherited" from the abstract parent bean. You should note that the abstract bean configuration has no relationship to the abstract DAO implementation that we created in Listing 8-6. One is a convenience for the implementation of the DAO, and the other is a convenience for its configuration. Either could exist without the other, and the properties of the abstract bean configuration do not have to (and do not) correspond to the properties available in the AbstractMailDaoImpl implementation.

Figure 8-1 shows an example of the resulting plain-text e-mail that will be sent by the basic e-mail DAO implementation.

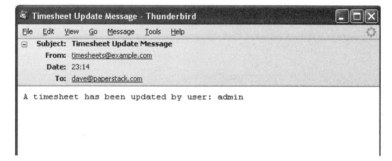

Figure 8-1. *The plain-text e-mail*

For the sake of the simplicity of the examples, the recipient, sender, and subject of the e-mail are all specified explicitly in the configuration of the e-mail beans. In a real-world application, you would almost certainly retrieve these details from the model passed to the bean's action method. For example, in a real timesheet application, you might send e-mail to the timesheet's owner based on a property of the timesheet object itself, or the owner and subject could be passed as additional parameters to the sendTimesheetUpdate() method. You will need to update the rcptAddress configuration property to a real e-mail address before testing this application!

Sending Formatted HTML

The plain-text e-mail is a useful tool. It is readable in all e-mail clients, including those that are not a part of any graphical user interface. It can be seen on all platforms, and if you are sending legitimate content, it is less likely to be treated as spam than more content-rich forms. Its only deficiency is that it is aesthetically rather unsatisfying. Although I would urge you to use plain-text e-mail of this sort when possible, there are some circumstances when rich content is appropriate, and still more when there will be demands for rich content regardless of its objective value.

You might imagine that it would be possible to create HTML content and send this in place of the text of the simple example, and you would be right—up to a point. The problem is that some e-mail clients will accept this as formatted content but others will treat the message as plain text, showing the raw markup to the user. As a result, you will produce rich content for some users and mangled content for others—not a desirable circumstance.

The solution is to use the MIME capabilities of Spring to create a message in which the message headers explicitly describe the message as containing marked-up content for rendering. Almost all users will be able to receive this content correctly. However, we still have the problem of creating the HTML markup and adding the dynamic data to it (often the markup will be created by designers entirely separate from the development team). So for this we will use the Velocity markup language covered briefly as a view technology in Chapter 6.

Listing 8-9 shows a Velocity macro for rendering an HTML e-mail roughly equivalent to the one sent as plain text in the previous section.

Listing 8-9. *A Velocity Macro for Sending a Simple HTML E-mail*

```
## Sent whenever a timesheet is updated
<html>
    <body>
        <h3>Timesheet updated</h3>
        <p>User ${timesheet.consultant.accountName} has
            updated one of their timesheets.</p>
    </body>
</html>
```

Velocity uses a syntax similar to the expression language used by JSPs and the standard tag library (JSTL) for representing content for replacement. The Velocity markup engine is provided with the macro from Listing 8-9 and a suitably named timesheet object. The part of Listing 8-9 marked in bold will be equivalent to calling the getConsultant() method on the timesheet object, and the getAccountName() method on the resulting UserAccount object. The resulting variable (the timesheet owner's account name) will be substituted into the HTML when the message is sent.

Listing 8-10 shows the implementation of this version of the DAO.

Listing 8-10. *The Implementation of Our Simple DAO for Sending HTML-Formatted Mail*

```
public class VelocityMailDaoImpl extends AbstractMailDaoImpl {
    private JavaMailSender mailSender;
    private String velocityMacroPath;
    private VelocityEngine velocityEngine;

    public void sendTimesheetUpdate(final Timesheet timesheet) {
        final MimeMessagePreparator preparator =
            new MimeMessagePreparator() {
                public void prepare(MimeMessage mimeMessage)
                    throws Exception
                {
                    final MimeMessageHelper message =
                        new MimeMessageHelper(mimeMessage);
                    message.setTo(rcptAddress);
                    message.setSubject(subject);
                    message.setFrom(fromAddress);
                    final Map<String, Object> model =
                        new HashMap<String, Object>();
                    model.put("timesheet", timesheet);
                    final String text = VelocityEngineUtils
                            .mergeTemplateIntoString(velocityEngine,
                                    velocityMacroPath, model);
                    message.setText(text, true);
                }
            };
        this.mailSender.send(preparator);
    }

    @Required
    public void setMailSender(JavaMailSender mailSender) {
        this.mailSender = mailSender;
    }

    @Required
    public void setVelocityEngine(VelocityEngine velocityEngine) {
        this.velocityEngine = velocityEngine;
    }
```

```
    @Required
    public void setVelocityMacroPath(final String velocityMacroPath) {
        this.velocityMacroPath = velocityMacroPath;
    }
}
```

Again we draw the addressing and subject information from the properties of the parent class, and we require a `MailSender` implementation (though here it must be a `JavaMailSender`, while the previous implementation accepted any `MailSender` implementation).

These parts are similar, but the creation of the message is somewhat more complicated. First, we create an anonymous instance of a `MimeMessagePreparator` to format the message. This is a symptom of the complexity of the standard JavaMail library that Spring uses to perform MIME operations. When a message is sent, the preparator's `prepare` method is passed a `MimeMessage` and the preparator must populate it. Nonetheless, within this method there are some similarities with Listing 8-7.

To create the body of the message, we populate a map object with the entities that will be needed by the Velocity macro in order to render the e-mail. For this example, this is the timesheet only, and the key value inserted into the map is the first part of the name used in Listing 8-9 to identify the substitution value (where the other parts of the name were the names of the bean properties to obtain).

Listing 8-11 shows the configuration of this enhanced DAO implementation for sending formatted e-mails.

Listing 8-11. *The Configuration of Our Simple DAO Implementation for Sending HTML-Formatted Mail*

```
<bean id="velocityEmailDao"
    class="com.apress.timesheets.mail.VelocityMailDaoImpl"
    parent="abstractEmailDao">
    <property name="velocityEngine" ref="velocityEngine"/>
    <property name="velocityMacroPath"
        value="velocity/timesheet/update.vm"/>
</bean>
```

The notable differences are the requirements for a `velocityEngine` bean (used to invoke the appropriate Velocity formatting) and the path to the Velocity macro file of Listing 8-9.

Listing 8-12 shows the configuration details required for the Velocity engine bean required by Listing 8-11.

Listing 8-12. *The Configuration Details for Velocity in Spring*

```
<bean id="velocityEngine"
    class="org.springframework.ui.velocity.VelocityEngineFactoryBean">
    <property name="velocityProperties">
        <value>
```

```
resource.loader=class
class.resource.loader.class=org.apache.velocity.runtime. ➥
resource.loader.ClasspathResourceLoader
        </value>
    </property>
</bean>
```

The purpose of this bean is essentially to provide a more IOC-oriented implementation of existing Velocity classes, but it also allows us to override some default properties. We have used this to specify that the markup files to be used should be loaded from the class-path instead of from an explicitly specified path.

The resulting e-mail is shown in Figure 8-2.

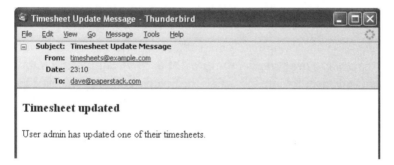

Figure 8-2. *The formatted e-mail*

The `text/html` content type is applied to the message by the `MimeMessageHelper`'s `setText` method; setting the second Boolean parameter to `true` specifies that an HTML message is being created. If the flag is set to `false` or the single parameter version of the `send` method is used, the content type is set to `text/plain`. The specific formatting mechanism used to create the content does not need to be Velocity. Other templating tools such as FreeMarker can be used, or the content can be created from code for particularly simple cases. If the content is not to be modified at all, it can be read directly from an HTML file.

Including Inline Images and Attachments

The previous section shows how e-mail can be formatted as HTML, but what about including external content in the e-mail? If we want to add graphics to the e-mail, how should we go about doing this?

One option is to use references to externally hosted material, and this will work in some cases, but it has some disadvantages. The first minor objection is that you will need to host the content for as long as the content of the e-mail will remain valid. The users should not find that their e-mail becomes unreadable just because your website is unavailable (if they are temporarily offline, for example). The more major objection is that many e-mail clients will not automatically download offline content. There are various reasons for this that are unimportant to us, because the net result is that we cannot predict how our e-mail will appear to all users.

The solution is to include the content within the e-mail itself and to reference it from the HTML. An example of the HTML used to reference an inline image is shown in Listing 8-13 (but note that this technique works for any inline content, not just images).

In addition to explicitly referenced inline binary content such as images, we can include unreferenced attachments in our message. The user's mail client will typically make these available for download upon receipt, so if the purpose of your e-mail is purely to transfer a file, the binary should be included as a file, not as inline content. Our example sends the same image in both modes.

The code marked in bold in Listing 8-13 is an image tag referencing an image to be included in the message.

Listing 8-13. *A Velocity Macro Containing a URI Referencing Inline Content*

```
## Sent whenever a timesheet is updated
<html>
    <body>
        <h3>Timesheet updated</h3>
        <p>User ${timesheet.consultant.accountName} has updated one
            of their timesheets.</p>
        <p>Image attached. Should be equivalent to the following image:</p>
        <p><img src="cid:inlineImage"/></p>
    </body>
</html>
```

The `cid:` prefix is a URI representing message content (*CID* stands for *common image descriptor*). The `inlineImage` following this is the identifier we will be using to associate the link with the correct inline content. Naturally, you must select a unique name to identify unique content items. The naming format follows the RFC 1738 URL address specification, but I would recommend that you constrain yourself to simple letters and numbers.

Listing 8-14 shows the implementation of our DAO to send the timesheet update with both the HTML content and images.

Listing 8-14. *Our DAO Implementation Supporting Both Attachments and Inline Images*

```
public class VelocityImageMailDaoImpl extends AbstractMailDaoImpl {
    private JavaMailSender mailSender;
    private String velocityMacroPath;
    private VelocityEngine velocityEngine;
    private Resource attachment;
    private Resource image;
```

```java
public void sendTimesheetUpdate(final Timesheet timesheet) {
   final MimeMessagePreparator preparator = new MimeMessagePreparator() {
      public void prepare(MimeMessage mimeMessage) throws Exception {
         final MimeMessageHelper message = new MimeMessageHelper(
                 mimeMessage, true);
         message.setTo(rcptAddress);
         message.setSubject(subject);
         message.setFrom(fromAddress);
         message.addAttachment(attachment.getFilename(), attachment);
         final Map<String, Object> model = new HashMap<String, Object>();
         model.put("timesheet", timesheet);
         final String text = VelocityEngineUtils
                 .mergeTemplateIntoString(velocityEngine,
                         velocityMacroPath, model);
         message.setText(text, true);
         message.addInline("inlineImage", image);
      }
   };
   mailSender.send(preparator);
}

@Required
public void setMailSender(final JavaMailSender mailSender) {
   this.mailSender = mailSender;
}

@Required
public void setVelocityEngine(final VelocityEngine velocityEngine) {
   this.velocityEngine = velocityEngine;
}

@Required
public void setVelocityMacroPath(final String velocityMacroPath) {
   this.velocityMacroPath = velocityMacroPath;
}

@Required
public void setAttachment(final Resource attachment) {
   this.attachment = attachment;
}
```

```
@Required
public void setImage(final Resource image) {
   this.image = image;
}
}
```

Broadly speaking, this code is similar to the example given in Listing 8-10. The differences are in the attachment of the images. First, we add an attachment to the message. This can be done at any point within the prepare method. We then add the message text. Finally, we add an inline image. The ordering of the last two steps is mandatory: the body text that contains URIs referencing inline content must be added to the message *before* the inline images themselves are added.

In Listing 8-14, I have specified the attachment and image properties as accepting a Resource object in preference to file paths. This allows the greatest flexibility in the type of resource definition that can be provided, and so in Listing 8-15 I have specified the properties as paths relative to the classpath.

Listing 8-15. *The Configuration of the Image-Aware DAO Implementation*

```
<bean id="velocityImageEmailDao"
   class="com.apress.timesheets.mail.VelocityImageMailDaoImpl"
   parent="abstractEmailDao">
   <property name="velocityEngine" ref="velocityEngine"/>
   <property name="velocityMacroPath"
      value="velocity/timesheet/attachments.vm"/>
   <property name="attachment" value="classpath:strawberry.jpg"/>
   <property name="image" value="classpath:strawberry.jpg"/>
</bean>
```

■**Note** If you have a large number of files, you may want to use an alternative mechanism to add the files to your outgoing message. A flat directory structure containing the template files and images could be checked at runtime, allowing the images to be attached programmatically with CIDs based on their (necessarily unique) file-names. If generated files (for example, PDFs created by using the view technologies described in Chapter 6) are to be attached, the path to the file and a suitable unique identifier can be passed in with the model information.

In this case, as in many others, the use of a classpath-relative resource ensures that the application will be easy to port to other environments and other platforms. The rest of the configuration details in Listing 8-15 are similar to those of the other HTML example in Listing 8-11, except for the specific Velocity macro file to be loaded and the DAO implementation class.

As Figure 8-3 shows, most e-mail clients treat inline content and attachments as quite distinct parts of the message. Indeed, it is possible for the body of the message to consist of plain text but still include separate attachments.

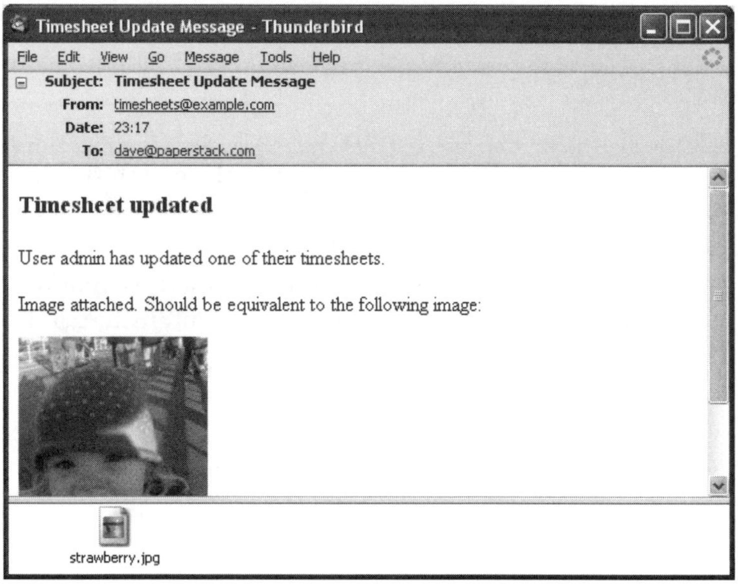

Figure 8-3. *The formatted e-mail with an attachment and an inline image*

Conclusion

In this chapter, you have seen how a Spring application can create e-mail content on-the-fly, injecting the specific formatting (and, indeed, the specific formatting mechanism) into the bean responsible for sending messages.

In the next chapter, you will see the provision for remoting mechanisms, allowing our application's service layer to be accessed by external systems without going through the web front end.

CHAPTER 9

■■■

Remoting

From time to time, you will want to transfer data between Java application processes. Sometimes these will be running on the same machine, but typically they will be running on physically distant machines. *Remoting* is the general term for the technologies that allow you to invoke methods on Java classes residing in other processes and on distant machines.

Various remoting mechanisms can collectively be used to transfer data between application servers—from server to client, from client to server, and from client to client. In this chapter, you'll learn about some of the mechanisms available in Spring, and you'll look at a simple example of remote access from a Spring-based client application to a service layer running in a Spring-based application server.

Remoting Mechanisms

Java provides innate support for a good selection of remoting mechanisms, and the Spring framework provides comprehensive support for them. Where possible, Spring provides the minimal amount of intrusion into your application architecture; in ideal circumstances, the configuration merely amounts to the initialization of an additional bean, but some protocols, particularly those that are not specific to the Java platform, require you to provide additional information in configuration files.

The need to provide mappings between Java classes and interfaces and the protocol arises from the differences of capabilities of various languages. For example, the multiple-inheritance capabilities of C++ do not exactly correspond to the single-inheritance-of-functionality and multiple-inheritance-of-interfaces model supported by Java. In these circumstances, the translation between the two models must be made tediously explicit.

When a Java-specific protocol is used, configuration can be simpler, but if custom objects are to be passed over the link, both ends must have access to implementation classes. In several of our examples, we will pass our entity objects over the link, and so it is necessary to have a copy of the core library available to both the client and the server implementations.

Figure 9-1 shows the relationships among the main libraries (`timesheet-core`, `timesheet-client`, and `timesheet-webapp`) in our example application, highlighting that the two instances of the core library implementation communicate only via the client and web application components.

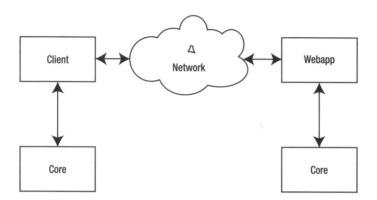

Figure 9-1. *The relationships between the libraries*

RMI

The Java remote method invocation (RMI) protocol is available as a standard part of the JSE environment. For the Java developer, RMI is probably the default choice in any situation where you can guarantee that the applications at both ends of the connection will always be Java based.

Spring's support for RMI-based remoting is particularly convenient. To make an interface accessible over RMI, you will need to configure an additional bean to create an RMI registry and associate it with the service bean. Any objects passed into or returned from the exported service methods must be made serializable (RMI uses serialization to pass parameter values over TCP socket connections).

The benefit of RMI in Spring is its simplicity of implementation. Its deficiency is that this is not an especially portable mechanism (Java RMI is not compatible with C# RMI, for example), so this is not a good choice if you want to make a service available to independently developed client applications.

Because of this ease of implementation, a common usage of RMI services is to create rich administrative applications. This allows administrative staff to have a desktop application for updating a web application. Because the RMI client calls into the same service layer that is being used by the web front end, the amount of software development required is reduced, and the scope for introducing new problems (and corrupting data in unexpected ways) is also limited.

It is possible to "tunnel" the RMI wire protocol (JRMP) over an HTTP connection, but this feature is only infrequently used because some aspects of the service behavior will then be dependent on intervening network infrastructure such as proxy servers and firewalls.

Implementing an RMI Server

The server application is, largely, the existing timesheet web application. We will be exposing only one small part of it, the user account service, the methods of which are defined by the UserAccountService interface. This is shown in Listing 9-1.

Listing 9-1. *The User Account Service to Be Made Available by RMI*

```
public interface UserAccountService {
    UserAccount findUser(String username);
    void createUser(UserAccount account);
    void deleteUser(UserAccount account);
    void updateUser(UserAccount account);
    List<UserAccount> listUsers();
}
```

We will be calling into the listUsers() method of Listing 9-1, which returns a list of UserAccount entities. You should note that the UserAccount entity has been made serializable in order to support this behavior. However, in practice, the requirements of serializability are completely compatible with the requirements for Hibernate-persisted entities, so only trivial changes (if any) are normally necessary in our type of environment.

Aside from the objects to be passed into or returned from the service, the rest of the implementation is irrelevant; the implementation bean is exposed via RMI, but the client needs only a copy of the interface and the implementation of the parameter objects.

Listing 9-2 shows the addition to the applicationContext.xml configuration file to import the configuration of the RMI server capability.

Listing 9-2. *Importing the Spring RMI Configuration*

```
<import resource="classpath:timesheet-remote.xml"/>
```

Listing 9-3 shows the configuration of the bean that then achieves this.

Listing 9-3. *The Configuration of the RMI Service Exporter*

```
<bean class="org.springframework.remoting.rmi.RmiServiceExporter">
    <property name="serviceName" value="UserAccountService"/>
    <property name="service" ref="userAccountService"/>
    <property name="serviceInterface"
        value="com.apress.timesheets.service.UserAccountService"/>
    <property name="registryPort" value="1001"/>
</bean>
```

The RMI service exporter configured in Listing 9-3 performs two tasks: creating and instantiating the RMI registry and registering the user account service bean with it by a given name.

The `serviceName` property defines the name by which clients will access the service. This has no connection with the class names or the bean IDs used by Spring. The `service` property references the bean implementation to be exported.

The service interface references the interface whose methods are to be made available over RMI. This must be explicitly specified, and your bean implementation must therefore implement at least one interface in order to be made into an RMI service. If this is not compatible with your design for some reason, you will have to create an additional bean implementation honoring a suitable interface that delegates method calls to the original service bean. Spring cannot autodetect and export service methods because of the risk of accidentally exposing inappropriate (insecure or privileged) methods such as property setters to untrusted external parties. The interface is the only mechanism by which you can define the basic set of methods to be exported.

Finally, the `registryPort` specifies the port on which the registry will accept queries from RMI clients. When a client connects, it will connect to the registry on this port and negotiate with it for a channel to the service in question.

Implementing an RMI Client

The client application should have access to the same interface definitions as the server, and to the same parameter implementations. In the example application, you will see that I have achieved this by giving the client Maven project a dependency on the core project containing these implementations. Although this actually gives us access to the service implementation also, we do not use these local copies of the service, as you will see if you reconfigure the client and the server to execute on physically different networked machines!

■Note Strictly speaking, it is possible to avoid the need to have copies of the interface and parameter objects in the client's classpath; it is possible to configure RMI to download these upon demand. However, for most purposes, this introduces unnecessary complexity, and I do not recommend the approach.

Listing 9-4 shows the remarkably simple context configuration necessary to make the user account service exported from the server available from the client. Spring uses Java's proxying facility to hide the RMI method calls behind a generated object that implements the specified interface.

Listing 9-4. *The Client Proxy to the Service Bean*

```
<bean id="userAccountService"
    class="org.springframework.remoting.rmi.RmiProxyFactoryBean">
    <property name="serviceUrl"
        value="rmi://localhost:1001/UserAccountService"/>
```

```
    <property name="serviceInterface"
        value="com.apress.timesheets.service.UserAccountService"/>
    </bean>
</beans>
```

The serviceUrl property defines the network location of the service we are connecting to. This is composed of the protocol (RMI), the hostname (localhost in my example, but you can site the client and server on different platforms if you change this configuration detail), and the port upon which you are connecting, which must correspond to the registry port specified in Listing 9-3 (both the client and the server will default to port 1099 if none is explicitly specified). The final part of the URL is the name of the service configured with the serviceName property in Listing 9-3. This is arbitrarily selected by the person configuring the service.

The serviceInterface property specifies the fully qualified class name of the interface defining the API to the service. The implementation of this interface must be present on the client as well as on the server because it is the template used to create the proxy object that will represent the remote implementation.

Listing 9-5 shows an implementation of the client.

Listing 9-5. *The RMI Client Application*

```
public class RmiExample {
    public static void main(String... args) {
        // Get the local configured context
        final ApplicationContext ctx =
            new ClassPathXmlApplicationContext("timesheet-client.xml");

        // Retrieve a bean (the proxy to the remote service)
        final UserAccountService service =
            (UserAccountService)ctx.getBean("userAccountService");

        // Extract data from the bean (via the remote service)
        final List<UserAccount> users = service.listUsers();

        System.out.println("User List");
        System.out.println("=========");
        for( final UserAccount user : users ) {
            System.out.println(user.getAccountName());
        }
    }
}
```

This uses a single context configuration file named `timesheet-client.xml` that configures the single bean of Listing 9-4. This implementation uses the RMI service to obtain a list of the `UserAccount` objects known to the remote system (the process of serializing a Hibernate entity will force the loading of any lazily loaded properties) and then iterates over the list displaying the usernames of the accounts.

Spring's Own HTTP-Based Remoting Mechanism

Spring provides its own mechanism for remoting: the HTTP invoker. As this name suggests, this is available purely for the purpose of building web services. Its sole advantages over RMI are that it is marginally simpler to configure and is explicitly intended for use over HTTP. In principle, it is also possible for third-party clients to invoke Spring's mechanism, but in practice, its relative obscurity and its use of the Java serialization mechanism in encoding objects sent over the network makes this a more theoretical than practical feature.

Even among Java developers, those who are unfamiliar with Spring are unlikely to have encountered Spring's HTTP invoker. It also requires the client implementation to use Spring libraries—although this is a relatively minor issue because the Spring IOC approach makes Spring's own implementations easy to integrate with other frameworks regardless of their architectural philosophies.

Implementing a Spring HTTP Invoker Server

The Spring HTTP invoker receives incoming HTTP requests from the client, parses them into its internal format, converts them to service invocations, makes the invocation, and encodes the results as a response page for processing by the client.

To get access to the incoming requests, the invoker must therefore be mapped to URLs in the web application's namespace. This is done in the normal Spring manner by configuring a `DispatcherServlet` to pass the incoming Java EE web requests to the Spring request handlers.

In principle, we could use the same dispatcher servlet that we established for handling conventional web requests in Chapter 6, but this would add some complexity to the URL-mapping configuration and require us to intermingle the web controllers with the remoting request handlers. Instead, as shown in Listing 9-6, we configure a custom dispatcher for these requests and map it to incoming requests on the `invoker` path of the application context.

Listing 9-6. *Configuring the Dispatcher for the Invoker Service*

```
<servlet>
    <servlet-name>invoker</servlet-name>
    <servlet-class>
```

```
org.springframework.web.servlet.DispatcherServlet
      </servlet-class>
      <init-param>
          <param-name>contextConfigLocation</param-name>
          <param-value>classpath:invoker-servlet.xml</param-value>
      </init-param>
      <load-on-startup>5</load-on-startup>
   </servlet>
...
   <servlet-mapping>
      <servlet-name>invoker</servlet-name>
      <url-pattern>/invoker/*</url-pattern>
   </servlet-mapping>
```

Individual services are mapped to paths beneath this one, so that our eventual URL will have the form http://*server:port/context*/invoker/*service*.

Listing 9-7 shows the mapping of the service name within this path to the HttpInvokerServiceExporter implementation that will handle the incoming requests and forward them to the service.

Listing 9-7. *Configuring the Invoker Service Exporter*

```
<bean name="/userAccountService" class=
"org.springframework.remoting.httpinvoker.HttpInvokerServiceExporter">
   <property name="service" ref="userAccountService"/>
   <property name="serviceInterface"
       value="com.apress.timesheets.service.UserAccountService"/>
</bean>
```

We supply this with a reference to the service that we are exporting, which is again the user account service. We also supply the service interface that we are exporting—again, as with RMI, this is mandatory because otherwise we might accidentally expose inappropriate service methods to the caller.

The path on which the service is accessed is defined by the web application context bean name and is appended to the dispatcher path. Assuming that the server is running locally on port 8080, and that the web application context is timesheet, the full path to this service will therefore be http://localhost:8080/timesheet/invoker/userAccountService. This is how we will configure the client in the next section.

Implementing a Spring HTTP Invoker Client

The Spring HTTP invoker client establishes an HTTP connection to the remote server, transmits the encoded service call, and awaits a response from the server. The client creates a proxy object to represent the remote service that implements the supplied interface (corresponding to the remote service interface). The class used to instantiate these proxy objects behaves as a standard Spring factory bean, so we can use it to populate other beans' properties with instances of the service, or obtain implementations directly from the Spring context.

Listing 9-8 shows the configuration of the Spring HTTP invoker client. We define an HttpInvokerProxyFactoryBean bean and supply it with the path to remote service and the interface to implement.

Listing 9-8. *Configuring the Spring Invoker Client Proxy Factory*

```
<bean id="invokerUserAccountService" class=
"org.springframework.remoting.httpinvoker.HttpInvokerProxyFactoryBean">
    <property name="serviceUrl"
        value="http://localhost:8080/timesheet/invoker/userAccountService"/>
    <property name="serviceInterface"
        value="com.apress.timesheets.service.UserAccountService"/>
</bean>
```

Listing 9-9 shows the usage of the factory bean. Here we are obtaining a bean instance from the application context by calling the context's getBean method, but we could alternatively inject a reference to the factory into any UserAccountService bean property.

Listing 9-9. *Invoking the Remote HTTP Invoker Service from the Client*

```
final UserAccountService service =
    (UserAccountService)ctx.getBean("invokerUserAccountService");

final List<UserAccount> users = service.listUsers();

System.out.println("(Invoker) User List");
System.out.println("====================");
for( final UserAccount user : users ) {
    System.out.println(user.getAccountName());
}
```

Hessian and Burlap

Hessian and Burlap are remoting mechanisms created by Caucho Technology, creators of the Resin application server. Hessian is based around binary data, and Burlap around XML data. Both were designed for the provision of web services over HTTP and HTTPS, but both can now be used over ordinary TCP sockets. Burlap's implementation has a particularly small footprint with no reliance on external libraries, so it is simple to deploy and well suited to constrained memory environments (such as JME devices).

Hessian and Burlap provide something of a halfway house between the complexity of SOAP and the simplicity of RMI. These protocols are not as well known among Java developers as RMI, and they are much less prominent in general than SOAP. The ease of configuration of the client and server components is comparable with RMI. The cross-platform support (for clients) is comprehensive.

In my opinion, Burlap is a good choice when the client device is memory constrained. Hessian is a good choice if you want to publish a web service, at minimal inconvenience to yourself, but which can still be supported by developers of third-party clients.

Implementing a Hessian Server

Hessian is similar in design to the Spring HTTP invoker and is therefore configured in a similar manner. Again, for convenience we give it its own dispatcher servlet (configured in Listing 9-10) to allow its services to have their own bean definition context and their own request path.

Listing 9-10. *Configuring the Dispatcher for Hessian*

```
<servlet>
    <servlet-name>hessian</servlet-name>
    <servlet-class>
org.springframework.web.servlet.DispatcherServlet
    </servlet-class>
    <init-param>
        <param-name>contextConfigLocation</param-name>
        <param-value>classpath:hessian-servlet.xml</param-value>
    </init-param>
    <load-on-startup>3</load-on-startup>
</servlet>
...
<servlet-mapping>
    <servlet-name>hessian</servlet-name>
    <url-pattern>/hessian/*</url-pattern>
</servlet-mapping>
```

Hessian does not use Java serialization to transmit custom objects across the network connection. Normally this would not present a problem, but Hibernate's use of proxy collection objects in conjunction with lazy loading can cause some problems, because the unpopulated lazily loaded collection object can be materialized on the client link—without access to the Hibernate session—resulting in a LazyInitializationException when its contents are accessed. There are three basic ways this problem can be addressed:

- If the Hibernate JAR file is not made available on the client, no attempt will be made to use Hibernate's custom implementations, and the collection contents will be forcibly materialized as they are sent over the link.

- The user can use the Hibernate class's static initialize() methods to "manually" materialize the contents of collections within service methods before they are returned to the client. This is potentially inefficient if the same service methods will be used internally by the server where no such workaround is required.

- An alternative service class can be implemented to avoid returning Hibernate objects, either by returning all data as standard types, or by creating custom data transfer objects (DTOs) to wrap the data that would otherwise be passed as Hibernate entities.

We will use the last of these three methods. The alternative interface that will be implemented to provide the service on the server, and for which a proxy will be generated on the client, is shown in Listing 9-11.

Listing 9-11. *Defining the Remote Service Interface for Hessian*

```
public interface HessianUserAccountService extends Remote {
    public List<String> listUserNames() throws RemoteException;
}
```

This simple interface will be implemented by a wrapper delegating to the existing UserAccountService bean as shown in Listing 9-12. Calls to the listUserNames() method will return the accountName property of the accounts returned by the wrapped service's listUsers() method.

Listing 9-12. *The Hessian Service Implementation*

```
public class HessianUserAccountServiceImpl
    implements HessianUserAccountService
{
    private UserAccountService service;

    public List<String> listUserNames() {
        final List<UserAccount> list = service.listUsers();
        final List<String> names = new ArrayList<String>();
        for( final UserAccount account : list ) {
            names.add(account.getAccountName());
        }
        return names;
    }
}
```

```
    @Required
    public void setUserAccountService(final UserAccountService service) {
        this.service = service;
    }
}
```

This delegating bean is configured within the servlet-specific bean definition file shown in Listing 9-13. Its sole configuration parameter is a reference to the service bean that it wraps.

Listing 9-13. *Configuring the Hessian Service Bean and Exporter*

```
<bean name="hessianUserAccountService"
    class="com.apress.timesheets.hessian.HessianUserAccountServiceImpl">
    <property name="userAccountService" ref="userAccountService"/>
</bean>

<bean name="/userAccountService"
    class="org.springframework.remoting.caucho.HessianServiceExporter">
    <property name="service" ref="hessianUserAccountService" />
    <property name="serviceInterface"
        value="com.apress.timesheets.hessian.HessianUserAccountService"/>
</bean>
```

Listing 9-13 also shows the configuration of the exporter. This Spring wrapper for the Hessian server component is near identical to the corresponding exporter for Spring's HTTP invoker mechanism. The pathname is defined by the bean name. The exporter passes incoming requests to a specified service bean that must implement the specified service interface. The only significant difference in configuration is our use of a service wrapper and corresponding interface to avoid the conflict with Hibernate lazy loading.

Implementing a Hessian Client

The Hessian client configuration also corresponds closely to the HTTP invoker's client configuration. The client bean is provided with the path to the remote service, and calls to the factory materialize proxy instances that implement the supplied service interface. Listing 9-14 shows this configuration.

Listing 9-14. *Configuring the Hessian Client Proxy Factory*

```
<bean id="hessianUserAccountService"
    class="org.springframework.remoting.caucho.HessianProxyFactoryBean">
    <property name="serviceUrl"
        value="http://localhost:8080/timesheet/hessian/userAccountService"/>
    <property name="serviceInterface"
        value="com.apress.timesheets.hessian.HessianUserAccountService"/>
</bean>
```

Accessing the remote service from client code is then near identical. Listing 9-15 shows the retrieval of a proxied instance of the custom service interface from the bean definition context.

Listing 9-15. *Invoking the Remote Hessian Service from the Client*

```
final HessianUserAccountService service =
   (HessianUserAccountService)ctx.getBean("hessianUserAccountService");

final List<String> users = service.listUserNames();

System.out.println("(Hessian) User List");
System.out.println("====================");
for( final String user : users ) {
   System.out.println(user);
}
```

Compare Listing 9-15 with the corresponding one for the use of the HTTP invoker in Listing 9-9 or the RMI example in Listing 9-5. The application logic for the client in all of these cases is purely a matter of obtaining a bean from the context and calling methods on it in the normal manner. The implementation is completely independent of the underlying transport, which easily can be swapped out for a local implementation by changing the configuration file. This trend continues with the rest of the client implementations that you'll see in this chapter, and I will show only the acquisition of the client service instance and the invocation of the service method in examples from here on.

Implementing a Burlap Server

Hessian and Burlap both originate with the same organization, Caucho Technology. From a configuration point of view within Spring, only the class names differ. The practical difference is that the underlying protocol for Burlap is XML, whereas Hessian uses a binary format. Listing 9-16 shows the usual creation of a dispatcher servlet.

Listing 9-16. *Configuring the Dispatcher for Burlap*

```
<servlet>
   <servlet-name>burlap</servlet-name>
   <servlet-class>
org.springframework.web.servlet.DispatcherServlet
   </servlet-class>
   <init-param>
      <param-name>contextConfigLocation</param-name>
      <param-value>classpath:burlap-servlet.xml</param-value>
   </init-param>
   <load-on-startup>4</load-on-startup>
```

```
</servlet>
...
<servlet-mapping>
   <servlet-name>burlap</servlet-name>
   <url-pattern>/burlap/*</url-pattern>
</servlet-mapping>
```

Burlap's implementation corresponds so closely to Hessian's that it suffers from the same problem when transporting Hibernate entity classes across the network. We therefore use the same technique to avoid this problem, creating a new interface and wrapper for the Burlap implementation.

Listing 9-17 shows the interface that we are using. The use of a distinct interface from the one given in Listing 9-11 for Hessian is purely for the sake of clarity. We could have defined and used the same interface and wrapper implementation for both examples.

Listing 9-17. *Defining the Remote Service Interface for Burlap*

```java
public interface BurlapUserAccountService extends Remote {
   public List<String> listUserNames() throws RemoteException;
}
```

Listing 9-18 shows the wrapping service implementation. Again, this corresponds exactly to the Hessian wrapper created for the same reason in Listing 9-12.

Listing 9-18. *The Burlap Service Implementation*

```java
public class BurlapUserAccountServiceImpl
   implements BurlapUserAccountService
{
   private UserAccountService service;

   public List<String> listUserNames() {
      final List<UserAccount> list = service.listUsers();
      final List<String> names = new ArrayList<String>();
      for( final UserAccount account : list ) {
         names.add(account.getAccountName());
      }
      return names;
   }

   @Required
   public void setUserAccountService(final UserAccountService service) {
      this.service = service;
   }
}
```

Listing 9-19 shows the configuration of the user account bean from Listing 9-18 and the Burlap exporter.

Listing 9-19. *Configuring the Burlap Implementation and Exporter Beans*

```
<bean name="burlapUserAccountService"
   class="com.apress.timesheets.burlap.BurlapUserAccountServiceImpl">
   <property name="userAccountService" ref="userAccountService"/>
</bean>

<bean name="/userAccountService"
   class="org.springframework.remoting.caucho.BurlapServiceExporter">
   <property name="service" ref="burlapUserAccountService" />
   <property name="serviceInterface"
      value="com.apress.timesheets.burlap.BurlapUserAccountService"/>
</bean>
```

The Burlap exporter's configuration has no practical distinction from Hessian's aside from the implementation-specific BurlapServiceExporter class.

Implementing a Burlap Client

The Burlap client bean configuration shown in Listing 9-20 corresponds almost exactly to the Hessian bean's configuration in Listing 9-14. We define the Burlap-specific proxy factory bean, supplying the path to the remote Burlap service and the name of the interface that it implements.

Listing 9-20. *Configuring the Burlap Client Proxy Factory*

```
<bean id="burlapUserAccountService"
   class="org.springframework.remoting.caucho.BurlapProxyFactoryBean">
   <property name="serviceUrl"
value="http://localhost:8080/timesheet/burlap/userAccountService"/>
   <property name="serviceInterface"
value="com.apress.timesheets.burlap.BurlapUserAccountService"/>
</bean>
```

The client implementation is similarly straightforward, pulling the materialized bean directly from the context and calling the service method on it as shown in Listing 9-21.

Listing 9-21. *Invoking the Remote Burlap Service from the Client*

```
final BurlapUserAccountService service =
   (BurlapUserAccountService)ctx.getBean("burlapUserAccountService");

final List<String> users = service.listUserNames();
```

As you can see, aside from the specifics of the protocol used and their relative size (Burlap being the lighter of the two), Hessian and Burlap are completely interchangeable with only minor configuration differences. Swap *Hessian* for *Burlap* in the configuration file, and you have pretty much done all that is required!

SOAP

The SOAP protocol is almost the exact opposite of Java RMI. Whereas Java is effectively limited to Java-to-Java communications, SOAP was designed from the outset for communication between heterogeneous platforms and languages.

■**Note** Officially, *SOAP* doesn't stand for anything. Originally it stood for *Simple Object Access Protocol*. Subsequently it has been referred to as *Service-Oriented Access Protocol* (a better description, as I would defy anyone to genuinely consider the SOAP technology stack *simple*), but as of version 1.2 the acronym was officially dropped by the W3C standards group. The name was considered to be misleading not because it was not simple, but because it was not constrained to be used purely for accessing objects; it can be used for message passing and as a remote procedure call mechanism.

SOAP is a term that covers various mechanisms, their common feature being that they are XML based and platform independent. In theory, the SOAP protocol is completely independent of the underlying transport. The example usually offered is of sending SOAP messages via SMTP. This is sometimes carried out in practice (I once built an application that did exactly this), but it is very much the exception. The majority of SOAP-based applications send their messages over either HTTP or HTTPS. Although there is nothing intrinsically wrong with this usage, at the height of its popularity SOAP was often selected for the slightly misguided reason that it could be sent over the un-firewalled port 80!

In practice, you should be using SOAP if you need the full breadth of its features—or if you need to consume external services that are presented to you as a SOAP API. The advantage of SOAP is its comprehensive platform independence and its mature support for features such as transactionality and user authentication.

The disadvantages of SOAP are its complexity and its performance. The underlying mechanism of transmitted XML is simple, but the breadth of document types and specifications covered by SOAP is bewildering and can make the creation of even a relatively simple service very time-consuming. The use of XML, a human-readable text-oriented format, leads to a performance disadvantage when transmitting complicated data. This can be ameliorated by the use of an optimization mechanism, but this then adds yet more complexity to the design.

The Spring support for SOAP is mostly oriented to the use of the JAX-RPC library for conducting remote procedure calls over SOAP, but there is additional support for creating and consuming other service types in the Spring WS library.

Spring WS allows for and encourages the use of "top-down" SOAP design. The user specifies an XML schema description for the methods that he will be exporting, and then creates corresponding service description files, interfaces, and services to support them. This all requires a very good understanding of SOAP—more than I think is appropriate for a beginners text; we will focus purely on the use of the JAX-RPC libraries because this has the most in common with the other remoting technologies that we have considered in this chapter. Note that I do not propose to teach you how to use even JAX-RPC in this chapter because the subject matter is far too complex—only how to integrate it with the Spring framework.

Implementing a JAX-RPC Server

Spring does not attempt to implement or provide a complete SOAP JAX-RPC server implementation. Instead, you are expected to use, and to some extent configure, an existing server. The most popular Java SOAP server implementation is Apache Axis. Unfortunately, Axis expects to be configured as a servlet in its own right, instantiate the target service object, translate incoming requests, and pass them to the service methods directly.

Rather than try to subvert the process on the server side, Spring plays a relatively low profile here. You will configure Axis for a Spring service pretty much exactly as you would for any other environment—although Spring does allow you to avoid the need to generate the skeleton classes for the server. The Axis servlet's configuration is shown in Listing 9-22.

Listing 9-22. *Configuring the Axis Servlet*

```
<servlet>
   <servlet-name>axis</servlet-name>
   <servlet-class>
      org.apache.axis.transport.http.AxisServlet
   </servlet-class>
   <load-on-startup>6</load-on-startup>
</servlet>
...
<servlet-mapping>
   <servlet-name>axis</servlet-name>
   <url-pattern>/service/*</url-pattern>
</servlet-mapping>
```

Axis uses a proprietary Web Service Deployment Descriptor (WSDD) file to instruct Axis in how to present the service API to client applications as a Web Services Description Language (WSDL) file, and to determine what service implementation to pass requests to. Axis provides tools to create WSDD files from service classes, and Listing 9-23 shows the pertinent part of this file. The full file is provided with the example source code from the Source Code/Download area of the Apress website (www.apress.com).

Listing 9-23. *Excerpt of the Axis Service Definition in the server-config.wsdd File*

```
<service name="SoapUserAccountService"
    provider="java:RPC" style="rpc" use="encoded">
    <parameter name="wsdlTargetNamespace" value="urn:Timesheet"/>
    <parameter name="wsdlServiceElement" value="SoapUserAccountServiceService"/>
    <parameter name="schemaUnqualified" value="urn:Timesheet"/>
    <parameter name="wsdlServicePort" value="SoapUserAccountService"/>
    <parameter name="className"
        value="com.apress.timesheets.soap.SoapUserAccountServiceEndpoint"/>
    <parameter name="wsdlPortType" value="SoapUserAccountService"/>
    <parameter name="typeMappingVersion" value="1.2"/>
    <parameter name="allowedMethods" value="*"/>
    <parameter name="scope" value="Session"/>

    <arrayMapping
        xmlns:ns="urn:Timesheet"
        qname="ns:ArrayOf_soapenc_string"
        type="java:java.lang.String[]"
        innerType="cmp-ns:string"
        xmlns:cmp-ns="http://schemas.xmlsoap.org/soap/encoding/"
        encodingStyle="http://schemas.xmlsoap.org/soap/encoding/"
    />
</service>
```

SOAP has its own slightly obscure terminology, but essentially Listing 9-23 defines a remote service made available via the Axis servlet defined in Listing 9-22. The remote service exposes the methods of the SoapUserAccountService interface, to which it appends the name Service to give the confusing remote service name SoapUserAccountServiceService. The service implementation is defined as being the SoapUserAccountServiceEndpoint class.

The SoapUserAccountService interface in Listing 9-24 defines the service method that we will be making available. Previously, with Burlap and Hessian we avoided using the standard service's interface because of a problem arising from transferring the collection classes across the network with too great a fidelity. Here we have the opposite problem: the consumer of this interface may not have corresponding collection classes available to them at all—or if they do, they may exhibit subtly different semantics. Instead, we use the explicitly supported array type and return Strings, whereas with the Caucho technologies we could use an ArrayList as long as it was not a Hibernate-specific implementation.

Listing 9-24. *The Remote Service Interface for the JAX-RPC Service*

```
public interface SoapUserAccountService extends Remote {
   public String[] listUserNames() throws RemoteException;
}
```

The implementation class implements the service, but also extends the
ServletEndpointSupport class. Our service class (the endpoint) will be instantiated and
invoked directly by the Axis servlet, so we need to provide a mechanism for accessing the
service bean in the Spring context. Listing 9-25 shows how we obtain the bean by dependency lookup from the endpoint's onInit() method.

Listing 9-25. *Implementing the JAX-RPC Endpoint Service*

```
public class SoapUserAccountServiceEndpoint
   extends ServletEndpointSupport
   implements SoapUserAccountService
{

   private UserAccountService service;

   @Override
   protected void onInit() throws ServiceException {
      service = (UserAccountService)
         getWebApplicationContext().getBean("userAccountService");
   }

   public String[] listUserNames() {
      final List<UserAccount> list = service.listUsers();
      final String[] names = new String[list.size()];
      for( int i = 0; i < names.length; i++ ) {
         names[i] = list.get(i).getAccountName();
      }
      return names;
   }
}
```

The use of the ServletEndpointSupport class also avoids the need to generate the various
skeleton and stub classes that would normally be created for an Axis SOAP JAX-RPC service
implementation. All that is required are the Axis servlet, the WSDD file configuring it (placed in
the WEB-INF directory), the service interface, and the endpoint implementation class. Relatively speaking, this is quite simple for a SOAP service.

Implementing a JAX-RPC Client

Happily, the JAX-RPC client looks a lot more like the remote clients that we have looked at in the rest of this chapter. To access the remote service, you define a JaxRpcPortProxyFactoryBean to create proxy objects implementing the remote interface. This configuration is shown in Listing 9-26. You are not constrained to use Axis only, so you must specify the service factory class to use. As usual, you specify the interface that the proxy will honor on behalf of the remote service. Axis provides a tool to generate classes, including the service interface from a WSDL file, but here as the creators of the remote service it is available to us directly. You must specify the path to the WSDL file defining the remote service (which contains the endpoints defining the server to connect to when accessing services) and the namespace used to specify the services within the WSDL file. Finally, you specify the name of the interface (*port* in SOAP terminology) that your client will access on the remote service.

Listing 9-26. *Configuring the SOAP JAX-RPC Client Proxy Factory*

```
<bean id="soapUserAccountService"
    class="org.springframework.remoting.jaxrpc.JaxRpcPortProxyFactoryBean">
    <property name="serviceFactoryClass">
        <value>org.apache.axis.client.ServiceFactory</value>
    </property>
    <property name="serviceInterface"
        value="com.apress.timesheets.soap.SoapUserAccountService"/>
    <property name="wsdlDocumentUrl"
value="http://localhost:8080/timesheet/service/SoapUserAccountService?wsdl"/>
    <property name="namespaceUri" value="urn:Timesheet"/>
    <property name="serviceName" value="SoapUserAccountServiceService"/>
    <property name="portName" value="SoapUserAccountService"/>
</bean>
```

The namespaceUri, serviceName, and portName properties specified in Listing 9-26 must correspond with their respective counterpart wsdlTargetNamespace, wsdlServiceElement, and wsdlPortType properties from the WSDD file of Listing 9-23 (which will in turn be represented by corresponding entries in the WSDL file generated by Axis). The wsdlDocumentUrl property of Listing 9-26 is specified by the usual web application server connection details and context, the mapping of the Axis servlet to the server's URL namespace, and the service element's name property from Listing 9-22. The ?wsdl suffix is used by Axis to determine that a WSDL file is being requested (which it generates dynamically).

The code used to access the remote SOAP service, shown in Listing 9-27, is not substantially different from the code used to access our other remote services after everything is configured directly. From the point of view of the application code, the remote service is just a bean like any other.

Listing 9-27. *Invoking the Remote SOAP JAX-RPC Service*

```
final SoapUserAccountService service =
(SoapUserAccountService)ctx.getBean("soapUserAccountService");

final String[] users = service.listUserNames();
```

CORBA

CORBA stands for *Common Object Request Broker Architecture*. It was one of the first successful protocols in bridging heterogeneous environments. Although it is a binary rather than XML-based suite of protocols, its feature list has a certain amount in common with SOAP: it is supported by a wide selection of platforms. It is well supported by Java, perhaps because CORBA was at the height of its popularity just as Java was becoming popular as a mainstream development language.

CORBA suffers from some of the problems of complexity that SOAP labors under. It is also subject to some compatibility problems between different implementations of CORBA. On the whole, it is becoming something of a legacy architecture—plenty of existing systems demand it, but new architectures are relatively unlikely to incorporate it for any other reason. In view of this, I have not included a CORBA example in this chapter, but the Java support for CORBA mostly uses the RMI classes and is therefore quite similar in configuration. Where it differs, the Spring classes beginning with the `JndiRmi` prefix in the `org.springframework.remoting.rmi` package provide the necessary support.

JMS

JMS stands for *Java Message Service* and is the Java EE API for exchanging data with messaging platforms. As such, it is not a remoting mechanism in the same sense as the others mentioned in this section of the chapter, but messages sent and received via JMS can be used to invoke and provide services. Any messaging platform for which JMS drivers exist is supported by Spring, including commercial systems such as IBM WebSphere MQ and Microsoft Message Queuing (MSMQ). There is also a reference implementation in Java.

The major advantage of JMS over the other mechanisms is that it provides support (and this in turn is often supported by the underlying platforms) for two-phase commit via JTA to tie operations such as database operations atomically to messaging operations.

Conclusion

In this chapter, we have discussed the selection of remoting mechanisms supported by Spring and the advantages and disadvantages of each. We have implemented examples of the JAX-RPC, Spring HTTP invoker, Hessian, Burlap, and RMI remoting technologies.

In the next chapter, you will look at the support offered by Spring for testing regimes, the creation of suitable unit tests for the major layers of an application, and the ways in which inversion of control as an approach to application design both supports and is driven by the creation of good unit tests.

CHAPTER 10

■■■

Testing

Like it or not, testing is a vital part of the application development process. All programs have bugs—they vary only in quantity and quality. Testing your applications is therefore an inevitable process, and the only question is how to carry it out.

There are various philosophies of testing. In the bad old days, testing was pretty much exclusively carried out as a manual process after the development phase had been completed, following laborious scripts and detailing the departures from the original specification.

Testing has evolved somewhat since that point. Rigorous testing still requires this manual process, but it is generally a phase that occurs after a substantial body of automatic tests have been carried out. This is not to say that all projects always carry out automated testing, but those that don't inevitably find that this omission is a false economy.

The real advantage of automated tests is that they are readily reproducible. The error in an application tested manually may originate from user error, from an idiosyncratic set of operator actions (for example, use of the Return rather than the Enter key), or from timing sensitive sequences of operations.

To be sure, there are still errors that are difficult to reproduce during automated testing, but unlike manual tests, automated tests can be run over and over again until the problem reoccurs. In contrast, human operators become recalcitrant or plain exhausted after a few iterations of a complicated script.

Another advantage of using automated tests is that they can be written and run as the application is developed—while the developer's recollection of *what* the code is intended to do and *how* the code is supposed to do it is still fresh. By identifying and fixing bugs in tandem with the development process, we can reduce the time to fix the problem as well as raise the overall quality of the end product.

This chapter differs from the previous ones in that it is not primarily about developing Spring-based application code. Instead, it focuses on the tools and techniques that we can use to test code that we have already written. Fortunately, code written with Spring is readily testable. The application of the principle of inversion of control gives us fine control over the environment that our code runs within. Spring also provides some useful helper classes that allow us to test components' interactions with the Spring libraries.

Unit Testing

Unit testing is the process of testing the smallest practical components of our code—usually particular classes or methods—in isolation from the rest of the application's implementation.

Because unit tests are isolated from the rest of the code base, errors discovered at this level allow us to readily identify the specific code causing the problem, often to within a handful of lines of simple code. It also isolates the conditions in which the bug occurs; the developer creates all the inputs and tests the outputs of the logic for its results. A failing test can therefore lead to only three conclusions:

- The inputs to the code are incorrect.

- The assumptions of the test are incorrect.

- The code is incorrectly implemented.

The first two points are easily checked, and will not vary from run to run, so the identification of the bug rarely takes long. You should write unit tests as you write code. As well as aiding you in tracking down implementation bugs, unit tests allow you much more scope for refactoring in code creation. Changes that break implementation logic will also break your unit tests. Fix these problems, and you can be confident that the application as a whole will still work as intended. The ability to refactor code at will allows you far greater freedom to tidy up implementation details, remove redundant code, and eliminate duplication from your code base, making support and further development far simpler.

Test-Driven Development

Unit tests can be written after you create each method or after you create each class. They should not be created after creating a batch of classes, because your memory of the specific implementation details will start to atrophy the longer you leave it. But creating tests after the code implementation is not the only option; you could also create the tests first.

This technique of creating unit tests to test the code that you have not yet written is known as *test-driven development* and is one of the most successful parts of the various agile approaches. Designing the test in advance forces you to decide exactly how the code will behave before you start to write it, which in turn forces you to think more carefully about the most appropriate implementation.

Although it is difficult to prove, it also seems to be the case that testable code is often better-designed code. Certainly, loosely coupled code is more easily testable, so the use of test-driven design will probably make your implementation more loosely coupled and thus more reusable.

Finally, by writing the test in advance, you will not be tempted to assume that an implementation is obviously correct. "Obviously correct" implementations usually turn out to contain a surprisingly large number of bugs.

Mock Objects

If you have not created unit tests before, you may be wondering how you can create a unit test for code that has dependencies on other objects. If the code is to be isolated from other implementation details, how can we supply it with objects that have their own implementations?

The solution to this paradox is the use of mock objects. *Mock objects* are fake implementations of the dependency. The particular type of mock object you use will depend on your circumstances: they can be stubbed implementations of your own objects, generated implementations with scripted behavior, or standard classes provided to replace more-complicated ones that would normally be generated by a framework environment. We will look at examples of all three types of mock objects in this chapter.

Testing the DAO Layer

The dependencies of a DAO are the implementation classes of the data store that it wraps. For the most part, these will be databases, but our application also provides DAOs for sending e-mail, and other stores such as message queues are possible.

We will now look at some tests for the DAOs created in Chapter 4, starting with the database-based user account DAO. The user account DAO provides user account information drawn from the database. We looked at two alternative implementations of the DAO based on JDBC and on Hibernate, and we will create tests for both of these. We will use the JUnit framework to run our tests.

JUnit test suites must extend the TestCase class. When run within the JUnit framework, the setUp() method will be invoked before each test. After each test, the tearDown() method will be invoked. These two methods allow us to initialize and reset resources to be used in the tests.

Individual unit tests are methods beginning with the word *test* and returning void. The test methods should take no parameters but may throw an exception. An example that will always fail is shown in Listing 10-1. The TestCase class provides various methods to test for conditions or to force failure or success of the test. If an exception is thrown by the method, the test is assumed to have failed.

Listing 10-1. *A JUnit Test Method That Will Always Fail*

```
public void testAlwaysFails() {
    fail();
}
```

The Maven environment will automatically attempt to run all of the tests contained in any class inheriting from the TestCase class. Because we have two equivalent DAOs for the database functionality, we will provide a class to describe the tests, and derive from this two implementation-specific tests that differ only in their setUp() and tearDown() methods. Maven presumes that any class with a name beginning or ending in *Test* in the src/main/ test source code directory of a project is a test case to be run. We will therefore name our test case UserAccountDaoTestHelper to avoid its methods being executed prematurely.

The abstract test class in Listing 10-2 contains tests to exercise all of the UserAccountDao interface's methods. A test derived from this class must provide an implementation of the DAO itself, against which the tests will run. It must also provide an implementation of a ConfigHelper interface. This is the mock database that our application will run against.

Listing 10-2. *The Intermediate Database DAO Test Case*

```
package com.apress.timesheets.dao;

import java.util.ArrayList;
import java.util.List;
import junit.framework.TestCase;
import com.apress.timesheets.entity.UserAccount;
import com.apress.timesheets.entity.UserRole;

public abstract class UserAccountDaoTestHelper
    extends TestCase
{

    private UserAccountDao dao;
    private ConfigHelper helper;

    public void testSaveUserRoles() {
        final UserAccount account = new UserAccount("testuser3");
        final UserRole admin = new UserRole("admin");

        account.getRoles().add(admin);
        dao.create(account);

        helper.clear();

        assertNotNull(account.getId());
        assertNotNull(admin.getId());
```

```
    final UserAccount retrievedAccount = dao.read(account.getId());
    assertNotNull(retrievedAccount);
    assertNotNull(retrievedAccount.getRoles());
    assertEquals(1, retrievedAccount.getRoles().size());

    final UserRole retrievedRole =
        retrievedAccount.getRoles().iterator().next();
    assertEquals(admin.getId(), retrievedRole.getId());
}

// READ, UPDATE, DELETE
public void testReadById() {
    final UserAccount account = new UserAccount("testuser4");
    dao.create(account);
    helper.clear();

    assertNotNull(account.getId());

    final UserAccount retrieved = dao.read(account.getId());
    assertNotNull(retrieved);
    assertEquals(account.getId(), retrieved.getId());
    assertEquals(account.getAccountName(),
        retrieved.getAccountName());
}

public void testReadByName() {
    final UserAccount account = new UserAccount("testuser5");
    dao.create(account);
    helper.clear();

    assertNotNull(account.getId());

    final UserAccount retrieved = dao.read(account.getAccountName());
    assertNotNull(retrieved);
    assertEquals(account.getId(), retrieved.getId());
    assertEquals(account.getAccountName(),
        retrieved.getAccountName());
}
```

```java
public void testList() {
    final List<Long> ids = new ArrayList<Long>();
    for(int i = 0; i < 10; i++) {
        final UserAccount account = new UserAccount("testuser6:"+i);
        dao.create(account);
        helper.clear();
        assertNotNull(account.getId());
        ids.add(account.getId());
    }

    final List<UserAccount> accounts = dao.list();
    assertNotNull(accounts);
    int index = 0;
    for( final UserAccount retrieved : accounts ) {
        final Long expected = ids.get(index++);
        assertNotNull(retrieved);
        assertEquals(expected, retrieved.getId());
    }
}

public void testUpdate() {
    final UserAccount account = new UserAccount("testuser7");
    dao.create(account);
    helper.clear();
    assertNotNull(account.getId());

    final UserAccount update = new UserAccount();
    update.setId(account.getId());
    update.setAccountName("Updated");
    dao.update(update);
    helper.clear();

    final UserAccount retrieved = dao.read(account.getId());
    assertNotNull(retrieved);
    assertEquals(account.getId(),retrieved.getId());
    assertEquals(update.getAccountName(),
        retrieved.getAccountName());
}

public void testDeleteByAccount() {
    final UserAccount account = new UserAccount("testuser8");
    dao.create(account);
```

```
        helper.clear();
        assertNotNull(account.getId());

        dao.delete(account);
        helper.clear();

        final List<UserAccount> retrieved = dao.list();
        assertNotNull(retrieved);
        assertEquals(0,retrieved.size());
    }

    public void testDeleteById() {
        final UserAccount account = new UserAccount("testuser9");
        dao.create(account);
        helper.clear();
        assertNotNull(account.getId());

        dao.delete(account.getId());
        helper.clear();

        final List<UserAccount> retrieved = dao.list();
        assertNotNull(retrieved);
        assertEquals(0,retrieved.size());
    }

    public UserAccountDao getDao() {
        return dao;
    }

    public void setDao(UserAccountDao dao) {
        this.dao = dao;
    }

    public ConfigHelper getHelper() {
        return helper;
    }

    public void setHelper(ConfigHelper helper) {
        this.helper = helper;
    }
}
```

We will now follow how the UserAccountDAO and ConfigHelper properties interact with a specific test method implementation, testReadById() highlighted in bold in Listing 10-2.

When we call the readById() method of a UserAccountDao implementation, we assume that previous calls to the create() method have successfully established an entity in the database and assigned a suitable primary key value to it. Calling the readById() method should then retrieve the corresponding entity for the primary key that we provide. Our test is implemented to check this behavior. First we instantiate a UserAccount bean, as shown in Listing 10-3.

Listing 10-3. *Instantiating the UserAccount Bean for the Test*

```
public void testReadById() {
    final UserAccount account = new UserAccount("testuser4");
```

Having established the bean, we then call the DAO's create() method in order to persist the bean to the database and assign a primary key value to the bean's id property. This is shown in Listing 10-4.

Listing 10-4. *Creating the Bean in the Database*

```
dao.create(account);
```

The purpose of our test is to establish that the data survives the round-trip to the database and back, so we need to eliminate any cached copies of the data from the underlying storage method. This is shown in Listing 10-5. Note that we are using the helper object to manipulate the mock database implementation.

Listing 10-5. *Clearing Any Cached Copies of the Bean*

```
helper.clear();
```

Having cleared the cache, we must first check that the primary key value was assigned to the bean successfully—implying, if not proving, that it was persisted successfully. We call one of the TestCase parent class's assertion methods to indicate that we expect the id property to have been assigned a value. This is shown in Listing 10-6.

Listing 10-6. *Asserting Our Expectation of a Non-null id Value*

```
assertNotNull(account.getId());
```

The test of Listing 10-6 is indicative of success, but not proof, and so we will now use the assigned primary key to retrieve the appropriate entity from the database by calling the DAO's read() method in Listing 10-7.

Listing 10-7. *Retrieving the Entity by Primary Key*

```
final UserAccount retrieved = dao.read(account.getId());
```

Having retrieved a copy of the entity from the database, we now need to check several things. Listing 10-8 checks that an entity is retrieved, that it has the same primary key as that assigned during the call to create(), and that the retrieved account entity has been created with the same account name as the one originally persisted.

Listing 10-8. *Asserting Our Expectations of the Retrieved Bean's Properties*

```
assertNotNull(retrieved);
assertEquals(account.getId(), retrieved.getId());
assertEquals(account.getAccountName(),
    retrieved.getAccountName());
}
```

Having examined one of the unit test methods in detail, we will now take a closer look at the implementation of the helper class and the mock objects used to construct the DAO itself for the two UserAccountDao implementations.

The JDBC Unit Test

The ConfigHelper implementation sets up the mock object that will be supplied to the JdbcUserAccountDaoImpl implementation class. The unit test for the JDBC-based UserAccount class is shown in Listing 10-9.

Listing 10-9. *The Unit Test Implementation Class for the JDBC-Based User Account DAO*

```
public class JdbcUserAccountDaoTest
    extends UserAccountDaoTestHelper
{
    public void setUp() throws Exception {
        final JdbcConfigHelper helper = new JdbcConfigHelper();
        helper.setUp();
        setHelper(helper);

        final JdbcUserAccountDaoImpl dao =
            new JdbcUserAccountDaoImpl();
        dao.setJdbcTemplate(helper.getTemplate());
        setDao(dao);
    }
}
```

All of the test methods are inherited from the helper test case implementation shown in Listing 10-2. The only difference between the actual unit test implementation and its parent is the configuration carried out during the test harness's invocation of the setUp() method prior to the calls to each of the various test methods.

First, we create a new helper object. This in turn is managing the mock object that we will be supplying to the DAO class. This helper object is split out from the unit test so that the parent class can be provided with an abstract interface that provides a clear() method. This interface is shown in Listing 10-10 and illustrates that the parent class knows nothing of the concrete helper's implementation details other than that any cached data can be cleared.

Listing 10-10. *The ConfigHelper Interface*

```
public interface ConfigHelper {
    public void clear();
}
```

The concrete helper implementation sets up an embedded in-memory database using HSQL from scratch, including the creation of the necessary tables. This is carried out when its setUp() method is called. The helper is provided to the parent test suite implementation to allow it to flush the cache (in fact, the JDBC implementation does not provide any caching, so this is an empty method implementation). The creation, setup, and provision of this helper to the parent is shown in Listing 10-11.

Listing 10-11. *Creating, Configuring, and Assigning the Helper Class*

```
final JdbcConfigHelper helper = new JdbcConfigHelper();
helper.setUp();
setHelper(helper);
```

The helper creates and makes available an instance of the JdbcTemplate object required by our DAO. We therefore create the DAO instance and assign the template obtained from the helper to the appropriate property of the DAO implementation. Finally, we make the DAO implementation itself available to the parent class. These three operations are shown in Listing 10-12.

Listing 10-12. *Creating, Configuring, and Assigning the DAO Implementation*

```
final JdbcUserAccountDaoImpl dao = new JdbcUserAccountDaoImpl();
dao.setJdbcTemplate(helper.getTemplate());
setDao(dao);
```

Note that the final call to the parent class's setDao() method to assign the DAO implementation takes a reference to the UserAccountDao interface, not the JdbcUserAccountDaoImpl implementation class. The parent test case is completely agnostic about the implementation details, and thus performs exactly the same operations when carrying out the tests regardless of the specific implementation being used.

Listing 10-13 shows the full implementation of the helper class used to create and populate the mock HSQL database, configure the template object connected to it, and clear the cache.

Listing 10-13. *The JdbcConfigHelper Class Implementation*

```
package com.apress.timesheets.dao.jdbc;

import java.sql.Connection;
import java.sql.Statement;
import javax.sql.DataSource;
import org.springframework.jdbc.core.JdbcTemplate;
import org.springframework.jdbc.datasource.DriverManagerDataSource;
import com.apress.timesheets.dao.ConfigHelper;

public class JdbcConfigHelper implements ConfigHelper {

    private static final String DRIVER = "org.hsqldb.jdbcDriver";
    private static final String URL = "jdbc:hsqldb:mem:JdbcDaoTest";
    private static final String USERNAME = "sa";
    private static final String PASSWORD = "";

    private static final String[] DDL = new String[] {
"drop schema public cascade",

"create table Period (id bigint generated by default as identity"+
" (start with 1), endTime timestamp, note varchar(255), rate numeric,"+
" startTime timestamp, rateType_id varchar(255), primary key (id))",

"create table RateType (id varchar(255) not null, primary key (id))",

"create table Timesheet (id bigint generated by default as identity"+
" (start with 1), created timestamp, note varchar(255), startDate"+
" timestamp, useraccount bigint not null, primary key (id))",

"create table Timesheet_Period (Timesheet_id bigint not null,"+
" periods_id bigint not null, unique (periods_id))",
```

```
    "create table UserAccount (id bigint generated by default as identity"+
    " (start with 1), accountName varchar(255) not null, primary key"+
    " (id), unique (accountName))",

    "create table UserRole (id bigint generated by default as identity"+
    " (start with 1), roleName varchar(255) not null, primary key (id),"+
    " unique (roleName))",

    "create table account_role (user bigint not null, role bigint not"+
    " null, primary key (user, role))",

    "alter table Period add constraint FK_PERIOD_RATE_TYPE foreign key"+
    " (rateType_id) references RateType",

    "alter table Timesheet add constraint FK_TIMESHEET_USER foreign key"+
    " (useraccount) references UserAccount",

    "alter table Timesheet_Period add constraint FK_PT_TIMESHEET foreign"+
    " key (Timesheet_id) references Timesheet",

    "alter table Timesheet_Period add constraint FK_PT_PERIOD foreign key"+
    " (periods_id) references Period",

    "alter table account_role add constraint FK_AR_ROLE foreign key (role)"+
    " references UserRole",

    "alter table account_role add constraint FK_AR_ACCOUNT foreign key"+
    " (user) references UserAccount"
};

    private JdbcTemplate template;

    public void setUp() throws Exception {
        final DataSource ds =
            new DriverManagerDataSource(DRIVER,URL,USERNAME,PASSWORD);
        template = new JdbcTemplate(ds);
        buildDatabase(ds);
    }

    private void buildDatabase(final DataSource ds) throws Exception {
        final Connection c = ds.getConnection();
        try {
```

```
            final Statement tableCreation = c.createStatement();
            for(final String ddl : DDL) {
                tableCreation.execute(ddl);
            }
        } finally {
            c.close();
        }
    }

    public void clear() {
        // No cacheing involved
    }

    public JdbcTemplate getTemplate() {
        return template;
    }

    public void setTemplate(JdbcTemplate template) {
        this.template = template;
    }
}
```

The bulk of the implementation in Listing 10-13 is primarily concerned with initializing the mock database tables, and some of its verbosity can effectively be reduced by pushing the table creation statements into an external file.

The Hibernate Unit Test

The test implementation for the Hibernate-based user account DAO shown in Listing 10-14 is similar to the JDBC example of Listing 10-9.

Listing 10-14. *The Hibernate DAO*

```
public class HibernateUserAccountDaoTest
    extends UserAccountDaoTestHelper
{
    @Override
    protected void setUp() throws Exception {
        final HibernateConfigHelper helper =
            new HibernateConfigHelper();
        helper.setUp();
        setHelper(helper);
```

```
      final HibernateUserAccountDaoImpl dao =
         new HibernateUserAccountDaoImpl();
      dao.setHibernateTemplate(helper.getTemplate());
      setDao(dao);
   }
}
```

As Listing 10-14 shows, we initialize the helper and assign it to the parent (to allow the Hibernate cache to be cleared as necessary). HibernateConfigHelper makes HibernateTemplate available rather than JdbcTemplate. The DAO implementation is instantiated, and HibernateTemplate retrieved from the helper is injected into it. The DAO is then provided to the parent test case. The steps are equivalent to Listing 10-9, although some of the implementations are different.

The HibernateConfigHelper implementation itself is also similar to, though slightly less verbose than, the JdbcConfigHelper implementation. The Hibernate-based ConfigHelper implementation is shown in Listing 10-15.

Listing 10-15. *The HibernateConfigHelper Implementation*

```
package com.apress.timesheets.dao.hibernate;

import org.hibernate.*;
import org.hibernate.cfg.*
import org.hibernate.dialect.HSQLDialect;
import org.springframework.orm.hibernate3.*;
import
org.springframework.transaction.support.TransactionSynchronizationManager;
import com.apress.timesheets.dao.ConfigHelper;
import com.apress.timesheets.entity.*;
import com.apress.timesheets.security.AcegiUserDetails;

public class HibernateConfigHelper implements ConfigHelper {

   private HibernateTemplate template;

   public void setUp() throws Exception {
      final AnnotationConfiguration configuration =
         new AnnotationConfiguration();
      configuration.setProperty(Environment.DRIVER,
            "org.hsqldb.jdbcDriver");
      configuration.setProperty(Environment.URL,
            "jdbc:hsqldb:mem:HibernateDaoTest");
```

```
        configuration.setProperty(Environment.USER, "sa");
        configuration.setProperty(Environment.DIALECT,
            HSQLDialect.class.getName());
        configuration.setProperty(Environment.SHOW_SQL, "true");
        configuration.setProperty(Environment.HBM2DDL_AUTO,
            "create-drop");
        configuration.addAnnotatedClass(UserRole.class);
        configuration.addAnnotatedClass(UserAccount.class);
        configuration.addAnnotatedClass(Period.class);
        configuration.addAnnotatedClass(RateType.class);
        configuration.addAnnotatedClass(Rate.class);
        configuration.addAnnotatedClass(Timesheet.class);
        configuration.addAnnotatedClass(AcegiUserDetails.class);
        final SessionFactory sessionFactory = configuration
                .buildSessionFactory();

        final String[] schema = configuration
                .generateSchemaCreationScript(new HSQLDialect());
        for (final String table : schema) {
            System.out.println("SCHEMA: " + table);
        }

        this.template = new HibernateTemplate(sessionFactory);

        final Session session = SessionFactoryUtils.getSession(
                sessionFactory, true);
        TransactionSynchronizationManager.bindResource(sessionFactory,
                new SessionHolder(session));
    }

    public void tearDown() throws Exception {
        final SessionFactory factory = template.getSessionFactory();
        final SessionHolder sessionHolder = (SessionHolder)
TransactionSynchronizationManager.unbindResource(factory);
        SessionFactoryUtils.closeSession(sessionHolder.getSession());
    }

    public void clear() {
        template.flush();
        template.clear();
    }
```

```
    public HibernateTemplate getTemplate() {
        return template;
    }

    public void setTemplate(HibernateTemplate template) {
        this.template = template;
    }
}
```

The Hibernate configuration object can generate a database schema without the need for a separate script, so this implementation is slightly less verbose than the corresponding JDBC-based implementation. However, it does require that the annotated entity classes be registered with the configuration object, sacrificing much of the brevity that would otherwise result. As the domain model grows, this slight advantage would become more pronounced. Again, the apparent verbosity can be improved slightly by moving the configuration into an external file. The configuration parameter required to enable schema creation is the create-drop option. This is shown in Listing 10-16.

Listing 10-16. *Configuring Hibernate to Automatically Create the Database Schema*

```
configuration.setProperty(Environment.HBM2DDL_AUTO,"create-drop");
```

Because Hibernate caches objects, there is an implementation in the body of the clear() method to remove cached items, shown in bold in Listing 10-15.

Unit Tests versus Integration Tests

The underlying mock object used in the two preceding examples was itself a database implementation. This goes against the grain of what I was saying earlier about the need to test components in isolation from the actual implementation of their dependencies. We have clearly used an *actual* implementation of a database in the test implementations. Strictly speaking, therefore, this is not a unit test—it is an integration test. I talk more about these in the section "Integration Testing" later in this chapter. Why have I chosen to do this?

Databases provide a layer of enormously complicated functionality; as a result, the number of ways in which a DAO implementation can interact with its underlying layer is vast. We can create a mock object to emulate the one specific way in which we really interact with the database, and that would be a legitimate unit test, but unfortunately it makes the test extremely brittle. A correct change to the implementation will require a corresponding change to the mock object. In the end, we would be testing not that the unit behaved in the way that it was supposed to, but that it was implemented in the way we anticipated. The behavior could be entirely erroneous.

So in the case of the database-based unit tests, I have chosen a halfway house. The mock object is itself a database, but it is an extremely limited embedded database. It will hopefully behave a lot like the real database implementation (such as MySQL, PostgreSQL, Oracle, or

SQL Server) that we might use in the production environment, but it is self-contained within the testing environment, will run quickly, and allows us to control the table structure and contents from the test implementation.

■Note Tests that must be changed with every modification, that run slowly against a real database, or that require manual configuration prior to the test execution will not be run and will therefore become out of synch with the application logic. If your unit tests are not being run by the developers, the tests serve no useful purpose. You should be pragmatic about ensuring that performance and convenience are met when creating unit tests.

I chose to present this hybrid test as a first example because database-based DAO implementations often contain a large part of an application's implementation detail and it is important to have a flexible, effective, and fast test of these components even if we have to compromise a test design principle to get it. In the next section on the e-mail–based tests, we create a purer but less flexible unit test based on proper mock objects.

The E-mail DAO Tests

Chapter 8 introduced three distinct implementations of the e-mail DAO. The first sent a plain-text message, the second an HTML-formatted message, and the third an HTML-formatted message with image attachments. Our unit test needs to cater to all three circumstances, and we therefore need mock implementations of the mail sender used by the DAOs.

All that is required of the mock mail sender is that instead of attempting to send the messages to an external mail server, it retains them in memory so that after the DAO method execution, the unit test can retrieve them and confirm that their contents correspond with what we intended to send. The interface methods that our implementation must provide are shown in Listing 10-17.

Listing 10-17. *The Methods of the JavaMailSender API*

```
// These from MailSender
void send(SimpleMailMessage simpleMessage)
   throws MailException;

void send(SimpleMailMessage[] simpleMessages)
   throws MailException;

// These from JavaMailSender which implements MailSender
MimeMessage createMimeMessage();
```

```
MimeMessage createMimeMessage(InputStream contentStream)
   throws MailException;

void send(MimeMessage mimeMessage)
   throws MailException;

void send(MimeMessage[] mimeMessages)
   throws MailException;

void send(MimeMessagePreparator mimeMessagePreparator)
   throws MailException;

void send(MimeMessagePreparator[] mimeMessagePreparators)
   throws MailException;
```

Unfortunately, no standard object exists to perform this task. We shall therefore roll our own mock object. Unlike the database-backed examples of the previous section, however, we are creating a pure mock object. Listing 10-18 shows the mock MailSender implementation.

Listing 10-18. *A Mock MailSender Implementation*

```
package com.apress.timesheets.mail;

import java.io.InputStream;
import java.util.*;
import javax.mail.*;
import javax.mail.internet.MimeMessage;
import org.springframework.mail.*;
import org.springframework.mail.javamail.*;

public class MockJavaMailSender implements JavaMailSender {

   private Session session;

   private List<Message> mimeMessages = new ArrayList<Message>();
   private List<SimpleMailMessage> simpleMessages =
      new ArrayList<SimpleMailMessage>();

   public MimeMessage createMimeMessage() {
      try {
         final Provider provider =
            new Provider(Provider.Type.TRANSPORT,"smtp",
```

```
MockTransport.class.getName(),"Apress","1.0");
        session = Session.getInstance(new Properties());
        session.setProvider(provider);
        return new MimeMessage(session);
    } catch( final NoSuchProviderException e) {
        throw new RuntimeException("Mock JavaMailSender provider failed",e);
    }
}

public MimeMessage createMimeMessage(final InputStream inputStream)
    throws MailException
{
    throw new UnsupportedOperationException(
        "Mock object does not support this method");
}

public void send(final MimeMessage message) throws MailException {
    mimeMessages.add(message);
}

public void send(final MimeMessage[] messages) throws MailException {
    for( final Message message : messages ) mimeMessages.add(message);
}

public void send(final MimeMessagePreparator preparator)
    throws MailException
{
    try {
        final MimeMessage message = createMimeMessage();
        preparator.prepare(message);
        mimeMessages.add(message);
    } catch(Exception e ) {
        throw new MockMailException(e);
    }
}

public void send(final MimeMessagePreparator[] preparators)
    throws MailException
{
```

```
    try {
      for( final MimeMessagePreparator preparator : preparators ) {
        final MimeMessage message = createMimeMessage();
        preparator.prepare(message);
        mimeMessages.add(message);
      }
    } catch(Exception e ) {
      throw new MockMailException(e);
    }
  }

  public void send(final SimpleMailMessage message) throws MailException {
    simpleMessages.add(message);
  }

  public void send(final SimpleMailMessage[] messages) throws MailException {
    for( final SimpleMailMessage message : messages ) {
      simpleMessages.add(message);
    }
  }

  public List<Message> getMimeMessages() {
    return mimeMessages;
  }

  public List<SimpleMailMessage> getSimpleMessages() {
    return simpleMessages;
  }

  public int getMessageCount() {
    return mimeMessages.size()+
        simpleMessages.size();
  }

  public void clear() {
    mimeMessages.clear();
    simpleMessages.clear();
  }
}
```

Because the JavaMail API uses a static factory method to associate MIME message objects with the underlying e-mail transport (usually SMTP), we need to register a custom transport with JavaMail in the createMimeMessage() method. We omit the implementation of the version of createMimeMessage(InputStream) method entirely because it is not used by our implementation. But an appropriate exception is generated so that if refactoring causes the method to become part of the code path of a class under test, we will not flounder around trying to determine the cause of mysterious failures!

The rest of the methods take the populated MimeMessage or SimpleMailMessage instances for transmission and instead store them in lists for later retrieval by the unit test. Additional utility methods are provided to access these lists, to obtain the count of messages contained within them, and to clear them of their contents upon test completion.

Listing 10-19 shows the environment that our three mail DAO test methods will operate within. We establish standard parameters for the sender, recipient, and subject of the e-mails that will be applied to the e-mails to be transmitted. We establish the mock instance of the JavaMailSender to be supplied to the DAO implementations (shown in bold in Listing 10-19), and we create a suitable timesheet object that will be passed to the MailDao's sendTimesheetUpdate method for each case. We also provide a tearDown() method that will clear the mock JavaMailSender's message stores after each test has completed.

Listing 10-19. *The Environment of the Unit Test*

```java
private static final String FROM = "from@example.com";
private static final String TO = "to@example.com";
private static final String SUBJECT = "subject";

private final MockJavaMailSender mailSender = new MockJavaMailSender();
private Timesheet timesheet;

@Override
protected void setUp() throws Exception {
   final UserAccount account = new UserAccount("username");
   final Calendar startDate = Calendar.getInstance();
   timesheet = new Timesheet(account,startDate);
}

@Override
protected void tearDown() throws Exception {
   mailSender.clear();
}
```

With the environment defined, we can now examine the simplest of the three tests. Listing 10-20 shows the test of the `SimpleMailDaoImpl` implementation of the `EmailDao` interface.

Listing 10-20. *The SimpleMailDaoImpl DAO Implementation*

```
public void testSimpleMailDao()
    throws MessagingException,IOException
{
    final SimpleMailDaoImpl impl = new SimpleMailDaoImpl();
    impl.setFromAddress(FROM);
    impl.setRcptAddress(TO);
    impl.setSubject(SUBJECT);
    impl.setMailSender(mailSender);

    impl.sendTimesheetUpdate(timesheet);

    assertEquals(1,mailSender.getMessageCount());
    final List<SimpleMailMessage> received = mailSender.getSimpleMessages();
    assertEquals(1,received.size());
    final SimpleMailMessage message = received.get(0);
    assertEquals(1,message.getTo().length);
    assertEquals(TO,message.getTo()[0]);
    assertEquals(FROM,message.getFrom());
    assertEquals(SUBJECT,message.getSubject());
    assertEquals("A timesheet has been updated by user: username",
        message.getText());
}
```

The first part of the test implementation creates and populates the `SimpleMailDaoImpl` implementation to be tested. The second part calls the `sendTimesheetUpdate` method, the behavior to be tested. The third part retrieves the "sent" message from the mock mail sender, and checks to see whether it contains the correct information.

Our assumption is that the real `MailSender` implementation (provided as a part of the Spring framework) is reliable and trustworthy, so that if the message is correct when it is passed to the mail sender, the message will be transmitted correctly. To be sure, third-party implementations are sometimes incorrect—but if we have doubts, we can add tests of the third-party implementations to verify their behavior.

Listing 10-21 shows the test corresponding to the `VelocityMailDaoImpl` implementation of the `EmailDao` interface.

Listing 10-21. *Testing the VelocityMailDaoImpl Implementation*

```
public void testVelocityMailDao()
   throws Exception
{
   final VelocityEngineFactoryBean factory = new VelocityEngineFactoryBean();
   final Properties props = new Properties();
   props.setProperty("resource.loader", "class");
   props.setProperty("class.resource.loader.class",
"org.apache.velocity.runtime.resource.loader.ClasspathResourceLoader");
   factory.setVelocityProperties(props);
   factory.afterPropertiesSet();
   final VelocityEngine engine = (VelocityEngine)factory.getObject();

   final VelocityMailDaoImpl impl = new VelocityMailDaoImpl();
   impl.setFromAddress(FROM);
   impl.setRcptAddress(TO);
   impl.setSubject(SUBJECT);
   impl.setVelocityEngine(engine);
   impl.setVelocityMacroPath("velocity/timesheet/update.vm");
   impl.setMailSender(mailSender);

   impl.sendTimesheetUpdate(timesheet);

   assertEquals(1,mailSender.getMessageCount());
   final List<Message> messages = mailSender.getMimeMessages();
   assertEquals(1,messages.size());
   final Message message = messages.get(0);

   final Address[] senders = message.getFrom();
   assertEquals(1,senders.length);
   final InternetAddress from = (InternetAddress)senders[0];
   assertEquals(FROM,from.getAddress());

   final Address[] recipients = message.getAllRecipients();
   assertEquals(1,recipients.length);
   final InternetAddress to = (InternetAddress)recipients[0];
   assertEquals(TO,to.getAddress());

   final String subject = message.getSubject();
   assertEquals(SUBJECT,subject);
```

```
    final String content = (String)message.getContent();
    assertTrue(
content.contains("User username has updated one of their timesheets."));
}
```

Although this test is complicated by the need to configure a Velocity engine and provide this to the implementation, the test takes the same form. We treat the Velocity engine as "infrastructure" that can be assumed reliable. Because it is easier to use the real thing than create a mock object, we do so.

The test is also made slightly more complicated by the need to extract the sender, recipient, subject, and content details from the MimeMessage. Rather than try to parse the HTML generated by the default Velocity template that we are using, or to rewrite the template itself, we treat the message as a string and check that it contains the desired text somewhere. This does not absolutely test the message contents for correctness (the HTML might be malformed, causing the text to be hidden from the recipient), but is sufficient for our purposes. Unit tests cannot test everything; we would add a more detailed test only if later problems with the HTML content suggested that the additional effort was worthwhile.

Listing 10-22 shows the test for the third implementation of the EmailDao that incorporates attachments into the message body.

Listing 10-22. *Testing the VelocityImageMailDaoImpl Implementation of the EmailDao Interface*

```
public void testVelocityImageMailDao()
    throws Exception
{
    final VelocityEngineFactoryBean factory =
        new VelocityEngineFactoryBean();
    final Properties props = new Properties();
    props.setProperty("resource.loader", "class");
    props.setProperty("class.resource.loader.class",
"org.apache.velocity.runtime.resource.loader.ClasspathResourceLoader");
    factory.setVelocityProperties(props);
    factory.afterPropertiesSet();
    final VelocityEngine engine = (VelocityEngine)factory.getObject();

    final VelocityImageMailDaoImpl impl =
        new VelocityImageMailDaoImpl();
    impl.setFromAddress(FROM);
    impl.setRcptAddress(TO);
    impl.setSubject(SUBJECT);
    impl.setVelocityEngine(engine);
```

```
impl.setVelocityMacroPath("velocity/timesheet/attachments.vm");
impl.setMailSender(mailSender);

final ClassPathResource image =
   new ClassPathResource("strawberry.jpg");
impl.setImage(image);
impl.setAttachment(image);

impl.sendTimesheetUpdate(timesheet);

assertEquals(1,mailSender.getMessageCount());
final List<Message> messages = mailSender.getMimeMessages();
assertEquals(1,messages.size());
final MimeMessage message = (MimeMessage)messages.get(0);

final Address[] senders = message.getFrom();
assertEquals(1,senders.length);
final InternetAddress from = (InternetAddress)senders[0];
assertEquals(FROM,from.getAddress());

final Address[] recipients = message.getAllRecipients();
assertEquals(1,recipients.length);
final InternetAddress to = (InternetAddress)recipients[0];
assertEquals(TO,to.getAddress());

final String subject = message.getSubject();
assertEquals(SUBJECT,subject);

boolean messageTextSent = false;
boolean messageInlineImageSent = false;
boolean messageAttachmentSent = false;

final MimeMultipart multipart =
   (MimeMultipart)message.getContent();
for(int i=0; i< multipart.getCount();i++) {
   final MimeBodyPart part =
      (MimeBodyPart)multipart.getBodyPart(i);
   if( partType(part,"multipart/related")) {
      final MimeMultipart mm =
         (MimeMultipart)part.getDataHandler().getContent();
```

```
            for(int j = 0; j < mm.getCount(); j++) {
                final BodyPart bp = mm.getBodyPart(j);
                if( partType(bp,"text/html")) {
                    messageTextSent = true;
                } else if( partType(bp,"image/jpeg")) {
                    messageInlineImageSent = true;
                }
            }
        } else if( partType(part,"image/jpeg")) {
            messageAttachmentSent = true;
        }
    }

    assertTrue(messageTextSent);
    assertTrue(messageInlineImageSent);
    assertTrue(messageAttachmentSent);
}
```

Here the complexity of extracting and verifying image data is severe enough that I have settled for checking that the expected components of the message are present—though they may be corrupted. Again, we will make the test more complex only if we have reason to believe that there is a problem with the transmitted content. For now, we presume that the external libraries operate as specified.

As you have now seen, the creation of mock objects can itself be a moderately complicated procedure. Sometimes it is unavoidable. For many cases, however, there are simpler options. We can generate mock implementations automatically, or we can use mock implementations provided with the libraries. In the next couple of sections, you will see both of these approaches.

Testing the Service Layer

The service layer usually provides a thin veneer of functionality between the presentation layer and the various DAO implementations. There may be additional business logic, but its outputs are based purely on parameters passed in and obtained from calls to DAO methods.

Listing 10-23 shows part of our implementation of the UserAccountService interface.

Listing 10-23. *An Implementation of the findUser Method*

```
public UserAccount findUser(final String username) {
    return userAccountDao.read(username);
}
```

This method calls straight through to the DAO. Although we could in principle implement this method in some other way, we are unlikely to do so in practice. We can therefore implement our test as a check that the service method calls into the corresponding DAO method, and that the return value of the latter is returned from the former.

Because of this test's greater simplicity, it is possible to use tools for automatically generating mock objects instead of manually crafting our own mock implementation of the UserAccountDao. There are several Java-based tools for generating mock objects, the most popular of which are jMock (www.jmock.org) and EasyMock (www.easymock.org). I have used EasyMock throughout my examples because its use of Java 5 language features gives it a slight edge in terms of code readability.

Listing 10-24 shows the full implementation of the unit test for the UserAccountService implementation.

Listing 10-24. *An EasyMock-Based Unit Test Suite*

```java
package com.apress.timesheets.service;

import static org.easymock.EasyMock.createMock;
import static org.easymock.EasyMock.expect;
import static org.easymock.EasyMock.replay;
import static org.easymock.EasyMock.verify;

import java.util.ArrayList;
import java.util.List;

import junit.framework.TestCase;

import com.apress.timesheets.dao.SecurityDao;
import com.apress.timesheets.dao.UserAccountDao;
import com.apress.timesheets.entity.UserAccount;
import com.apress.timesheets.security.AcegiUserDetails;

public class UserAccountServiceTest extends TestCase {
    private UserAccountService service;
    private SecurityDao mockSecurityDao;
    private UserAccountDao mockUserAccountDao;

    @Override
    protected void setUp() throws Exception {
        final UserAccountServiceImpl impl = new UserAccountServiceImpl();
        mockSecurityDao = createMock(SecurityDao.class);
        mockUserAccountDao = createMock(UserAccountDao.class);
```

```java
        impl.setSecurityDao(mockSecurityDao);
        impl.setUserAccountDao(mockUserAccountDao);
        impl.setSecurityDao(mockSecurityDao);
        impl.setUserAccountDao(mockUserAccountDao);
        this.service = impl;
    }

    public void testFindUser() {
        // Prepare test data
        final String username = "test";
        final UserAccount account = new UserAccount(username);

        // Script the mock object's expectations
        expect(mockUserAccountDao.read(username)).andReturn(account);
        replay(mockUserAccountDao);

        // Run the test. The mock object will fail the test if its
        // script is not followed.
        final UserAccount actualAccount = service.findUser(username);
        verify(mockUserAccountDao);
        assertTrue(actualAccount == account);
    }

    public void testCreateUser() {
        // Prepare test data
        final String username = "test";
        final UserAccount account = new UserAccount(username);
        final AcegiUserDetails acegi = new AcegiUserDetails(account,"password");

        // Script the test
        expect(mockSecurityDao.createUser(account)).andReturn(acegi);
        replay(mockSecurityDao);

        // Run the test
        service.createUser(account);
        verify(mockSecurityDao);
    }

    public void testDeleteUser() {
        final String username = "test";
        final UserAccount account = new UserAccount(username);
```

```
        mockSecurityDao.deleteUser(account);
        replay(mockSecurityDao);

        service.deleteUser(account);
        verify(mockSecurityDao);
    }

    public void testUpdateUser() {
        final String username = "test";
        final UserAccount account = new UserAccount(username);

        mockUserAccountDao.update(account);
        replay(mockUserAccountDao);

        service.updateUser(account);
        verify(mockUserAccountDao);
    }

    public void testListUsers() {
        final String username = "test";
        final UserAccount account = new UserAccount(username);
        final List<UserAccount> accounts = new ArrayList<UserAccount>();
        accounts.add(account);
        expect(mockUserAccountDao.list()).andReturn(accounts);
        replay(mockUserAccountDao);

        final List<UserAccount> actual = service.listUsers();
        verify(mockUserAccountDao);
        assertNotNull(actual);
        assertEquals(1,actual.size());
        assertEquals(account,actual.get(0));
    }
}
```

No additional mock objects needed to be created. EasyMock generates all of the mock classes that we require. Rather than inheriting from a special base class to gain access to the EasyMock methods, we make static calls into an EasyMock utility class. These methods are statically imported—a Java 5 feature highlighted in bold—to remove the need to explicitly reference the EasyMock class.

The service implementation requires access to a UserAccountDao implementation and a SecurityDao implementation. Both of these are created by calling the EasyMock createMock method on the class types in the setUp method. The setUp method also creates the service instance to be tested and assigns these mock controls to it.

Each of the test methods follows the same basic outline: the test data is prepared, the mock controls are scripted, the service method is invoked, and the expectations are checked. Two parts of this process require further explanation. The scripting of the mock controls (the mock DAOs) is carried out by executing methods on the mock object itself. Listing 10-25 shows an example from the testFindUser() method.

Listing 10-25. *Scripting the Mock Control in the testFindUser Method*

```
// Script the mock object's expectations
expect(mockUserAccountDao.read(username)).andReturn(account);
replay(mockUserAccountDao);
```

The call to the read() method on the mock UserAccountDao object informs the control that when the service call is made, we will expect it to invoke this method on the DAO (exactly what you see in Listing 10-23). This is wrapped in an expect() method call that allows us to specify what the mock object will actually return when this is done (an instance of the account object). The mock object starts out in a "scripting" mode that allows these method calls to be defined. The call to replay() at the end of Listing 10-25 then switches the control into a mode where it matches subsequent calls against the script established in Listing 10-24. A call to the read() method will now return the specified account object. As shown in Listing 10-26, we now make a call to the service itself.

Listing 10-26. *The Actual Service Call to Be Tested*

```
final UserAccount actualAccount = service.findUser(username);
```

The service implementation will (we hope) make the corresponding call to the DAO to receive from it the account object specified in Listing 10-25, and return that. So, subsequent to this call, the actualAccount reference shown in Listing 10-26 should refer to the same object as the account reference passed into the andReturn() method of Listing 10-25.

Finally, we validate the resulting state, as shown in Listing 10-27. We call an EasyMock method to verify that the expected methods were called on the mock object, and we use a normal JUnit assertion to verify that the service returns the correct account object instance.

Listing 10-27. *Validating the Results of the Service Method Call*

```
verify(mockUserAccountDao);
assertTrue(actualAccount == account);
```

The usage of mock class generation demonstrated here is not exclusively applicable to testing the service layer. You can use a generated mock class anywhere that you need a mock class to stand in as the container of data that would otherwise be passed to, or obtained from, other components. The checks to determine ordering of method calls can be disabled or enabled as appropriate, and numerous additional facilities allow you to apply other tests to the method calls, their parameters, and their return values.

Testing the Presentation Layer

Testing the presentation layer components is not notably different from testing the service layer. Again, we have a layer that predominantly performs its actions by calling through to another layer (although here we are one level higher up calling into the service layer instead of into the DAO layer).

The source code available from the Source Code/Download area of the Apress website (www.apress.com) includes an EasyMock-based test of a Spring MVC controller and its validation class. Testing a Spring Web Flow implementation class presents an additional challenge, however.

The configuration of the test shown in Listing 10-28 is very much as you would expect: the only real departure from the sort of mock object–based testing we have seen before is the creation (shown in bold) and use of the MockRequestContext object. This object is provided as a standard part of the Web Flow libraries specifically to make testing easier.

Listing 10-28. *Testing a Spring Web Flow Action Class*

```
private final EventFactorySupport support =
   new EventFactorySupport();
private CreateUserAction action;

@Override
protected void setUp() throws Exception {
   action = new CreateUserAction();
   action.setFormObjectName("command");
   action.setFormObjectClass(CreateUserForm.class);
}

public void testEdit() throws Exception {
   // Setup test data
   final MockRequestContext context = new MockRequestContext();

   // Carry out the action
   final Event event = action.edit(context);

   // Verify success
   assertNotNull(event);
   final String successEventId = support.success(action).getId();
   assertEquals(successEventId,event.getId());
}
```

Although it would be possible for us to implement the object by using a generated or custom created mock class, we have a problem: the population of the context object from the request parameters is normally carried out within the implementation of the action class's parent classes, and a similarly opaque method call within the action class getFormObject is used to retrieve the populated command object from the context itself. This detail is hidden within the Web Flow library classes. Even if we knew exactly what methods were called upon the context during the getFormObject method invocation, we would have no guarantee that the exact details would not change in a future implementation—making our test dependent on a specific version of an external library and potentially hindering us in the use of future versions.

The testEdit() method of Listing 10-28 makes limited use of the context, but the need is much more conspicuous in Listing 10-29, where the contents of the RequestContext object will be used to determine the UserAccount object to manipulate in the calls into the service classes (the scripting of which is shown in bold).

Listing 10-29. *Testing the CreateUserAction's Save Method*

```java
public void testSave() throws Exception {
    // Setup test data
    final MockParameterMap params = new MockParameterMap();
    params.put("username", "example");
    final MockRequestContext context = new MockRequestContext(params);
    action.bind(context);
    final UserAccount account = new UserAccount("example");

    // Script the test
    final UserAccountService service = createMock(UserAccountService.class);
    action.setUserAccountService(service);
    service.createUser(matchesNamedAccount(account));
    replay(service);

    // Carry out the action
    final Event event = action.save(context);

    // Verify success
    verify(service);
    final String successEventId = support.success(action).getId();
    assertEquals(successEventId,event.getId());
}
```

By using the provided MockRequestObject, we can avoid the need to know any of these details. And because the provider of the library has provided the mock implementation, we can reasonably assume that changes in the implementation details of one will be reflected by appropriate changes to the other.

Spring Mock Classes

The Spring framework provides a small suite of standard mock objects to aid in the creation of unit tests. Tools such as EasyMock are adequate for the creation of basic unit tests, but the Spring standard mock classes can make some tests less verbose, while allowing for more-sophisticated test behavior. Table 10-1 enumerates the standard mock object implementations provided with the Spring framework.

Table 10-1. *The Standard Spring Mock Object Classes*

Mock Class	Description
ExpectedLookupTemplate	Can be substituted for the JndiTemplate helper class in applications that use JndiTemplate instances to access JNDI.
SimpleNamingContext	Provides a simple JNDI context so code that looks up JNDI resources directly (without using JndiTemplate) can be provided with suitable mock objects.
MockExpressionEvaluator	A substitute for the ExpressionEvaluator JSTL class when testing custom JSP tags.
MockFilterConfig	Used to provide the configuration parameters when testing Java EE filter implementations (avoids the need for a servlet container and a deployment descriptor).
MockHttpServletRequest	A mock version of the HttpServletRequest object supplied to servlets and JSPs (and to controller classes via the dispatcher).
MockHttpServletResponse	The counterpart of the MockHttpServletRequest, this is a mock version of the HttpServletResponse object supplied to servlets and JSPs.
MockHttpSession	Used to provide a mock HttpSession object to web application components.
MockMultipartFile	Used to provide a mock multipart file-upload object to fake the results of a multipart form upload. Typically, this would be set into the MultipartFile attribute(s) of a form bean.
MockMultipartHttpServletRequest	Used to provide a mock request object to controllers expecting to receive multipart form uploads. This allows you to check that the multipart file is correctly bound to form properties or otherwise extracted from the request object correctly.
MockPageContext	Used to fake the PageContext object when testing custom JSP tags.
MockServletConfig	Used to supply configuration parameters to servlets under test (avoids the need for a servlet container and a deployment descriptor).

This suite of tests is heavily oriented toward the testing of the presentation components because these are the classes that are likely to have the heaviest dependency on the "normal" Java EE way of doing things. For example, it is often desirable to configure a Java EE application by using JNDI resources. Because this is a process of dependency lookup, legacy code will be difficult to inject with the resource, but the `SimpleNamingContext` mock class can be used in a stand-alone environment to supply appropriate mock substitutes for the "real" resources being looked up.

Integration Testing

Unit testing requires you to test the components in isolation. The reverse—testing the behavior of the components when connected—is *integration testing*. Integration testing ensures that the various component APIs can exchange data. Various errors can be introduced if these methods are not tested together. For example, misassumptions about the purpose of a method are sometimes apparent only when a class provides real data, rather than dummy data, to the other components.

Integration testing does not require any technologies specific to Spring, and there are no special techniques required. Integration testing is about verifying the behavior of the application as a whole so the internal details should not be relevant. When you need to perform partial integration tests (for example, testing from the web application layer down to a dummy database layer), the techniques shown already are applicable.

Web Testing

There are various tools to allow you to create tests of a web application. Two that I recommend are HttpUnit (http://httpunit.sourceforge.net/) and Selenium (www.openqa.org/selenium/). These tools approach the problem of automating the testing of a GUI designed for manual operation in two different ways. Both HttpUnit and Selenium tests can be integrated into Maven builds.

HttpUnit allows your unit test to connect directly to a web application without using a browser. You use the HttpUnit libraries to create a JUnit test case that specifies the inputs to provide and the outputs expected from each page of the application. These tests provide an excellent test to confirm that the back-end components correctly interpret the incoming web requests, but they are less effective in testing that the correct content is displayed to the user. Although there is some support for it, debugging and testing JavaScript-based issues is particularly difficult when using HttpUnit.

Selenium allows you to create a test of the application by creating JavaScript-based scripts to drive the browser directly. The approach is considerably more complicated than the HttpUnit technique, but you have the advantage of using the same browser that your end users will be using. Any quirks in the rendering engine or script interpretation that would otherwise cause problems will result in an error in the script. For example, if a bug in the generated HTML prevents a button from rendering properly, the script will fail as a result of the missing button, whereas the HttpUnit script might successfully submit the associated form regardless.

Regression Testing

Regression tests are not a particular type of test; they are merely tests created in order to verify that a resolved bug has been fixed. Regression tests are intended to ensure that bugs that have been fixed are not accidentally reintroduced as a result of later changes to the implementation.

For every unique bug that is fixed in the application after it has officially "gone live," a corresponding regression test should be created and included in the test suite. It is a lamentable fact that many applications have bugs that reoccur time and time again precisely because no regression suite has been created for them. In most cases, bugs will arise as a result of mistakes in the code, and the regression test is merely an addition to the existing unit test suite to catch the special case that was missed during development.

A comprehensive unit test suite in conjunction with a growing regression test suite will lead to an application whose quality never decreases over time, avoiding the notorious "bit rot" that sometimes seems to affect older applications as they fail to adapt to their changing environment.

Conclusion

In this chapter, you have looked at the techniques and tools available to you to correctly test your Spring application's components. If you follow Spring's IOC techniques, you will find it easy to create comprehensive test suites that increase the quality of your code and increase the ease with which you can make architectural changes.

■■■

The Spring IDE Plug-in for Eclipse

The Spring IDE plug-in for Eclipse enhances the Eclipse environment by providing a variety of features that make it easier to work with Spring projects. The Spring IDE provides tools for creating, validating, viewing, and editing your Spring configuration files. A particularly attractive feature is the provision of *autocompletion* when editing bean definitions.

Although the Spring IDE is a separate project from Spring itself, there are developers who participate in both projects, so there is excellent support for the latest Spring features. In this appendix, I discuss the installation of the Spring IDE and then briefly present the features related to editing and viewing bean and Spring Web Flow definitions.

It is not possible to discuss all of the Spring IDE features in depth in this appendix. I would recommend installing and working with the plug-in initially as an aid to the creation of bean definition files. The autocompletion feature works in a manner nearly identical to the Java source autocompletion features. After you are familiar with these aspects of the plug-in, you should visit the Spring IDE website (`http://springide.org/`) to learn more about the tool.

Installing the Plug-in

Although it is possible to download the Spring IDE components and install them manually, by far the easiest way to install the Spring IDE into Eclipse is to use the built-in Software Updates feature of the Eclipse environment.

Version 2 of the Spring IDE supports versions of Spring up to and including Spring 2.1 and up to version 1 of Spring Web Flow. You will need at least version 3.2 of the Eclipse IDE in order to use version 2 of the Spring IDE, but unless you already have an established 3.2 Eclipse environment, you should start with version 3.3 of Eclipse released as a set of integrated environments called Europa. I would not advocate a migration to Eclipse 3.3 unless you are confident that all of your plug-ins are compatible with the newer version; Spring IDE works well in the Eclipse 3.2 environment if you are in this position, so it is safer to stay with a known-good environment. To use Spring IDE to its fullest potential, you should install the Eclipse IDE for Java EE Developers Europa release because this includes Web Standard Tools (WST) components that support XML parsing—necessary for use of the bean editing support.

As Figure A-1 shows, the Software Updates feature is accessed from the Eclipse Help menu. Choose Software Updates ➤ Find and Install to start the installation wizard.

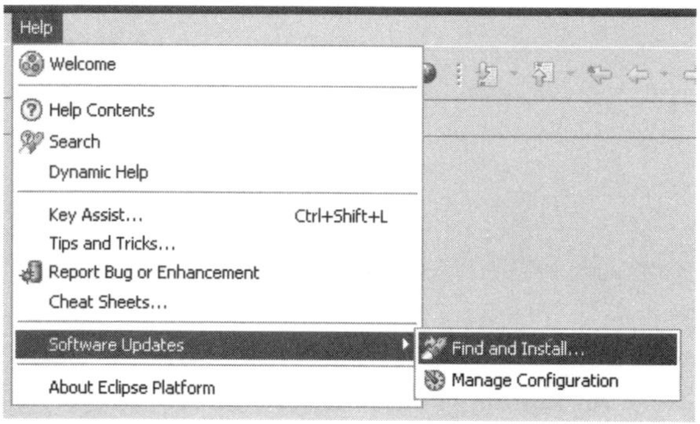

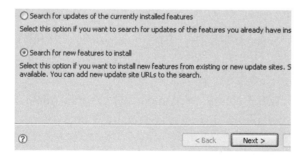

Figure A-1. *Starting the installation process*

The first page of the installation wizard, shown in Figure A-2, prompts you to select updates to existing features or to search for new features. To acquire the latest updates to an already-installed Spring IDE environment, you would select the first of these options. However, upon the initial installation you should select the Search for New Features to Install option and click the Next button.

Figure A-2. *Installing new features*

In the next wizard (not shown), click the New Remote Site button and then enter the details exactly as shown in Figure A-3.

Figure A-3. *Specifying the update site details*

The Name field in Figure A-3 is an arbitrary name that will be shown in subsequent pages of the installer, but the URL field is used to obtain the installation files and must be entered verbatim as `http://springide.org/updatesite/`.

After you click the OK button, the next page will show a list of the update sites known to the Eclipse update installer, with only the Spring IDE site selected (if any other entries are selected, deselect them). Click Finish, and the installer will check the Spring IDE site for the features that are available from it.

After the installer has obtained the list of features, they will be shown in the Updates dialog box. If you expand the tree view of features to install, the dialog should look much like Figure A-4, but with the Integrations features selected. If the page presents any error messages, deselect the tools that cannot be installed.

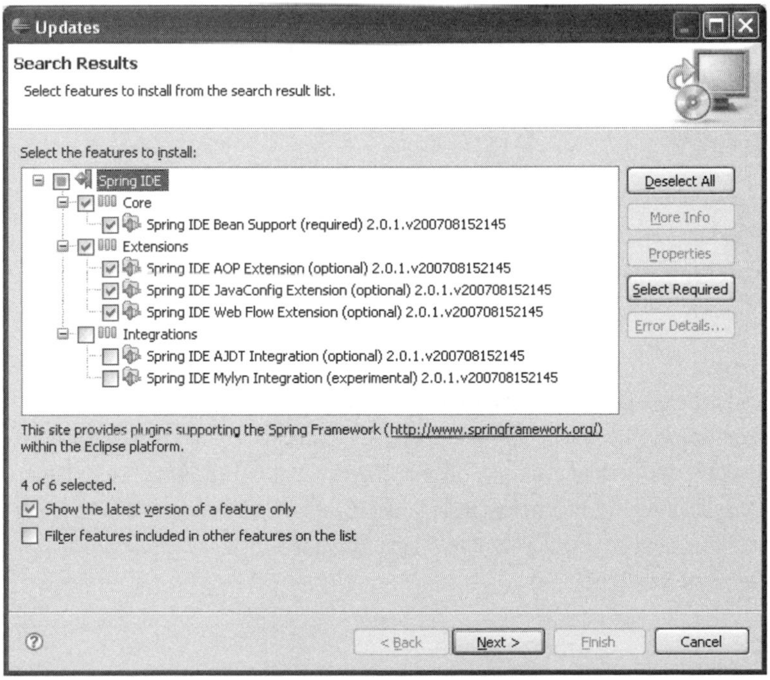

Figure A-4. *Selecting the feature set to install*

At the time of this writing, the AspectJ Development Tools component (AJDT) is not compatible with the Europa release of Eclipse, and the Mylyn integration tool is unlikely to be of immediate interest, so I have disabled their installation as shown in Figure A-4. Click Next, and you will be prompted to accept the license agreement for the tools. After you have accepted this, the installation will proceed. The installation files are not "signed," so you will need to click Install when a dialog warns you of this. Finally, select Yes when you are asked whether you would like to restart the Eclipse environment. The Spring IDE plug-in is now installed.

Managing Bean Configurations

As you have seen throughout this book, a large part of your work with Spring involves either the editing of conventional Java code (for which existing language support in most IDEs is adequate) or the editing of XML bean definition files. To gain the benefits of the Spring IDE in managing these files, you need to add the Spring Project Nature to your Eclipse projects.

Figure A-5 shows the standard Eclipse Project Explorer view of a set of projects generated by using Maven's `eclipse:eclipse` target. Currently these are decorated with two icons, a *J* symbol at the top right indicating that they are Java projects, and a standard warning symbol at the bottom left indicating that there are minor problems with the project configuration.

Figure A-5. *An Eclipse project without the Spring Project Nature*

■**Caution** Although you can generate Eclipse-compatible project definitions by using the Maven tool's `eclipse:eclipse` build target, it cannot currently generate Spring IDE–compatible projects. You will need to apply and configure the Spring Project Nature manually. Once configured, the `eclipse:eclipse` target will not overwrite these settings, but the `eclipse:clean` build target to remove stale project definitions *will* remove them, which is often undesirable, so you may want to avoid using this target unless your project configuration has become irretrievably corrupt.

Right-click on each project in turn and choose the Apply Spring Project Nature option from the context menu. After performing this action, you will see the decoration in the top-right corner change from the *J* to an *S*, indicating that this is now a Spring project (a Spring project is always a Java project also, so the *J* decoration is no longer required). The resulting look is shown in Figure A-6.

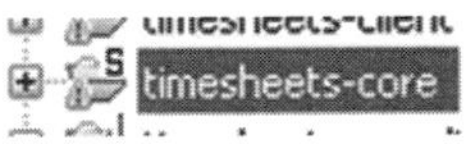

Figure A-6. *An Eclipse project with the Spring Project Nature*

If you open one of the projects, as shown in Figure A-7, you will see that an additional entry has been added to the project details in the Project Explorer. This will represent the Spring-specific configuration details of your project. However, it is not automatically populated with entries.

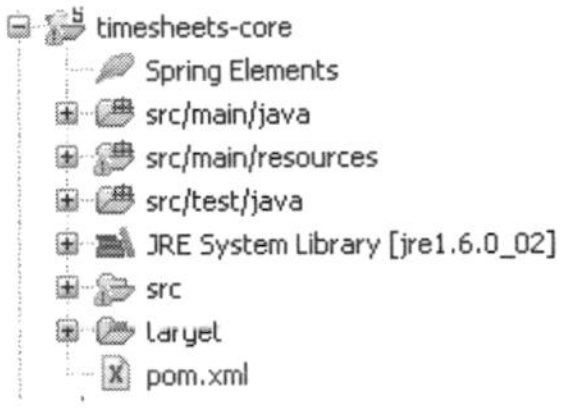

Figure A-7. *The Spring Elements node within a Spring project*

Although the Spring Elements option is shown by default as a branch of the Project Explorer, it can be opened as a view in its own right by choosing the Window ➤ Show View ➤ Other ➤ Spring ➤ Spring Explorer menu option.

To configure your bean configuration files for inclusion in the Spring Elements view, choose the Properties option from the Spring Elements leaf's context menu, or open the project's context menu, choose Properties, and select the Spring node in the tree on the left-hand side. Either way, you will be presented with a dialog box corresponding to Figure A-8.

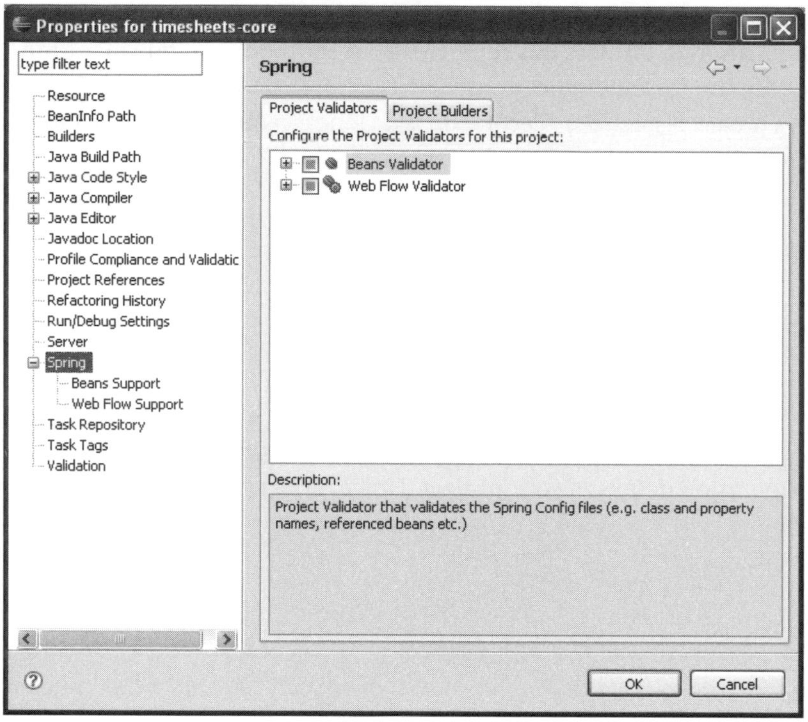

Figure A-8. *Configuring the Spring-specific project properties*

The default page for this menu option allows you to enable and disable the various types of validation that will be used to check your bean definition files for errors. Usually you will leave the default options for validation and for the (hidden) project builders options. However, on large projects you may find that the validation can make the IDE less responsive, so you may want to disable some of the more rigorous options in this situation.

Select the Beans Support option from the left-hand menu, and you will be presented with the Beans Support dialog box. Click the Add button to select the bean configuration files. This action tells the Spring IDE which bean configurations are relevant to your project (and indeed which XML files are bean configurations in the first place—the IDE does not attempt to autodetect bean configuration files). Figure A-9 shows the bean configuration files of the timesheets-webapp project selected from the Beans Support menu.

Returning from this dialog to the Project Explorer window shown in Figure A-10, the Spring Elements branch of the project's tree has been populated with the details of the configuration files, of the Spring beans defined within them, and of the properties assigned to those beans.

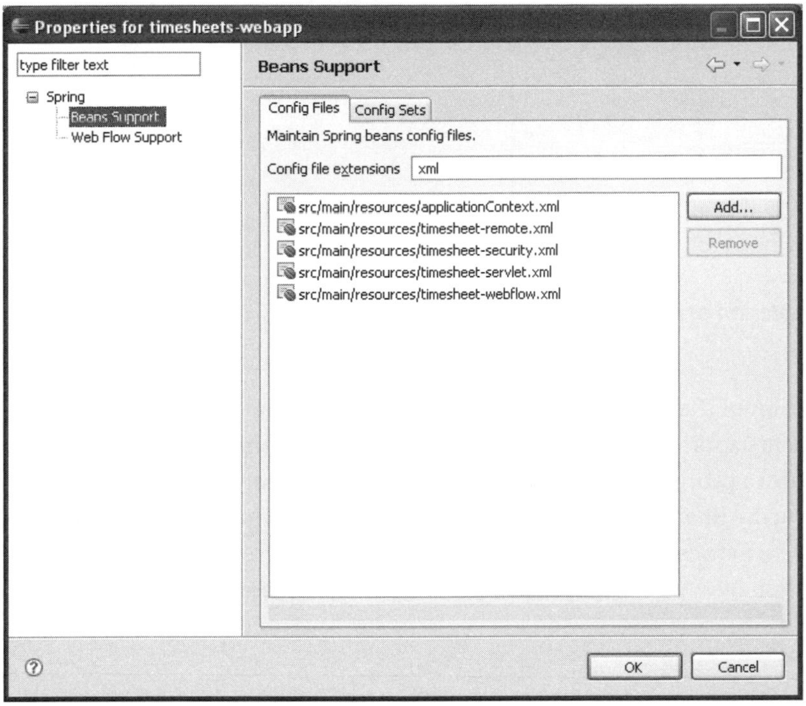

Properties for timesheets-webapp
type filter text
Spring
Beans Support
Web Flow Support
Beans Support
Config Files
Config Sets
Maintain Spring beans config files.
Config file extensions
xml
src/main/resources/applicationContext.xml
src/main/resources/timesheet-remote.xml
src/main/resources/timesheet-security.xml
src/main/resources/timesheet-servlet.xml
src/main/resources/timesheet-webflow.xml
Add...
Remove
OK
Cancel

Figure A-9. *Specifying the bean definition files for the project*

timesheets-webapp
Spring Elements
Beans
src/main/resources/applicationContext.xml
beans
org.springframework.beans.factory.annotation.RequiredAnnot
classpath:timesheet-security.xml
classpath:timesheet-aop.xml
classpath:timesheet-remote.xml
dataSource [org.apache.commons.dbcp.BasicDataSource]
driverClassName
org.hsqldb.jdbcDriver
url
jdbc:hsqldb:file:timesheet;SHUTDOWN=true
username
password
sessionFactory [org.springframework.orm.hibernate3.annotatio
securityDao [com.apress.timesheets.dao.hibernate.HibernateS
userAccountDao [com.apress.timesheets.dao.hibernate.Hibern

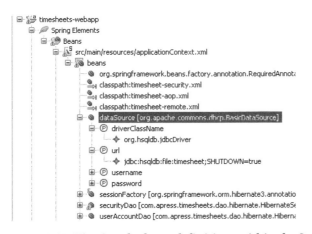

Figure A-10. *Viewing the bean definitions within the Spring project*

Prior to the installation of the Spring IDE, if you were to attempt to use autocompletion within one of the Spring bean definition files, you would be presented with the basic XML autocompletion options shown in Figure A-11. These are better than nothing, but are really of very limited help when creating these files.

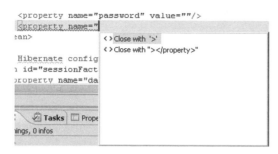

Figure A-11. *Autocompletion of a bean definition in a typical Eclipse Java EE project*

After the installation of the Spring IDE plug-in, you will find that autocompletion provides a much richer experience. Figure A-12 illustrates the options available when you use autocompletion on a property name. Without carrying out the registration of the bean configuration files via the Bean Support menu option described earlier, you will also have access to all of the bean names local to the file when populating references, and after registering the configuration files, you will have access to bean references throughout the suite of configuration files.

```
<!-- Determines how views are resolved to rendering impl
<bean class="org.springframework.web.servlet.view.UrlBas
    <property name="prefix" value="/WEB-INF/jsp/"/>
    <property name="suffix" value=".jsp"/>
    <property name="viewClass" value="org.springframework
</bean>

<!-- Determines how
<bean class="org.s
    <property name="
        <map>
            <entry key
            <entry key
            <entry key
            <entry key
```

    applicationContext - ApplicationObjectSupport
    attributes - UrlBasedViewResolver.setAttribute
    attributesMap - UrlBasedViewResolver.setAttr
    cache - AbstractCachingViewResolver.setCach
    contentType - UrlBasedViewResolver.setConte
    order - UrlBasedViewResolver.setOrder(int ord
    prefix - UrlBasedViewResolver.setPrefix(String
    redirectContextRelative - UrlBasedViewResolv
    redirectHttp10Compatible - UrlBasedViewReso

Figure A-12. *Autocompletion of a bean definition in a Spring project*

The Spring IDE is also "schema aware," allowing it to take advantage of the schema-based property specifications described in Chapter 3. Figure A-13 shows an example of autocompletion of a property defined in this manner.

The features described so far allow you to manage the process of creating the bean definitions, and the Spring Elements explorer branch (or the Spring Explorer view) provide some benefits in visualizing and navigating the configuration files. Double-clicking on the various nodes within the Spring Elements branch allows you to open a view on the corresponding configuration file positioned to the appropriate line for the detail that the node represents. Right-clicking provides a context menu that (where appropriate) allows you to open the Java source code corresponding to the bean in question.

Figure A-13. *Autocompletion of schema-based properties*

In addition to the normal Spring Explorer view of the beans, there is an Open Graph context menu option on the nodes within the Spring Explorer. Selecting this option presents a read-only graphical representation of the dependencies established by the definition files. Figure A-14 shows part of a graph of the bean dependencies established by the `timesheet-webapp` project's `applicationContext.xml` bean definition file.

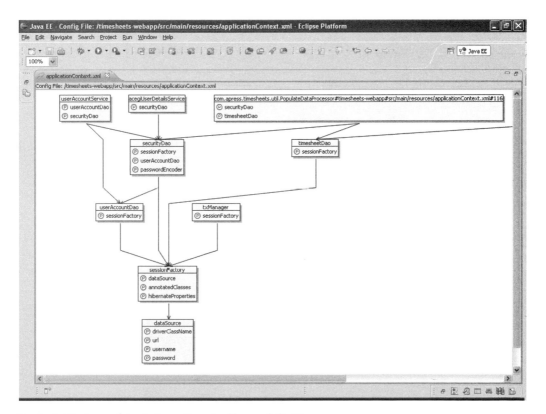

Figure A-14. *A graphical view of a set of bean definitions*

Managing Spring Web Flow Configuration

Having looked at the bean configuration files, we will now take a look at the support for the Spring Web Flow web application framework. The Spring IDE provides an option under the Spring properties dialog box. Figure A-15 shows this dialog.

The left menu is abbreviated because it has been accessed via the Spring Elements context menu instead of the top-level project's context menu; otherwise, the dialogs of Figure A-8 and A-15 are identical in their behavior. Figure A-15 shows the Web Flow Support leaf selected, and a Web Flow configuration file has been added via the Add button. So far this is similar to the addition of bean definition files on the Beans Support node of the same dialog.

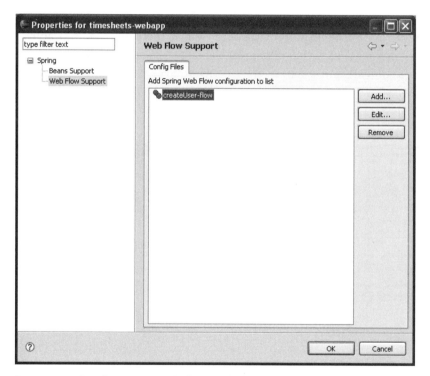

Figure A-15. *Configuring a web flow definition*

The configuration file selected in Figure A-15 is the flow definition file used to specify the interactions necessary to create a new user. We defined this file manually in Chapter 6.

The web flow has dependencies on the configured Spring beans. For example, our web flow defined in the `createUser-flow.xml` file invokes actions on a bean specified in the `timesheet-webflow.xml` bean definition file. Clicking the Edit button in Figure A-15 brings up the dialog box shown in Figure A-16, listing the bean definition files known to the project. Selecting appropriate bean definitions makes their contents available for access from the web flow definition.

Figure A-16. *Adding bean definition dependencies to a web flow definition*

With the web flow and its dependencies correctly specified, we get a similar range of benefits to those for bean definitions described earlier in the chapter—creating, validating, viewing, and editing your web flows. In Figure A-17, I have commented out a vital element of the web flow definition file. The error is flagged in the margin, and the first incorrect element has been underlined in red (a `view-state` element should not appear until a `start-state` element has been defined). Autocompletion is also provided for most of the elements and attributes of the file—and where bean-related information must be provided, the autocompletion can supply the valid options from the bean definition files that we associated with the web flow.

Figure A-17. *Validation errors in the web flow definition*

The same warning shown in Figure A-17 will appear as a problem for resolution in the standard Eclipse Problems view, as shown in Figure A-18. Working on Java source code, Spring bean definition files, and Spring web flow definition files becomes a part of the same work flow.

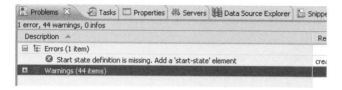

Figure A-18. *Web flow definition validation errors in the Problems view of the project*

If you select the context menu for the web flow definition in the Spring Elements tree, you will see an option for Open Graphical Editor. If you select this option for the createUser-flow.xml web flow, the graphical view of the web flow shown in Figure A-19 will appear. If you look back to Figure 6-2 in Chapter 6, you will see that this is a slightly more technical view of essentially the same state transition diagram.

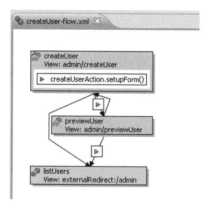

Figure A-19. *A graphical view of the createUser web flow*

This ability to view the state defined by the web flow is a useful feature when verifying your web flow against the initial design, but it is more than that. Unlike the bean definition graph, this is an editable diagram, and the changes you make will be represented in the underlying configuration file.

For example, if you double-click on the starting `createUser` state at the top of the graph, you will be presented with the View State dialog box shown in Figure A-20.

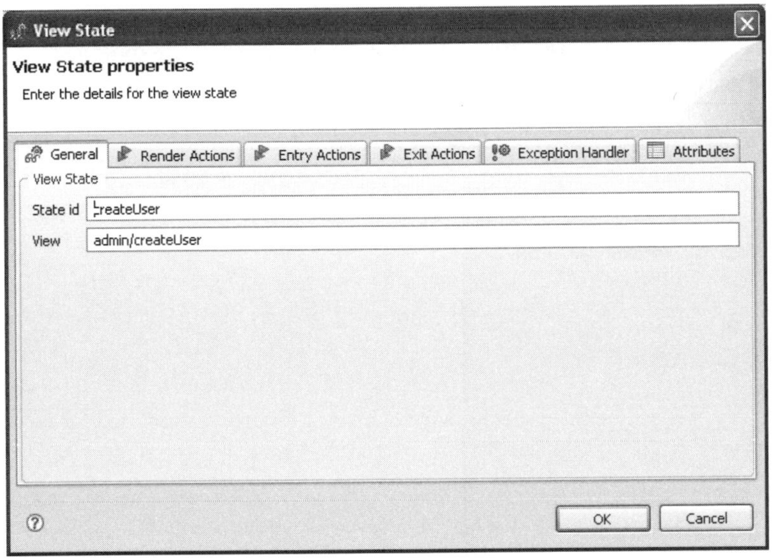

Figure A-20. *A dialog allowing you to edit details of the createUser view state*

This is an exact representation of the corresponding state definition reproduced in Listing A-1. The first line of Listing A-1 specifies the `id` property of the state and the name of the view that represents it, which are both visible in Figure A-20. The Render Actions tab hidden in Figure A-20 contains the values corresponding to the `render-actions` element of Listing A-1.

Listing A-1. *The Create User Flow Definition in XML Form*

```
<view-state id="createUser" view="admin/createUser">
   <render-actions>
      <action bean="createUserAction" method="setupForm"/>
   </render-actions>
   <transition on="preview" to="previewUser">
      <action bean="createUserAction" method="bindAndValidate"/>
   </transition>
   <transition on="cancel" to="listUsers"/>
</view-state>
```

The first of the transitions specified in Listing A-1 moves the flow from the createUser state when a preview event is raised. Double-clicking the arrow representing this transition (drawn between createUser and previewUser in Figure A-19) brings up the Transition dialog box shown in Figure A-21. The originating and destination states are visible in the diagram, and the event that causes the transition in question is shown in the dialog. This information can also be acquired by hovering the cursor over the box containing a green triangle symbol that decorates this transition line, but the dialog allows the details of the transition to be changed as well as viewed.

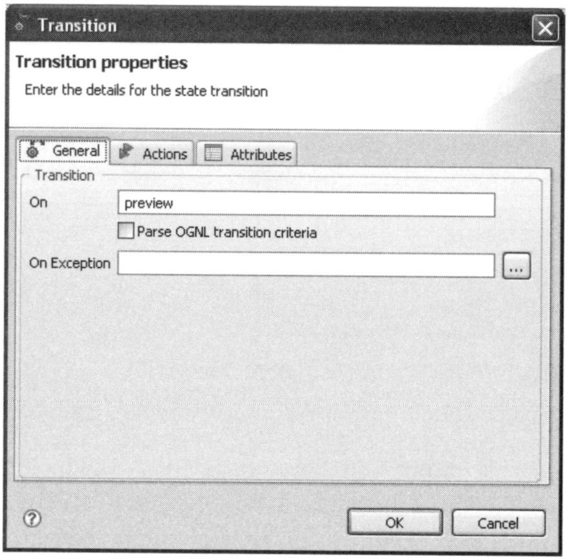

Figure A-21. *A dialog allowing you to edit details of the preview state transition*

In addition to editing the existing elements of the web flow definition, we can create new elements by using the graphical tool. On the right-hand side of the graph is a Palette tool that can be expanded by selecting it with the cursor. This contains a list of elements that can be dropped onto the graph, as shown in Figure A-22.

The palette contains all of the elements that can be created within the web flow definition files, so you can create any of the contents of the file by using the GUI tool if you wish.

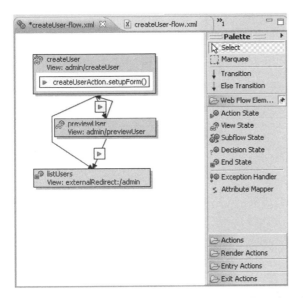

Figure A-22. *The palette allowing new web flow details to be created*

Using File-Creation Wizards

Three wizard tools are provided with the Spring IDE plug-in. The wizards are reached via the New ➤ Other ➤ Spring context menu option. They allow you to create the following:

- New Spring bean definition files

- New web flow definition files

- New projects with the Spring Project Nature

The bean definition wizard allows you to specify the name and location of the configuration file within the project and the set of XML Schema Definition declarations to include in the file (shown in Figure A-23). The wizard also allows you to add the new file to existing groupings of configuration files.

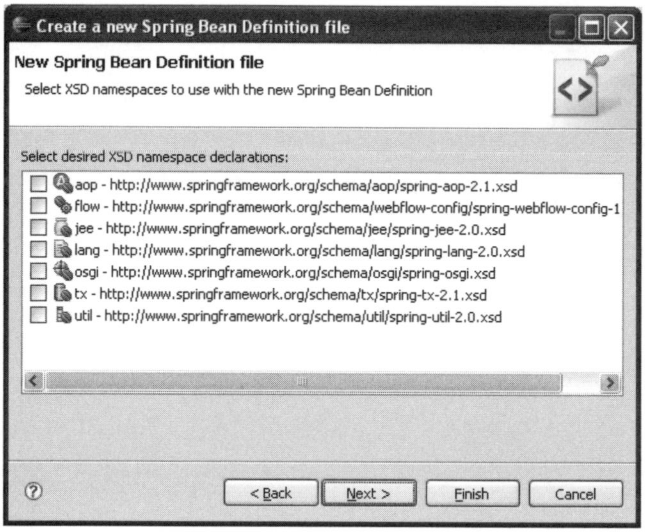

Figure A-23. *Adding XSD namespace declarations to a new bean definition file*

The flow definition file–creation wizard allows you to specify the name of the definition file and the set of Spring bean definition files that it depends on. The Spring project–creation wizard essentially allows you to specify only the project name, and is thus rather less versatile than the existing Java project wizards. Of the three, the two configuration file–creation wizards are the most useful because they enable you to avoid the error-prone task of copying boilerplate file content into the new files and of separately configuring the project to include them.

Conclusion

The Spring IDE is a rapidly growing tool that will soon justify a book dedicated to the subject if it has not already. It is not possible in a single chapter to give you more than a taste of the features that are offered, but even the limited parts of the Spring IDE that I have been able to cover here should give you more than enough reason to install and use the tool, and to investigate its capabilities further.

Index

forums.apress.com

FOR PROFESSIONALS BY PROFESSIONALS™

JOIN THE APRESS FORUMS AND BE PART OF OUR COMMUNITY. You'll find discussions that cover topics of interest to IT professionals, programmers, and enthusiasts just like you. If you post a query to one of our forums, you can expect that some of the best minds in the business—especially Apress authors, who all write with *The Expert's Voice*™—will chime in to help you. Why not aim to become one of our most valuable participants (MVPs) and win cool stuff? Here's a sampling of what you'll find:

DATABASES

Data drives everything.

Share information, exchange ideas, and discuss any database programming or administration issues.

INTERNET TECHNOLOGIES AND NETWORKING

Try living without plumbing (and eventually IPv6).

Talk about networking topics including protocols, design, administration, wireless, wired, storage, backup, certifications, trends, and new technologies.

JAVA

We've come a long way from the old Oak tree.

I lang out and discuss Java in whatever flavor you choose: J2SE, J2EE, J2ME, Jakarta, and so on.

MAC OS X

All about the Zen of OS X.

OS X is both the present and the future for Mac apps. Make suggestions, offer up ideas, or boast about your new hardware.

OPEN SOURCE

Source code is good; understanding (open) source is better.

Discuss open source technologies and related topics such as PHP, MySQL, Linux, Perl, Apache, Python, and more.

PROGRAMMING/BUSINESS

Unfortunately, it is.

Talk about the Apress line of books that cover software methodology, best practices, and how programmers interact with the "suits."

WEB DEVELOPMENT/DESIGN

Ugly doesn't cut it anymore, and CGI is absurd.

Help is in sight for your site. Find design solutions for your projects and get ideas for building an interactive Web site.

SECURITY

Lots of bad guys out there—the good guys need help.

Discuss computer and network security issues here. Just don't let anyone else know the answers!

TECHNOLOGY IN ACTION

Cool things. Fun things.

It's after hours. It's time to play. Whether you're into LEGO® MINDSTORMS™ or turning an old PC into a DVR, this is where technology turns into fun.

WINDOWS

No defenestration here.

Ask questions about all aspects of Windows programming, get help on Microsoft technologies covered in Apress books, or provide feedback on any Apress Windows book.

HOW TO PARTICIPATE:

Go to the Apress Forums site at **http://forums.apress.com/**.
Click the New User link.

You Need the Companion eBook

We believe this Apress title will prove so indispensable that you'll want to carry it with you everywhere, which is why we are offering the companion eBook (in PDF format) for $10 to customers who purchase this book now. Convenient and fully searchable, the PDF version of any content-rich, page-heavy Apress book makes a valuable addition to your programming library. You can easily find and copy code—or perform examples by quickly toggling between instructions and the application. Even simultaneously tackling a donut, diet soda, and complex code becomes simplified with hands-free eBooks!

Once you purchase your book, getting the $10 companion eBook is simple:

❶ Visit **www.apress.com/promo/tendollars/**.

❷ Complete a basic registration form to receive a randomly generated question about this title.

❸ Answer the question correctly in 60 seconds, and you will receive a promotional code to redeem for the $10.00 eBook.

2855 TELEGRAPH AVENUE | SUITE 600 | BERKELEY, CA 94705

Offer valid through 6/08.